Secrets from the Greek Kitchen

CALIFORNIA STUDIES IN FOOD AND CULTURE

Darra Goldstein, Editor

Secrets from the Greek Kitchen

*Cooking, Skill, and Everyday Life
on an Aegean Island*

David E. Sutton

UNIVERSITY OF CALIFORNIA PRESS

The publisher gratefully acknowledges
the generous support of the General Endowment Fund
of the University of California Press Foundation.

University of California Press, one of the most
distinguished university presses in the United States,
enriches lives around the world by advancing scholarship
in the humanities, social sciences, and natural sciences. Its
activities are supported by the UC Press Foundation and
by philanthropic contributions from individuals and
institutions. For more information, visit www.ucpress.edu.

University of California Press
Oakland, California

Library of Congress Cataloging-in-Publication Data

Sutton, David E., 1963–
    Secrets from the Greek kitchen : cooking, skill, and
everyday life on an Aegean island / David E. Sutton.
        pages   cm—(California studies in food and
culture; 52)
    Includes bibliographical references and index.
    ISBN 978-0-520-28054-0 (cloth : alk. paper)—
    ISBN 978-0-520-28055-7 (pbk. alk. paper)
    ISBN 978-0-520-95930-9 (e-book)
    1. Cooking, Greek.   I. Title.
    TX723.5.G8S88   2014
    641.59495—dc23
                                        2014006567

Manufactured in the United States of America

23 22 21 20 19 18 17 16 15 14
10 9 8 7 6 5 4 3 2 1

In keeping with a commitment to support
environmentally responsible and sustainable printing
practices, UC Press has printed this book on Natures
Natural, a fiber that contains 30% post-consumer waste
and meets the minimum requirements of ANSI/NISO
Z39.48–1992 (R 1997) (Permanence of Paper).

Contents

Illustrations

Video Examples

The video examples discussed in this book are available at www.ucpress. edu/go/greekkitchen. All videos were shot by David Sutton unless otherwise noted. Interested readers who want to go further in exploring Kalymnian cooking may find these and additional videos on YouTube at www.youtube.com/channel/UCZhvwUWSdxHSHM0Frx3J17Q/videos.

1. "Cutting Medley" (2005). Katerina Kardoulia cutting potatoes for a stew, Nina Papamihail cutting an onion for a salad, and Katerina's granddaughter, called Little Katerina Miha, cutting zucchini for an omelet.

2. "Polykseni Cutting Eggplant" (2008). Polykseni Miha slicing eggplant.

3. "Polykseni Making Mushroom Pies" (2008). Polykseni Miha and the author rolling phyllo dough.

4. "Evdokia Rolling Dough" (2011). Evdokia Passa rolling dough in her restaurant kitchen.

5. "Georgia Rolling Dough" (2001). Georgia Vourneli rolling dough for a leek pie. Video by Michael Hernandez.

6. "Katerina and the Can Opener" (2006). Katerina Kardoulia opening a can of tomato paste.

7. "Nina Making Octopus Stew" (2005). Nina Papamihail preparing an octopus dish in the kitchen of her summer home.

8. "Kitchen Choreography" (2006). Katerina Kardoulia and her daughter, Katina Miha, preparing several dishes for a Lenten meal while negotiating the limited space of Katerina's kitchen.

9. "Little Katerina Learning Cooking" (2006). Little Katerina Miha preparing a zucchini omelet for the first time, under the direction of her mother, Katina.

10. "Little Katerina Making a Salad" (2008). Little Katerina Miha making a salad for her father in her grandmother's kitchen.

11. "Little Katerina Describing a New Dish" (2012). Little Katerina Miha describing how she started making her own béchamel sauce instead of buying it from the store, and also how she prepares a dish with rice and vegetables.

Acknowledgments

This project benefited from the generous hospitality of a number of Kalymnians who shared their kitchens and ideas with me. In particular I'd like to thank Nomiki and Mihalis Tsaggaris, Popi Galanou, Pavlos Roditis, Yiannis Gavalas, Polykseni Miha, Polymnia Vasaneli, Nikolas and Katerina Maïlli, Irini and Savas Ergas, and Mihalis and Julia Koullias. Also thanks for hospitality and stimulating conversations in Athens to Susannah Verney and her lovely family.

Three families have been particularly central to this project. Without their help and friendship I can't imagine having gotten to this point. To Yiannis, Angeliki, and Dimitris Roditis I'm grateful for all of our many shared conversations and meals. Angeliki has been like a second mother to me, and ruminations with her over freshly squeezed orange juice, not to mention *avgozoumi* and other culinary treats, always got my day off to a good start. In Carbondale, Illinois, Yiannis's paintings are a constant reminder of his thoughtfulness, care, and shared love of talking about Kalymnian tradition and history, and I miss him tremendously since his passing in 2006. Dimitris, too, treated me like a brother, and I'm so pleased that he is learning the joys of fatherhood with such a delightful young son. Dimitris's lovely wife, Evdokia, and mother-in-law, Aleka Passa, have been extremely generous in welcoming me into their restaurant kitchen and putting up with my endless questions, even in the midst of preparing the day's meal for customers. And their *papoutsakia* definitely made it worth slipping from my vegetarianism.

Nina and Manolis Papamihail, as well as Nina's mother, Irini Psaromati, were always gracious hosts to me and my family. I had no inkling when Nina and my wife, Beth, first became friends how central her family would become to my research. I appreciate all our discussions over the years about the advantages and disadvantages of life on Kalymnos and in the United States. Nina's willingness to keep a three-month food diary, and allowing herself to be pestered on a regular basis about what she was making on any particular day, was truly saintly. I'm so glad I was able to be there for part of her long-awaited trip to the United States, and to follow her on her culinary journeys.

Finally, I especially want to thank Nikolas and Katina Miha and their children, Yiorgos, Vasilis, and Little Katerina, who have been my longest and most trusted friends on Kalymnos; I have had uncountable meals and conversations in their kitchen over the past thirty years. Visiting with them and becoming part of their daily lives has made returning to Kalymnos a great pleasure, and seeing the continuities and changes in cooking practices over three generations in their family has been truly fascinating. From the time they nicknamed me "Kyrios Gallorizos" for my early linguistic gaffe, I have felt part of the family, for, as Clifford Geertz wrote, to be teased is to be accepted. Katina has always been willing to give me the inside scoop on Kalymnian social and gender relations, and related her stories with characteristic style and humor. Of course, the center of the family for most of the time that I've known them was Katina's mother, Katerina Kardoulia. From the first day we met, when I was sent to help her collect pine cones for her leather-tanning operation (as part of the study abroad program on which I first traveled to Kalymnos), we both felt a connection in our shared attitude of openness and curiosity about the wider world, while not neglecting the importance of the "mundane" pleasures of good food, good tastes, and talk about food. No one was more central in making me feel at home on Kalymnos, and the many and varied conversations we have had and feelings that we've shared over the past thirty years on life, politics, religion, and family have become very much part of who I am. When Katerina died in late 2012 after a long battle with cancer, part of me went with her, and it is very hard to imagine Kalymnos without her central presence. While Katerina's husband, Yiorgos, died toward the beginning of this particular project, his hospitality and generosity to me over the years, and his many stories and prodigious memory of Kalymnos past were constant touchstones for me. Little Katerina, who is now no longer so little, has taken on the mantle of her grandmother while shaping her own ways in the world, and it has been a delight to get to know her and see her change over the years.

During the process of thinking about this project, I had the chance to present it in a number of different forums. I'm grateful for the opportunity provided by anthropology departments at Yale, Harvard, Indiana, Illinois, Sussex, Vermont, Concordia, Panteion, Mytilini, and Vytautas Magnus universities, as well as by the Center on Everyday Lives of Families at UCLA, and the Department of Food and Nutrition at New York University. Thanks for invitations and ensuing stimulating discussions (often lubricated by good meals, of course) go to David Howes, Jane Cowan, Vytis Ciubriskas, Akis Papataksiarchis, David Graeber, Michael Herzfeld, Alma Gottlieb, Martin Manalansan, Sid Mintz, Elinor Ochs, Margaret Beck, Amy Bentley, and Rhona Richman Kenneally.

I also had the good fortune to present early versions of this work at a Wenner-Gren conference in 2003. Thanks to Chris Gosden, Elizabeth Edwards, Ruth Phillips and the other participants for an intense and stimulating time. A similarly inspiring environment was provided by the European Institute Summer School Program in Tours. Thanks to Marc Jacobs, Harry West, and Peter Scholliers for their kind invitations and delightful discussions.

Jim and Renate Fernandez have been tremendous mentors and friends over the years of this project, and their home a haven of tasty and nourishing food, company, and conversation. Ever since Jim spoon-fed me while my arms were full with my newborn son Sam, I have been at least unconsciously aware of the connections among food, continuity, and cultural transmission. I appreciate all that Jim has taught me, in both the explicit and implicit ways of master and apprentice, in the craft of anthropology, and have enjoyed tremendously the many long discussions with Renate about food and the world of "nature," as seen from our differing but ultimately complementary perspectives.

A number of people carefully read all or parts of this manuscript, or simply provided intellectual sustenance over the years, and I'm particularly grateful for their input into the development of my thinking about issues of skill, transmission, and cooking. Thanks in no particular order go to Nick Doumanis, fellow lover of *barbounia;* Antonio Lauria, to my knowledge the best Marxist pasta-maker; Janet Dixon Keller and Charles Keller, for great conversations and kava too; Neni Panourgia, who cares about food and things Greek in deeply profound ways; Heather Paxson, with whom I've crafted a panel and many thoughts on the subject of skill; Ilana Gershon, who has been a delightful friend and confidant about the latest anthropological trends; Krishnendu Ray, for always-stimulating conversation and always bringing me together with the right person (often over a fabulous table); David Beriss, font of information about all things alimentary; Carole Counihan, whose work is an ongoing inspiration; Wendy Leynse, for helping me think about bringing children into the picture; Charles Stewart, for much-appreciated dialogues about history and historical consciousness; Faith Warn and Russ Bernard, two lovely friends and interlocutors about our shared passion for things Greek and Kalymnian; Fred Myers, whose thoughtfulness and guidance to a younger scholar were always appreciated; Yiannis Hamilakis, with whom I've shared many discussions about the growing field of sensory anthropology; Rick Wilk, always generous with ideas and culinary passions; and Nina Glick-Schiller and Steve Reyna, who push me to defend my positions, always in a loving way. I've also been grateful for the intellectual companionship of Renée Hirschon, Vassiliki Yiakoumaki, Rachel Black, Daniel Knight, Tony Webster, Juan Rodriguez, Jane Fajans, and Roberto Barrios.

Particular thanks as always to Peter Wogan, my anthropological muse, always ready to chew on a question of grammar or of theory. Without you, it just wouldn't be as much fun! And thank God for the disagreements. And the rules. And the goals. Amy Trubek has become a close colleague these past years, and her shared interests in everyday cooking have been a tremendous boon for my thinking about questions of skill, taste, the strange ways of molecular gastronomists, and other topics of concern. Both Peter and Amy have reminded me that the best anthropology grounds theorizing in everyday realities, questions, and curiosities and has at least something *surprising* to say. Eleana Yalouri's hospitality, friendship, and careful reading have all helped shape this project, and she and her husband, Karl, have provided many stimulating conversations and even some good arguments. I'm particularly grateful for their hospitality to my family, and even a much-needed yoga class. Eleana's shared interest in material culture and sensory anthropology, and our many discussions about the work of current luminaries like Daniel Miller and Tim Ingold, have been a real pleasure as well.

And special thanks to Leonidas Vournelis, my student and colleague with whom I wrote chapter 5, who has taught me too many things to count. But of course, that's why, as David Graeber would say, we owe each other favors and not debts. Leonidas's family has also contributed to this project. Georgia Vourneli was the first "guinea pig" to agree to be filmed preparing a *spanakopita,* and she inspired my thinking on a number of the issues developed herein. Thanks also to Hercules Vournelis and Dimitra Kampouri for providing the photograph that adorns the book cover. I also want to thank other students with whom I collaborated in one fashion or another, and who shared my passion for thinking about cooking as a subject of anthropological scrutiny, especially Michael Hernandez, with whom I got this project started, and who had a considerable impact on helping me see the methodological benefits of video ethnography; Meghan Fidler, whom I could always go to for trenchant thoughts on cooking techniques and their anthropological implications, not to mention the best udon soup this side of Tokyo; and Kaitlin Fertaly, who has picked up the torch of cooking ethnography with her own developing work in Armenian kitchens, and who provided "drink for thought" in the form of heavenly pomegranate wine. Lindsey Baker was instrumental in transferring my videos to YouTube, and I'm very grateful for all her hard work. Greg Wendt's help with the videos all along the way has been invaluable. And thanks to Eric Collier for his help with indexing.

I am grateful to my family for their help and support. My mother, Constance Sutton, couldn't believe I was writing another book about food, but she taught me all along to take women's ideas and activities seriously. She has been a constant interlocutor in my understanding of feminist anthropology, and has even come around to seeing food as interesting. My son Sam was a tremendous help with the videos, and with the difficult task of creating still photos from some of the videos. Sam also did the filming for a few of the videos during our trip to Kalymnos in 2009. Stay afloat! My son Max put up with my endless computer questions with patience and humor. And my wife, Beth, has shown tremendous faith in my anthropological projects and in my cooking over the years.

Finally, Kate Marshall, at University of California Press, provided much thoughtful guidance and direction and was lovely to work with. My thanks to her, Stacy Eisenstark, and the press staff.

Parts of chapter 4 were published in *Material Culture Review* (Sutton 2010). Parts of chapter 5 first appeared in *South European Society and Politics* (Sutton and Vournelis 2009), copyright Taylor and Francis. Parts of chapter 6 were published in *History and Memory* (Sutton 2008), and parts of chapter 2 in *Social Research* ("A Tale of Easter Ovens: Food and Collective Memory," *Social Research* 75: 157–80). All are reproduced here by permission of the publishers. The research for this book has been reviewed and approved by the SIUC Human Subjects Committee.

Introduction

Why Does Greek Food Taste So Good?

Tonight, only two *mezedes* [appetizers] are served: a bowl of freshly picked *yigantes*—gigantic white beans—oven-roasted with tomatoes, carrots, and parsley, and a slab of the undramatically named *dopio tyri* ("local cheese"), which turns out to be the richest cheese I've ever tasted on Thasos, its equal portions of goat's and sheep's milk held together by a tender membrane of rind. When I begin swooning over the cheese, pestering the men with inquiries, they point to a scarecrow sipping *tsipouro* in the corner. "That's the shepherd there," they tell me. . . . When we ask him about the cheese, he tastes a slice from his impossibly weathered fingertips. "It's not mine," he says. "This is some other man's cheese. There's too much goat in this one." With that, he nods and returns to his corner and his drink. (Bakken 2013, 14)

Nomiki is describing to me the making of a meat sauce for the dish pastitsio. She begins by listing the main ingredients, and then she comes to the spices, noting, "I added cinnamon, garlic, onion, pepper, bay leaf. . . . " Here she reaches into the pan to pull out a bay leaf and says, "I'm using my hand. It doesn't matter. Cooking requires hands." After listing a few more ingredients, she adds, "The ingredients don't go in all at once. One at a time. There's an order in cooking. You'll put in the cinnamon, then after a little bit the pepper, the salt, the bay leaf, one by one, so that you can hear the smell of each ingredient." (Author's fieldnotes, May 2006)

Both of these extracts capture something of the unique taste of Greek food, the first from a culinary memoir by poet Christopher Bakken and the second from my fieldnotes during my own research. Bakken's text captures the sense of "the taste of place," that the flavor of food is shaped by its environment and the profoundly local knowledge of process and small differences that are the stuff of endless conversation in Greece. As many Greeks will tell you, and as I have experienced myself, no matter how hard you try to reproduce the same dish outside its local context, you won't be able to because the sun, soil, and air will be different, leading to different flavors. If you have ever traveled and then tried to reproduce the flavors of your trip in your home environment, you will know that the results tend to be ghostly reflections of your memory of the original dish.

The extract from my fieldwork is a reminder that "taste" is not only embedded in the context of place, but in a cultural context in which the senses are enculturated in specific ways—in this case, through a stress not only on careful technique, but on the ways that all the senses need to work together in creating proper flavors. Synesthesia, the union of the senses, has always been a major feature of food practices on the island of Kalymnos in the eastern Aegean, where I have conducted research for the past two decades. The easy expression of this synesthesia encapsulated in the intriguing phrase "hear the smell" was only emphasized by Nomiki's comfortable tactile engagement with the ingredients as she dipped her hand confidently into the bubbling meat sauce to scoop out a bay leaf—captured and preserved on my video camera— while all at the same time emphasizing that cooking is far from a haphazard affair; cooking involves forethought and order.[1] If anything had impressed itself on me during my research in Kalymnian kitchens, it was that the flavor of food, and how that flavor was achieved, was a matter of deep concern to Kalymnians, women and men, young and old.

Indeed, even though men are not the primary cooks on Kalymnos, it became clear to me during my research that cooking matters to Kalymnian men in a fundamental way. It is fascinating to me to observe men talking to other men on Kalymnos about the details of cooking, details that they may never need to put into practice in their daily lives. Men on Kalymnos are typically accidental cooks; yet they will still express fascination with cooking processes and their variations—the way to cook an octopus, for example, by either removing or conserving its sea water, or the importance of adding feta cheese directly to a dish of green beans in tomato sauce so that the cheese absorbs the sauce. These are some of the topics that men spontaneously raise with other men, and that they pass on to young boys as part of a valued cultural knowledge of flavors on Kalymnos. Kalymnians care about cooking because flavor matters to them, because it represents one of their deeply held values—or at least so it had always seemed.

COOKING, DEAD OR STILL BREATHING? OR, WAS THE ANTHROPOLOGIST TOO LATE ONCE AGAIN?

This book is an ethnography of cooking knowledge and practices on Kalymnos, an island in the Dodecanese chain, just a few miles off the coast of Turkey. It explores the ways that cooking is transmitted, reproduced, and transformed among several generations of Kalymnian cooks. It poses this question: are cooking traditions passed down from one generation to the next, and if so, how?

Why should this matter, one may ask, to anyone except the Kalymnians with whom I worked? The question of the fate of cooking knowledge in our so-called "modern" world is a topic of ongoing concern, as many bemoan the supposed "death of cooking." Michael Pollan (2009), for example, suggests that we have moved from the kitchen to the couch, as cooking has become a spectator sport to watch on TV, but not to attempt to reproduce at home (as it was, presumably, in the days when food TV meant Julia Child). Similarly, a *New York Times* article notes that what used to be a "60-minute gourmet" column now has been trimmed to "30 minutes." "30 is the new 60," the author notes ruefully (Grimes 2004). Apparently, the only time that Americans spend more than half an hour in the kitchen these days is when they're cooking for their canine or feline companions. Considering my project, was I condemned to old-fashioned salvage ethnography, lamenting another "lost tradition" captured in writing just before its last flames flicker out in practice? Or are rumors of the demise of cooking greatly exaggerated?

The study of cooking knowledge and its transmission raises questions about the fate of tradition generally, and the potential loss of cultural and linguistic diversity that is feared to accompany the decline of all sorts of practices labeled "traditional." Some scholars and activists who wish to fight the loss of tradition through the preservation of "traditional" linguistic, ecological, or other knowledge seem to end up abstracting and objectifying it, as if knowledge were a freestanding object that can be treated with the tools of resource management. As Julie Cruikshank argues about the sensory practices and stories that are interwoven with the reproduction of knowledges among Tlingit and Athapaskans, creating the idea "that truthful knowledge can somehow be 'captured' and recovered in databases; such studies seem to do damage to northern visions when statements by knowledgeable people are stripped from evocative contexts and taped, transcribed, codified, and labeled."[2] In the realm of food, this approach is reflected in the seed banks that attempt to preserve the diversity of agricultural plant life separate from the knowledges and contexts in which these plants have been grown.

When we turn to cooking, we can see similar attitudes and approaches reflected in the vast dissemination of recipes on the Internet and in mass media, the kind of food programming that Pollan sees as leaving us deskilled couch potatoes, able to name and describe a *crudo* or the uses of a shiso leaf, but with no actual ability to produce such exotic, not to mention mundane, concoctions. Pollan holds that transmission of cooking knowledge has lost its traditional, female context with the rise of women in the workforce and the lure of the fast-food industry, while food programs on TV have not replaced such traditional female sources of transmission, but simply made us better able to know how to order in fancy restaurants: "As a chef friend put it when I asked him if he thought I could learn anything about cooking by watching the Food Network, 'How much do you learn about playing basketball by watching the N.B.A.?'" (Pollan 2009).

Recent times have also seen the rise of a movement known as molecular gastronomy, which claims to transform cooking by using laboratory science to "rationalize stylistic and aesthetic conceits" and "eradicate tacit knowledge from culinary practice" (Roosth 2013, 8, 7). In this view, the transmission of cooking knowledge is not something that is being lost by modernity and must be preserved by external, technical means. On the contrary, as practiced in France by Hervé This, one of its leading exponents, "vernacular skills transmitted intergenerationally—from parent to child or from chef to trainee—get left out of French cuisine as it is reinvented as rational and positivist."[3] He and his colleagues believe that cooking's "old wives' tales" will stand or fall based on their confirmation or disproof in his laboratory—or as another molecular gastronomist put it, "'Because for a lot of centuries our ancestors did this one [recipe] like that, [so] we do it like that and maybe it's wrong. It's wrong. And molecular gastronomy can explain why it's wrong.'"[4]

These ideas run parallel to those found in other domains of the contemporary food scene, such as the magazine *Cooks Illustrated,* which purports through extensive empirical testing to create recipes that are replicable and perfectible (a subject discussed further in the conclusion to this book). Note that whether traditional cooking knowledge is something to be preserved or discarded, it is seen as an object, like a recipe or a technique, which can be detached from its context and made to speak for itself, without distraction, in the objective setting of the scientific laboratory.

As an anthropologist who has been conducting fieldwork in Greece for more than two decades, I have a different view of tradition and its relation to tacit knowledge and its transmission. "Traditional knowledge" is not frozen in time; rather, it is deeply responsive to social and material environments, as those who study processes of learning and apprenticeship have long argued. The ethnography that follows is an argument for what is revealed about cooking when one starts from a more complex and contextual understanding of what ordinary people have been doing in kitchens. It is only when we move away from static notions of tradition that we can begin to understand and assess the actual impacts of something like the rise of food television on everyday cooking practices. If, as a generation of scholars has shown, learning always occurs in concrete contexts, deeply shaped by social, historical, and material environments, then we must seek to study cooking in its contexts rather than separate it from them.

Such an approach allows me to ask questions about tradition that include the following: Has cooking ever passed smoothly and directly from mothers to daughters? How does the choice of cooking tools and technologies shape everyday notions of identity and morality? Why might Kalymnians choose to cut vegetables in a way that cooking specialists would label "inefficient" and "dangerous"? I am not suggesting that Kalymnos represents an exotic repository of tradition to be contrasted to our "modern" ways of cooking—as we will see, Kalymnians struggle with some of the same contrasts. But I am suggesting that by taking seriously *everyday* practices and values in ordinary kitchens and presenting them for scrutiny, we can develop new perspectives on why people make the choices they do in their kitchens, and why those choices matter to them.

ENTERING THE KALYMNIAN KITCHEN

When I returned to Kalymnos in the summer of 2005 for the first time with a video camera, intending to record some of the processes and practices of Kalymnian kitchens, I found much that had changed since previous trips. Young women were dressed in the latest fashion, a rarity during my research in the early 1990s. The first big supermarkets, carrying diverse frozen foods and preprepared meals, had opened the previous year, while specialty stores offered wasabi mustard, Thai curries, and a variety of Mexican seasonings that had not existed previously. Cooking shows were now a regular feature on Greek TV stations, and they seemed popular with many Kalymnians. And the discourse of health, while not absent in the past, seemed to have been quantified; people discussed cholesterol numbers with confidence and precision.

One thing that struck me as both new and seemingly an echo of American concerns over loss of cooking skills was the succinct claim I heard repeated by many older Kalymnians: "The younger generation doesn't cook anymore." Nowadays claims that cooking is dead roll off the tongue of many Kalymnians, its passage seen as one of the ambivalent fruits of "modernity" that has been threatening to overtake the island during the decades that I have been doing fieldwork there, and no doubt for much longer. On a Greek sitcom about four single women seeking love and fulfillment titled *Alone through Carelessness,* I watched one of the heroines shopping diffidently in the pasta aisle of a supermarket. She is confronted by a more matronly-looking woman who says, "Pasta, pasta, all pasta. Don't you younger women know how to cook anything else? That's why men don't want to leave their mothers."

This statement suggests that such discussions are not merely descriptive but moral discourses, laced with gendered assumptions. As I argued in my earlier ethnography of Kalymnos, the balancing of "tradition" and "modernity" is seen as the most significant moral issue faced, individually and collectively (Sutton 1998). Here I am attempting to get at some of the real changes as well as continuities in people's lives. What has been striking to me since I began to examine the local meanings of "modernity" on Kalymnos was the pervasiveness of the discourse, how it invaded every aspect of daily life, from the hair color of children to the choice of what kind of pot to use for boiling one's stuffed grape leaves. This was true even before the commodification of food traditions that emerged in the first decade of the new millennium, as producers of foods such as cheese and honey as well as restaurateurs were increasingly encouraged and given institutional support to sell their products *as Kalymnian tradition*. Meanwhile, in the autumn of 2010, Greece's application to have the Mediterranean diet recognized as a UNESCO Intangible Cultural Heritage (an application made in conjunction with Spain, Italy, and Morocco) had been accepted. When I have presented my research to nonacademic audiences, one of the things they have wanted to know is, "What is happening to the Mediterranean diet?" and whether it is still prevalent or, perhaps, being swept aside by McDonald's and other global forces.

By 2011 food choices and cooking were being recontextualized by questions about the Greek debt crisis. On Kalymnos the priests were telling people to return to the practice of backyard gardening to supplement their food budget. Some people were talking about how to survive the crisis by reverting to a traditional bean-based diet (after the past twenty-five years have seen meat gain more prominence in the diet), while others suggested that careful shopping for cheaper cuts and better deals at the island's supermarkets would allow them to ride out the storm. In Athens, by contrast, the protesters, known as the "outraged," were not thinking about such small adjustments, but rather employed food metaphors to express their desperation and anger at the government and political parties. As reported in *The Guardian:*

> There is another mic here, and it's grabbed by a man wearing a mask of deputy prime minister Theodoros Pangalos: "My friends, we all ate together." He is quoting the socialist politician, who claimed on TV last year that everyone bore the responsibility for the squandering of public money. Pangalos may have intended his remark as the Greek equivalent of George Osborne's remark that "We're all in it together," but here they're not having it. "You lying bastard!" they roar back. "You're so fat you ate the entire supermarket." (Chakrabortty 2011)

Despite the direness of the economic situation as it related to cooking and eating, in the second half of the 2000s I noticed a flourishing of food TV in Greece. Beginning with indigenous cooking shows like *Vefa's Kitchen* and *Forgiveness with Every Bite* (analyzed in detail in chapter 5), by 2011 Greek channel lineups were crammed with both Greek programs (some following the model of successful shows in the United States and England like *Top Chef* and *Ramsay's Kitchen Nightmares*) and foreign shows featuring chefs like Jamie Oliver. And these shows were popular. It seemed that economic news had not yet dampened the pleasure Kalymnians took in discussing and analyzing their daily fare. More than that, kitchen choices of major proportions, like building an outdoor oven in one's backyard, or simple things like styles of can opener were seen not simply as superfluous frills but as existential choices, very much about how one saw one's relationship with the past and present, or with the ill-defined concept of "modernity."

HOW I CAME TO STUDY KALYMNIAN COOKING

I never imagined when I started out as a graduate student with an interest in Greece that twenty-five years later I would be writing a book about Kalymnian cooking. When I first did fieldwork on Kalymnos in the early 1990s, my graduate training had posed the question of historical change—the relation between "structure" and "event," or "rules" and "practices"—as the central question for anthropology to solve. My own research project was framed in terms of these concerns, but I also felt that the question of historical consciousness, or the felt relevance of the past in people's daily lives, might be important for understanding how the past shapes the present, and how the present inflects our memories of the past. I explored some of the ways that the past and the present are tangled up with one another in Kalymnian practices, such as the ritual throwing of thousands of pounds of dynamite at Easter, an "explosive" expression of complex Kalymnian attitudes about their relationship with the long history of outside occupation of the island. I looked at how debates over the proper place of tradition in contemporary life shape people's understanding of gender relations in the present in the memories and ongoing influence of the Kalymnian "first-daughter" inheritance system of female primogeniture, a system that is unique in Greece to Kalymnos and some of the neighboring islands. And I examined how debates over contemporary events such as the breakup of Yugoslavia became debates over "history." But I was also concerned with how these debates were shaped, sometimes unconsciously, by customary practices such as the naming of children after grandparents as a key aspect of the creation of cultural continuity (see Sutton 1998). As I pursued this project, I increasingly became aware of the significance of food in people's memories of the past. Food was in the margins of my notes as part of expressive anecdotes, but for Kalymnians it was clearly central to their memories, marked by the expression often directed to me, to "eat, so that you remember Kalymnos."

In reviewing these marginal notes I became increasingly intrigued by the Kalymnian perception of a strong interrelationship of food and memory, and noted the absence of anthropological reflection or analysis on the topic. This lack of anthropological interest at the time provided an impetus for me to pursue a "Proustian anthropology," which would take food memories as a jumping-off point for broader anthropological considerations. In *Remembrance of Repasts* (2001) I traced some of the ways that food memories tied together ritual and everyday life and were central to exchange relations, in which the memory of past acts of generosity were narrated for the ways that they could establish and solidify individual and collective identities. I was struck by the sensory dimensions of Kalymnian memories and posed questions about how anthropologists might get at sensory experience, a subject that has become an ongoing concern for me. I noted at the time the ways that a kind of casual synesthesia seemed to pervade Kalymnian cooking practices (as well as other aspects of life on Kalymnos), and explored the metaphors and other tropes by which Kalymnians themselves attempt to convey the tastes, textures, smells, and sounds of the kitchen.

When I was close to finishing writing *Remembrance of Repasts* I had another "revelatory moment" (Fernandez 1986)—or an "aha moment." My colleague Janet Dixon Keller suggested to me that cooking was very much a "memory process," and that I should consider cooking in a more systematic way. Of course, I thought, you can't think about food without thinking about cooking, but somehow cooking as a *topic of ethnographic exploration and analysis* had escaped my notice until that moment. This led me to write a largely speculative chapter on what an ethnography of cooking focused on "memory processes" might look like, raising questions of kitchen tools and technologies and their relation to embodied memory, of the role of recipes and other forms of objectification in the transmission of cooking, and of how different kinds of learning processes might shape the acquisition and retention of cooking knowledge. I was most excited by the fact that this inquiry led me to different approaches that I had not been familiar with before, in particular to studies of learning and apprenticeship, to phenomenology, to actor-network theory, and to various archaeological perspectives on tools and technology, and material culture studies more generally. As I read more, I got increasingly excited both because these diverse approaches seemed to illuminate the topic of cooking *and* because they had not been applied to cooking before. So as with food and memory, I have felt throughout this project that there was something to be gained by bringing together topics and approaches that hadn't been tried before—like trying out a new recipe—and seeing what resulted.

I began my ethnography of cooking with several small projects in southern Illinois, and with, for me, a major methodological innovation: prompted by my graduate student Michael Hernandez, I began filming people as they prepared everyday meals.[5] In using video I was inspired, in part, by the work of Patricia Greenfield on Maya weavers.[6] While visual anthropology has a history almost as long as the discipline itself, Greenfield was a relatively early proponent of using video to explore daily practices, particularly in the context of learning skills (her subjects were young Maya girls). Her work pointed me to the ways that video can get at how bodily habits themselves are culturally shaped, as she described the training that goes into mastering the difficult postures involved in balancing oneself to manipulate a backstrap loom. And her work pointed to the value of collecting video data over time, as she explored some of the changes in her subjects' practices as they matured and as their community adapted to changing socioeconomic circumstances.

The value of video was instantly apparent to me, as even for interviews it created a richness of presence lacking in audio recordings. But it also created for me a whole new type of data that provided information about the relationship between language and all kinds of practices, the use of tools in the kitchen, kitchen organization, and bodily movements and postures as cooks interact with noncooks or fellow cooks—an entire kitchen choreography. Returning to these videos allowed me to start thinking in much greater detail about questions of *how* people do things, the technical and aesthetic aspects of life that I had paid only scant attention to while focused on more purely social or symbolic questions.

In 2005 I began filming cooking on Kalymnos, and I have returned yearly or semiyearly since then to follow up and document some of the micro-changes that may be occurring in Kalymnian kitchens. These videos served not only to expand my appreciation for people's everyday practices (and, indeed, provided a better record of their linguistic devices as well), but when I presented my research to colleagues, video also seemed to bring my arguments to life and provide for engagement and lively discussion. Thus in this book I supplement my written descriptions with video footage from my research. I urge readers to become viewers as well, and to deepen and perhaps also to challenge my analysis through viewings of these videos.

PREVIOUS SCHOLARSHIP

No introduction would be complete without a ritual invocation of the scholarly and theoretical tradition in which one is working, while typically also showing that no one has studied this particular issue in this particular way before. My own version of this exercise humbly follows, divided into two sections, the first briefly reviewing general theoretical issues, with some thoughts on how they apply to food, and the second focused more specifically on previous approaches to studying food and particularly cooking.

Objects, the Senses, and Skill

Contemporary studies of objects or "material culture" have stressed an approach that acknowledges that "the representational aspects of material culture far from exhaust its uses or role within society" (Boivin 2010, 30). Thus, instead of seeing material culture as interesting to anthropologists purely because of its signifying or languagelike properties, recent work has focused on how all phenomena in the world are mixtures of both "social" and "material" effects, and the two cannot easily be distinguished or segregated from each other; nor should they be. Thus, chiles are not interesting because they "stand for" heat, or even masculinity, but because they take on certain meanings in the process of producing certain effects on the tongue and the body. Much of the debate in such theorizing is in working out the implications of these insights for anthropological practice, whether to speak of "materials" or "materiality," and what all this implies about "the agency of objects."[7] Here I simply want to make a few points.

Without reviewing the complex corpus of anthropologist-philosopher Bruno Latour, I take from him the important point that "objects" need to be part of our ethnographies in new ways—that is, neither as pure symbolic repositories of human thought, nor as technological determinants of human society. In between these two views, Latour suggests, we can analyze the way that "*any thing* that does modify a state of affairs by making a difference is an actor. . . . Thus the questions to ask about any agent are: Does it make a difference in the course of some other agent's action or not? Is there some trial that allows someone to detect this difference?" (2005, 71; emphasis in original). Latour asks us to imagine hitting a nail with or without a hammer to understand that hammers *make a difference* in human actions and projects. This is not, as Latour notes, to say that hammers *determine* any particular action, nor that they *symbolize* strength or power. Between these two possibilities, he suggests, "things might authorize, allow, afford, encourage, permit, suggest, influence, block, render possible, forbid, and so on" (2005, 72).[8]

In the following pages we will see cooking tools such as knives, rolling pins, brick ovens, and can openers that all *make a difference* in the daily lives, projects, and actions of Kalymnian cooks, and that need to be as much a part of our consideration in an ethnography of cooking as issues of gender identities, matrilocality, "globalization," and cultural values. Bringing such "objects" as cooking tools into our analytic consideration no more discounts these typical subjects of anthropological inquiry than an anthropology of "power," developed in the 1980s and 1990s, should displace concerns with kinship, ritual, or exchange, still clearly important facets of human social life. One goal of this book, however, is to suggest that "technology" need not be a stand-alone subspecialization within anthropology; rather, its consideration is very much part of what we want to understand about contemporary life, whether we are talking about potato peelers or smart phones. That these "objects" are still tied to "identities" is clear, but not only in the sense, once again, of being symbols of identity or status markers (though they can be that as well), but in the sense described by Marx in his image of *Homo faber*, that is, the way humans shape themselves in the course of producing objects: "By thus acting on the external world and changing it, he at the same time changes his own nature."[9] This is similar to Daniel Miller's notion of *objectification*: "In objectification all we have is a process in time by which the very act of creating form creates consciousness . . . and thereby transforms both form and the self-consciousness of that which has consciousness" (Miller 2005, 9). When this concept is applied to cooking, one could say that in transforming materials or ingredients into forms— the cooked dish—one is also engaged in a process of self-transformation, into that of the competent or incompetent cook.

A related approach to objects draws from Marcel Mauss (1954), who stressed the way that objects and subjects blur into each other, as the objects themselves become personified, taking on the histories and identities of their owners and recipients, while the identity of subjects becomes tied to the objects they possess, hence the notion of "biographical objects," or even "inalienable possessions."[10] As we will see, all of these approaches are useful in understanding objects in the Kalymnian kitchen, where old flour sifters or coffee grinders may be displayed on top of cabinets as a reminder of the previous owners or users of these objects as Kalymnians struggle to come to terms with notions of "tradition" and "modernity" in what I refer to as "existential memory work."

What of food itself as an object? Or as Jon Holtzman asks, how might we approach food "as food" (2009, 50)? Some have suggested that food's distinctiveness lies in its power to cross the boundaries between outside and inside, to begin as external and then become part of "us"— one of the reasons that food is so tied to notions of kinship or "shared substance."[11] Philosopher Jane Bennett—drawing on nutritional studies as well as on philosophers such as Nietzsche and Thoreau—argues for the importance of the "material agency" of food to alter our moods, affecting our dispositions as well as our "psychological, aesthetic, cognitive and moral complexions," suggesting that "edible matter is a powerful agent . . . that modifies the human matter with which it comes into contact" (Bennett 2010, 43–44). Holtzman takes a slightly different approach, suggesting that to study food as food is to study the intersection of multiple processes, nutritional, social, political, religious, emotional, and so on—that "what makes food *food* . . . is how it simultaneously ties together disparate threads of causality and meaning" (2009, 53). Holtzman also suggests that ordinary people, at least where he did fieldwork in northern Kenya, don't tend to parse out the different aspects of food that anthropologists tend to treat separately. While I like the holism suggested by such a view, I think the same might be said of many other topics of anthropological study as well, death or money, for example. Of course, food doesn't have to be unique among objects to be interesting, and Holtzman's point is well taken that food can be studied *as food* rather than mainly as a window onto some other thing (class, globalization) seen as more important.

Another approach to food as an object is suggested by Joy Adapon in her application of Alfred Gell's theory of art as agency in her ethnography *Culinary Art and Anthropology* (2008). If the essence of Gell's approach is that humans tend to impute agency when they encounter an "effect," Adapon applies this insight to food in showing how "we recognize culinary artistry by the power of the food to perform a perceptual change in the eaters, physically enhancing their experience of life" (34). As Adapon argues for Mexican cuisine, "Confronting a meal can also be thought of as confronting a person . . . and the food itself is the outcome of the cook's intentions" (38). This leads people to talk about transfers of emotion between persons and food—if someone is angry, tamales will not set because they are angry as well (39), and food resents being "rudely handled" (20). These personifications are examples of Gell's notion that an object is an "artwork" to the extent that "'it embodies intentionalities that are complex, demanding of attention and perhaps difficult to reconstruct fully'" (Gell, cited in Adapon 2008, 39). This is related to the notion that artworks, such as a complex meal, can be "traps" for the viewer-eater, as they suggest a complexity of intention and execution that the eater cannot fully reconstruct: How were they produced? With what feelings and intentions? There is a notion here that food "collaborates" with humans in producing certain effects (Janeja 2010, 20). But by the same token, as food circulates—that is, as it is eaten by different people—it has the possibility to "betray" the intentions of its creator (Janeja 2010, 20); its taste can be unpalatable to some or it can spoil, thus once again suggesting a notion of "agency" if not of actual intentionality.

Much as with objects, the senses themselves are no longer understood as passive recording devices, but as part of our active engagement with our socio-material environment. As David Howes puts it, attention to the senses allows us to explore "how meanings are transmitted and experienced through sensual modes of communication and . . . how perceptual relations are also social relations, making culture a lived, multisensory experience" (2003, 40). Moving beyond some of Paul Stoller's earlier claims that anthropologists "should spice [their ethnographic descriptions] with the sauce of sensuous observations," Howes argues that "sensuous experience is not opposed to reason, rather it is replete with logic and meaning, both personal and communal. Consequently, sensuous evocation is not just a way of enlivening ethnographic description, or of infusing scholarship with sensuality. It is an essential basis for exploring how peoples make sense of the world through perception" (2003, 43).

Perception, it should be noted, is not simply present-tense, but always involves a combination of what Howes refers to here as "perception" with memory and imagination, a mixture of tenses and temporalities that leads to the rich complexity of all embodied sensory experiences.[12] What is powerful in a synesthetic approach is that it sees the senses as a bridge between what we traditionally divide into "internal" or "subjective" and "external" or "objective" experiences. Sensory experience occurs at the borders between these Western dualisms, as numerous authors have attempted to capture. Thus, C. Nadia Seremetakis writes, describing what she sees as a Greek rural approach to the experience of the senses, "The sensory is not only encapsulated within the body as an internal capacity or power, but is also dispersed out there on the surface of things, as the latter's autonomous characteristics, which can then invade the body as perceptual experience" (1994, 6). Others have commented on how taste and smell seem to dissolve the boundaries between subject and object, problematizing the distinctions drawn from a more vision-based worldview (see Borthwick 2000 for a review).

Howes is one of a number of scholars who have transformed our understanding of sensory experience so that one can now speak of an "anthropology of the senses."[13] This scholarship has shown quite clearly that the typical Western view of the senses—including the notion that there are only five and that they can be ranked from "higher" to "lower"—is as limiting and limited as any other supposed commonsense dressed as "universal." Recent ethnographies have provided wonderful descriptions and analysis of the senses—movement in Japanese dance and Brazilian *capoeira,* the sense of balance in Ghana, the synesthetic experience of baskets and "acoustemologies" in the Amazon, and the smell and taste of environmental hazards in Canada, to name just a few.[14]

When it comes to studying the senses in relation to our human, cultural experience of food and eating, a number of recent approaches have been suggestive. There is a developing sense among anthropologists and other scholars of food that the study of taste, far from being peripheral to our understanding of culture, can in fact provide a new way of organizing our research into social life. I suggest the term *gustemology*, a gustemic way of knowing, living, and interacting, to capture this idea, drawing on Stephen Feld's coinage of the term *acoustemology* to make a similar point about sonic approaches to the world (2003). What I mean by gustemology goes beyond Pierre Bourdieu's more metaphoric use of "taste" (1984) to talk about social distinction, drawing inspiration rather from Sidney Mintz's use of sweetness to understand social life and the transformations that led to the notion of the "modern" individual consumer (1985), and Judith Farquhar's focus on bitterness as a key to understanding changing experiences in pre- and post-Maoist China (2002).[15] In both of these cases, it is because sweetness and bitterness are placed in a context in which taste matters deeply to people's daily lives and identities, and because these sensory experiences become part of the person through consumption, that taste can take on much broader and potentially more metaphoric applications. In a gustemological approach, taste takes on the quality of a total social fact, tied to multiple domains of social life.

But a gustemological approach should certainly not be limited to taste, and should recognize that "taste" is only one of the sensory aspects of flavor, which needs to include most obviously smell, texture, and temperature, but also sight and sound ("hear the smell," as Nomiki put it). Such parsing does not capture the fluidity and interconnectivity of these experiences, which even Proust tried to limit to "taste and smell" in his famous Madeleine reverie. A gustemological approach would both recognize the potential for far more tastes than the standard four (or now five, with the latecomer umami), and recognize that our experience of food (like all of life) is always inherently synesthetic.

If, as noted above, the senses are seen to bridge the internal and the external, they are deployed in relation to a social and material environment. As Elizabeth Edwards, Chris Gosden, and Ruth Phillips put it, "The forms that things are felt to take, the general sense of what it is possible to do with things, and the ways of being-in-the-world, derive from sensory interaction with the world" (2006, 5). In thinking about what it is possible to do with things in the sensorily rich Kalymnian kitchen, I have found it helpful to draw from notions of situated action and skill developed by anthropologists Jean Lave and Tim Ingold, among others. Both take us closer to understanding the mechanics of everyday practice through exploring the emergent qualities of action.

For Ingold, for example, skilled practice involves not the mind telling the body what to do according to a preconceived plan, but rather a mobilization of the mind/body within an environment of things that "afford" different possibilities for human use. This is a departure from traditional learning research in which, as Lave notes, "learning researchers have studied learning is if it were a process contained in the mind of the learner . . . ignor[ing] the lived-in world" (1996, 7). Skill, for Ingold, involves much more than the application of a sort of mechanical force to objects (what he sees as the model of technology); rather, it is an extension of the mind/body, often through the use of tools, requiring constant and shifting use of judgment and dexterity within a changing environment. The environment is not objectified as a "problem" that humans must "adapt" to; instead, it itself is part of the total field of activity, as in his example of a woodsman who, in chopping wood, consults the world with his senses for guidance, not a picture in his head. "The world is its own best model" (Ingold 2000, 12; see also Lave 1988). It is through such skilled practices, then, that forms are generated, rather than through the execution of a mental plan, though mental plans may provide guideposts for practices; in other words, they can allow you to assess your work at various moments.[16] This approach has implications for the transmission of skill as well, which once again is not a set of rules to be memorized. Skill must be learned through the sensuous and sensory engagement of a novice with the environment or with a skilled practitioner. This learning, as Lave argues, is part of all ongoing activity: "Situated activity always involves changes in knowledge and action . . . and 'changes in knowledge and action' are central to what we mean by 'learning'" (1996, 5).

Learning has tended to be referred to in classical anthropology as "enculturation," based on the "blank slate" notion of precultural children with minds waiting to be filled with cultural stuff—categories, ideas, and so on. Ingold suggests that we reframe this learning as an "education of attention," or, as he puts it, speaking of his father, "His manner of teaching was to show me things, literally to point them out. If I would but notice the things to which he directed my attention, and recognize the sights, smells and tastes that he wanted me to experience . . . then I would discover for myself much of what he already knew" (2000, 20). Learning from others involves copying, but rather than a transcription of knowledge from one head to another, it is a "guided rediscovery" (2000, 11) in a sensorily rich environment. It also involves people in sociality, as learning a skill often involves, as Rebecca Bryant puts it, "Learning to be the type of person who can do X" (Bryant 2005, 224). Harry West shows the co-presence involved in developing into the kind of person who becomes a cheese maker, in describing the children of cheese makers: "Each of them came of age in a world where dairying and cheese making were taken-for-granted facts of life. Each spent time in the stable and in the cheese room long before they sought to learn, and long before others sought to teach them. By the time they might have started learning, they seemingly already knew. They rarely ever asked how to do something and rarely were they explicitly told" (West 2013, 330; see also Grasseni 2009).

One can see here why a view of skilled practice might be compatible with an anthropology of materiality attuned to the senses. Like other recent scholars of material culture, Ingold does not view objects or the environment as passive ciphers to which humans simply add symbolic meaning (see also Myers 2001; Miller 2005). Rather, objects—because of their sensual properties—afford certain possibilities for human use; the semiotic and the material constantly cross-cut and convert into each other. Hiking boots, for example, by their material nature "afford" certain possibilities in relation to nature by "expanding the range of possible actions available to the body" (Michael 2000, 112). This in no way limits the meaning or uses of hiking boots, but it forces us, as analysts, to engage with the everyday problems that boots, or other material objects, are meant to engage with.

A Brief for More Ethnographies of Cooking

For a long time cooking seemed to be interesting only to anthropologists of the universally human. Thus, Claude Lévi-Strauss famously saw cooking as the key practice indicating the human transition from "nature" to "culture." Lévi-Strauss also suggested the importance of human-technology relations in this view of cooking: the more technology involved (boiling in a pot versus roasting directly on a fire, for example), the more "cultural." More recently, biological anthropologist Richard Wrangham updated and broadened Lévi-Strauss's claim for the centrality of cooking in his much-discussed *Catching Fire* (2010). Wrangham's argument boils down to cooking being the central motor of human evolution since its discovery, which he dates to approximately

1.8 million years ago.[17] It was the discovery of cooking, not warfare or some other social process, not even meat eating, that drove the changes from Habilines (*Homo habilis*) to *Homo erectus;* and it was improvements in cooking that led to more recent evolutionary changes. This is because the energy unlocked in cooked food and the time saved in digestion freed up human creative capacity for brain growth and, eventually, complex social relations. His arguments seem impressive, but when it comes to speculating on the implications of cooking for human social structure, Wrangham is on shakier grounds in claiming that the supposed universal division of labor in which men hunt and women cook was a necessary adaptation, which he describes as a "primitive protection racket" in which "having a husband ensures that a woman's gathered foods will not be taken by others; having a wife ensures the man will have an evening meal" (2010, 154). While I will be considering the implications of cooking for gender relations on Kalymnos in what follows, I part company with Wrangham's deterministic views of the implications of evolution on social structure to which his speculations (and indeed, they are speculations, as no evidence of social structure of *Homo erectus* is available) lead him.

Jack Goody, by contrast, focuses on social processes that have structured cooking over the past several millennia in Europe, Asia, and Africa. In his *Cooking, Cuisine and Class,* Goody makes an argument for the importance of key structural factors in shaping cooking, factors to which he has given attention in his many other works on the development of various societies. These factors include environmental and technological ones, such as the role of writing and cookbooks, hoe versus plow agriculture, and the preservation processes that allowed for the development of the food industry in the late nineteenth century. They also include the importance of class difference in allowing for the development of elite cuisines that were significantly different in *quality* rather than just in quantity, and indeed reflected other divisions of society conceptually and socially into "the high and the low" (Goody 1982, 97).

One would be wrong to claim that cooking has been ignored by anthropologists, and indeed if we broaden our terms from cooking to food in general, no one doubts that the study of food goes back to the very beginnings of the discipline.[18] However, despite the central place that scholars give to cooking in the story of what it means to be human, it's clear that for a long time the process of cooking simply did not pose any interesting *ethnographic* questions to the majority of anthropologists, and one can find no ethnographies with cooking as their central subject in the anthropological literature up to the turn of the twenty-first century. In part this could no doubt be laid at the feet of the tendency of male ethnographers simply to ignore activities associated with women. Western feminism's ambivalence about cooking—seen as simply another domestic chore like cleaning the bathroom, a source of oppression—meant that the rise of feminist anthropology in the mid-1970s didn't lead to any noticeable growth in studies of cooking. Indeed, pioneer feminist anthropologist Michelle Rosaldo, in claiming that "the wives of herders, agriculturalists and businessmen lead lives that are conceptualized in remarkably similar terms" (Rosaldo 1974, 29 n. 8), seemed to imply that "domestic" activities were relatively uninteresting anthropologically speaking, and it was only when women stepped into the so-called "public sphere" that they became involved in socially valued activities of "articulat[ing] and express[ing] social differences" (29).[19]

As feminists in anthropology and other fields began challenging the distinction between public and private, showing repeatedly how it does not capture the fluidity of people's lives, kitchen activities became a subject worthy of scrutiny. The key question that emerged was, Is cooking a source of women's oppression or empowerment? The answers were diverse depending on context, circumstance, and approach. In some cases cooking was an activity that brought women together and allowed them to extend their social networks and gain influence far beyond the immediate family; while in others cooking, even when it traveled beyond the home, was part of women's isolation from generally valued social goods, a chore and a task that men and other cultural agents could demand of women, and judge their failure to comply.[20] More recently, various scholars have shown the ways that cooking can be simultaneously oppressive *and* a "recipe for agency" (Counihan 2010, 128; see also Meah 2013). A number of scholars have avoided an either-or approach and begun to explore the potential of the kitchen as women's space for social commentary and for the transmission of personal and family histories.[21] Feminist social historians have drawn our attention to the ways cooking has become part of public discourse in the nineteenth and twentieth centuries, and to the gender, class, and race assumptions deeply embedded in many of the ways that cooking has been publicly framed in the United States in cookbooks and other popular media. These social historians have also pointed to the ways that cooking has been used, contradictorily, by women such as Fannie Farmer and Julia Child who were making claims to public authority and value.[22]

What I take from this previous scholarship is the need to pay attention to the contexts in which cooking occurs, both in the sense of the social relationships (gendered, generational) that surround cooking, and in the sense of the larger context of cultural values and public and media discourses that frame cooking choices and ideas about what makes for "proper food" and "good food." In any particular setting there may be competing values such as "healthy food," "fresh food," "tasty food," "convenient food," "traditional food," and "modern food," and how these different, often contradictory values play out in people's practices is a complex process for ethnographic exploration.[23] Finally, cooking may be about power, but it is not only about power between men and women; it also plays out among women (and among men) in intergenerational, neighborly, friendship, and other relations. And cooking is clearly *not only* about power, but expresses many different, culturally defined values including love, solidarity, control, creativity, joy, disdain, and friendly competition.[24] While my earlier work on Kalymnos tended to see women's intrafamily relationships as largely ones of solidarity, as mothers and daughters often cooperated against "outsider" husbands, exploring cooking has led me to a more complex view of female relationships and their multiple, shifting aspects.

Recently, studies have begun to explore the kitchen itself as a space of cultural contestation, and of processes of identity and memory formation—"kitchenspace" as Christie (2006, 2008) dubs it—while recognizing that this space may extend beyond the boundaries of the kitchen proper to "the indoor and outdoor spaces of food preparation" (Christie 2006, 654). Some cognitive scientists have looked at the workings of different sorts of semantic, biographical, and habit memory in the kitchen,[25] while cultural studies scholars have explored some of the ways that the design of technology and the material form of kitchen objects can shape their meanings and usages, as well as the memories associated with these objects. For example, Louise Purbrick's study of preservation practices associated with the objects used in cooking and serving food shows how considerations of materiality can open up onto wider social histories. She suggests this in exploring the introduction of Pyrex into British postwar homes. Through its ability to move between the kitchen and the dining room, to be used for cooking *and* for serving, Pyrex was integral in people's experience of a "servantless" home, in which women were supposed to experience labor as a kind of leisure, part of "a new propriety; it was a material expression of twentieth century ideologies of the good home that modernized, rationalized and to a certain extent a [sic] democratized without entirely abandoning, the past ideals of domesticity" (2007, 74).[26]

In my own cooking research in southern Illinois I worked with my student Michael Hernandez to explore how kitchen tools can become biographical objects that people use to tell their stories of their lives. We looked at the ways that objects like steel knives and cast-iron pans, because they both endure and change with time, seem to be apt vehicles for people to chart their own changing relationship with cooking and the larger social worlds that cooking indexed. We treated these objects as fetishes, in the positive sense of fetishism as a recognition of the "spirit in things" or the mixing of human and nonhuman intentionalities. We also began to think about cooking tools as ways of extending the human body into the world, and how the body itself becomes a tool in cooking, themes that I develop further in the present work.[27]

Recently, a number of scholars have made cooking the focus of book-length ethnographies. Jean-Claude Kaufmann (2010), for example, shows how questions of choice versus tradition are mediated through people's cooking practices in France, while Frances Short (2006) makes the case for a much wider definition of cooking to reflect the ways that people balance and negotiate multiple household demands in the process of providing family sustenance in Britain. Meredith Abarca describes how Mexican women employ "twists" in "making their distinctive meals original to them at the time of their invention" (2004, 10; see also Fertaly 2012). Abarca (2006) and Joy Adapon (2008) both use the concept of *sazón* to look at the cultural value given to the sense of taste in Mexico, and how in producing taste women can project their agency onto the wider world, even when marginalized economically, socially, or otherwise.

I have drawn on all these approaches in thinking about my own project. I believe that my innovation on these previous approaches is in focusing methodologically not only on the rich materials available from interview methods, but in adding to this the insights gleaned through long hours spent observing in Kalymnian kitchens, which allow me to analyze more directly the practices that others have relied on informant description to examine.[28] The point of observation, of course, is not that it is more objective than what people say, nor certainly is it to judge people's cooking against some explicit or implicit external standard (or even a self-imposed external standard), but to be able to gain a sense of how Kalymnians' diverse goals and values are reflected in and modified by their practices, their skilled use of tools and technology, their relation to previous iterations of any particular dish (written, passed down orally, seen on TV), and their relation to their kitchen as a space or an environment for cooking. This brings me to questions of methodology.

RECIPES FOR METHODS

Recent food scholarship has drawn on notions such as "food-centered life history," or more generally "food voice," which express experiences and viewpoints of women and others who tend to not leave traces in official discourses and records.[29] I have drawn on these notions, but my approach is both more general and more specific. More generally, cooking is integrated into daily life in diffuse and often surprising ways as Kalymnian women balance the myriad daily demands of family life and the many, often unexpected, exigencies and opportunities that arise. A discussion of cooking suddenly morphs into memories of World War II, a critique of politicians, a comparison or contrast with "the Turks," or an exegesis of religious themes. In light of my longstanding research on Kalymnos, I have tried to follow these conversations where they lead at times, in order to give a sense of the wider embedding of cooking in various aspects of Kalymnian social life rather than focus only on individual "life histories" through food. However, I have been interested in particular in intrafamily dynamics, and how cooking shapes not only relations among grandmothers, mothers, daughters, husbands, sons, and so on, but also how different life transitions are experienced through cooking: a daughter getting married and leaving the island, a mother dying, a young girl maturing while staying home or going off to college, men giving up migration patterns to "settle" on Kalymnos. Cooking practices can illuminate our understanding of these intrafamily dynamics and life stages.

Researchers interested in the anthropology of skill and the senses have pointed to the importance of digital video for capturing "the significance of repetitive but skilled action, and of . . . embodied technical knowledge."[30] No doubt video has its own particular implications that one has to be aware of. Katerina Miha, a teenager, always talked about my cooking videos in terms of the TV cooking shows she was familiar with, and the first time we made a video of her cooking, she tried to mimic the style of the leading Greek cooking show host, Vefa Alexiadou. The first time I turned on the camera, Nina—a middle-aged Kalymnian American woman—told me explicitly, "I don't want to talk into this thing." But my request to pretend it wasn't there seemed to mollify her, so that she never hesitated afterward. She did like to reflect in amazement on the idea that her kitchen had been seen "at Harvard" when I presented my research to a seminar there. Polykseni, a schoolteacher, used the video to give a formal statement about her respect for the research I have done on Kalymnos before getting down to the business of cooking. Rinyo, a middle-aged office worker, simply said she didn't want to be filmed, but would discuss her cooking practices while I used a voice recorder. By and large, however, I found that my subjects seemed to settle quickly into their routines as if the camera were not there, perhaps a reflection of how ubiquitous video cameras have become on Kalymnos.

I was grateful that some Kalymnians allowed me to film intimate scenes, such as some women cooking in their nightgowns. This reflected the fact, as well, that almost all of my subjects were Kalymnians whom I have known over a period of twenty years or more. I was not a stranger invading their homes with my camera, but a known presence among the families with whom I worked. Nevertheless, I remain conscious of the trust that my subjects have placed in me in allowing me such intimate access to their private domestic spaces, a trust I didn't want to betray by displaying scenes of family conflict for any casual YouTube viewer. At the same time, Kalymnians take considerable pleasure in the thought that their opinions will be transmitted to a wider world beyond the island, a reflection of notions of locality and globality and ideas about the role of hospitality in "bringing the world to our table" that I have analyzed in my previous work.[31]

WHAT FOLLOWS . . .

Jean Lave, reflecting on her long ethnographic engagement with questions of learning among Liberian tailors, writes that contrary to the notion that there is an identifiable relation between masters and apprentices, those who know and those who don't know, in fact "we are all apprentices, engaged in learning to do what we are already doing. . . . Further, learning to act on the basis of any craft, and for that matter, any problematic, requires practice to come to inhabit the practice and its conception of the world" (2011, 156). In approaching cooking as a deeply valued skill for Kalymnians, and as an ethnographic subject for myself, I am trying in this book to reflect a sense of daily practice that is always fluid, fraught with challenges that are culturally embedded in particular social, technical, aesthetic, and sensory worlds. Developing skill in the kitchen is a project without an end point, just as developing ethnographic understanding is a project that can yield only temporary satisfactions, ongoing questions, and new challenges. Through the various approaches I take in this book I am trying to capture this sense of cooking as a *skilled practice,* and examine what that might mean for its role and significance in Kalymnian lives. However, *capture* itself is the wrong word, for how to write about cooking skill without objectifying it into the very types of static and solid knowledge associated with formal education and capital C Culture? How does one trace relations of memory, identity, and the present without falling into sterile dichotomies—"Cooking is dead," "No, it's just changing"—of "tradition" and "modernity," the "global" and the "local"?

In the chapters that follow I alternate between general considerations of topics—the kitchen as an environment for practice, recipes and cooking shows, the politics of cooking knowledge or skill and its transmission—and sections focused on the specific stories of Kalymnian families, as seen through their daily cooking and its transformation over time as family members change roles, gain or lose knowledge, and view their cooking practice in different lights. These sections are not meant to alternate between general analysis and particular stories, or to reproduce invidious distinctions between the "analytical" and the "evocative." Rather, sections based on more general considerations are meant to provide contexts and comparisons, while individual stories will give a sense of the ways that Kalymnians live this shared background, and of some of ways that cooking practices transform through time. These may take the form of minor alterations—a new ingredient or technique added to an old recipe—or major breaks: a new outdoor oven or a death in the family. I think that both these minor and major transformations (as well as the repetitions that accompany them) are important in trying to get at a sense of the flow of people's everyday lives.

In the end, cooking is important because it is clearly tied up with cultural reproduction. Cooking is a process that involves knowledges: explicit verbal knowledges of recipes and ingredients as well as embodied knowledges of techniques and "tricks." Does cooking knowledge simply "pass from mother to daughter," a phrase that rolls off the tongue of many of my informants? Or is it filled with breaks, gaps, inventions, rediscoveries, and renewals, just like the secret male ritual knowledge much studied by anthropologists? How Kalymnians manage to produce what is recognizable to them as Kalymnian food while still incorporating all kinds of new tools, techniques, and ingredients is at the very heart of understanding the role of identity, memory, and embodied knowledge in the process of cultural transmission and transformation.

CHAPTER I

Emplacing Cooking

This chapter provides a short background sketch of life on Kalymnos in order to set the stage for my subsequent explorations of cooking. I develop ideas about food provisioning through some of my more recent ethnographic explorations of shopping and gifting on Kalymnos, and also briefly describe some aspects of Kalymnian marriage and family life relevant to thinking about cooking. Finally, I take a look at some of the key values that frame Kalymnian cooking discourses and practices.

Kalymnos has always been known for its barrenness, which, while not inimical to agriculture entirely, made agriculture secondary to sources of livelihood from the sea. While the days of the Kalymnian sponge trade, having been in decline since the 1970s, are now almost completely a memory (a "bitter" one at that [Warn 2000]), various sorts of fishing and especially the merchant marine continue to be options for those Kalymnians (men, almost exclusively) called by the sea. During my research in the 1990s, tourism was a much smaller part of the economy than it was on many of the neighboring Dodecanese islands, yet a number of factors have increased the visibility of tourism on Kalymnos during the first decade of the twenty-first century. The completion of an airport on the island means that it no longer requires a fourteen-hour boat ride from Athens to reach Kalymnos, though flights to Kalymnos so far are only from Athens. A spectacular discovery of fifth century B.C. artifacts in 2001 and the subsequent construction of a beautiful

EU-funded museum have also raised the tourist profile of the island. But perhaps the biggest impact on tourism has been the discovery of Kalymnos in the late 2000s by rock climbers, which has led to the staging of a yearly rock-climbing festival that draws renowned climbers from all over the world to the island, converting Kalymnos's legendarily arid landscape into a money-making attraction. As one Kalymnian whose wife owned a restaurant and pension noted, Kalymnos is one of the few places in the world where you can climb imposing cliffs by day and relax in the Aegean Sea in the evening. Kalymnos, which had been unknown to all but the most dedicated tourists, was getting all kinds of press from rock climbing, even an article with spectacular pictures in the in-flight magazine for Lufthansa as I flew from the United States to Athens. Kalymnians were promoting their local attractions, not only the landscape and rock-climbing opportunities offered by no other island, but also Kalymnian restaurants. I remember attending a seminar in 2008 sponsored by the Kalymnian restaurant association that encouraged restaurateurs to feature the preparations they had offered all along as "local"—like the Kalymnian version of a Greek "village salad" known as *mermizeli*.[1] By 2011 Kalymnian preparations were being featured in slow-food cookbooks, and several cooking shows (both Greek and American) had devoted segments or whole programs to Kalymnian specialties.

These new tourist opportunities notwithstanding, Kalymnos was feeling the pinch of the financial crisis in 2011. The main street of Kalymnos was littered with closed stores, mainly clothing stores. Kalymnians who had always had worked in the building industry or in the mayor's office were laid off. Increasing numbers of Kalymnians were following the long-hallowed tradition of migration from the island to Australia (the United States seemed to be drying up as a migrant destination), and some suggested to me that the population had dipped to nine thousand, draining the young from the island.[2] The main Kalymnians moving in the other direction seemed to be women moving back to the island because they had inherited property (matrilineally, see below) that could be turned into tourist accommodations.[3] One twenty-five-year-old told me that he had lucked into a job that spring, otherwise he would have joined many of his friends in seeking work in Australia. Some older Kalymnians had acquired Australian passports, even if not seeking work, because they looked to Australia as a backup if life in Greece became intolerable.

MATRIFOCALITY AND THE KALYMNIAN KITCHEN

Kalymnos shows a pattern shared through much of the Dodecanese island chain of matrilocal residence and matrilineal inheritance, practices that I traced in my earlier research in terms of their implications for female power (Sutton 1998). And while Kalymnos does have some "public" versus "domestic" distinctions, they are extremely blurry, with women taking an active role in the religious, economic, and political life of the island. And this is not a recent phenomenon (see Sutton 1999). One ongoing puzzle in my studies of Kalymnos was to understand the origins and role of female primogeniture in island life. This inheritance system was distinctive to Kalymnos and possibly a few other neighboring islands, and always intrigued me.[4] In my scholarly reading and talk with colleagues and specialists, I've become convinced that this may be the only place in the world with such an inheritance system, or at least the only one that has been recorded. So I was curious about how this "custom," as people referred to it on Kalymnos—the "custom of the first daughter"—might have influenced gender relations in the past. Equally intriguing was how its memory (it officially ended in 1948 after the Dodecanese became part of Greece, though with a slower diminution of the practice during the course of the second half of the twentieth century), often expressed in the claim "We used to have matriarchy on the island," might still have influences on people's practices. While such puzzles remain for me, what I found clearly was that the practice of giving the entire family inheritance to the first-born daughter (who also takes the name of the maternal grandmother) established a pattern of and a model for powerful women on Kalymnos that shaped life on the island for several centuries at least.[5]

I realized how much things had changed, however, in 2011 when talking with a woman in her twenties with two young boys. She told me that she was done with childbearing, and that there was no need to "make the daughter." When I asked about carrying on the grandmother's name, she dismissed this idea as the thinking of "the old mind-set," noting that she and her husband were happy with two boys, and that they would try to build houses for them when they grew up but it wasn't necessary: "If you have you give, but if you don't, there's nothing wrong with renting."

While first-daughter inheritance is now a memory, certain patterns remain that distinguish the island from mainland Greece, including a more equal inheritance of names between the mother's and the father's side than in patrilineal areas, and a strong matrilocal bias in postmarital residence. Mothers and daughters ideally still live together, sharing a large living space between two (or sometimes more) separate but interconnected households. Husbands enter the family as outsiders, and grandmothers, mothers, and daughters are, in many cases, allies in family struggles against fathers or husbands in family decisions about marital, financial, or other issues (Sutton 1998, chap. 5). This can play in interesting ways into cooking practices, where cooperation, negotiation, and affection can come up against claims to authority, hierarchy, and power, not just across genders but between women in the family. The current research project, which got me observing daily cooking in a much more detailed way than I had even in my earlier book about food and memory on Kalymnos, revealed family conflicts and tensions, as well as cooperation and alliances that I hadn't noticed in my earlier studies.

A brief description of the typical Kalymnian kitchen is in order. However, it's important to be aware that this is very much an ideal-typical description; as we'll see, Kalymnians negotiate their own practice in diverse ways. Nonetheless, it's also important to note that all Kalymnians seem to be aware of typical patterns and define their own practice in relation to what "other people" do. In some cases mothers and daughters live together but cook separately; in other cases they may live at a distance but still share meals. In most cases, actual practice combines some separation and some sharing of cooking and meals. The description I give here is of cases in which mothers and daughters are living adjacent to each other, sharing some parts of the living space, while other parts remain somewhat separated (for example, the mother may very rarely enter the daughter's bedroom).

As people's economic means expanded in the period from the 1970s to the early 2000s, they may have built more elaborate living areas with more "modern" furnishings, but they did not abandon many of their previous living arrangements, in particular the shared, two-family setup. In such a shared living space, the mother's kitchen may be quite small: a space large enough for a sink, a refrigerator, a small table, a wall cabinet for plates, and a two-burner stove run off a gas bottle. It is usually a small room separated from the main living area. Alternatively, a shack outside the house might be used as a primary area for processing and cooking, or a simple covered area that opens up into a courtyard could be used. The daughter's kitchen, by contrast, can be quite large, on the first floor of the daughter's living area, and typically is not a room separated by a divider, but opens on to a larger living space. The daughter's kitchen will include a full stove and oven, and a large amount of counter space with cabinets above and below. The mother's kitchen uses wall space for storage of pots, pans, implements, and often plates. By contrast, the daughter's kitchen will have those items placed in cabinets, and will instead use wall and counter space for decorative items, or sometimes for a kind of display of the tools of past generations.

What this setup in some cases allows is for the mother's kitchen to be the primary everyday kitchen for processing and cooking heavy, full meals, and the daughter's kitchen to be much more used for lighter, occasional cooking, cooking of sweets or casseroles, which use the oven, and the making of snacks and coffee. Because the mother's kitchen tends to be outside the house proper, the smells associated with cooking or cleaning fish, and the dirt associated with processing the food, do not enter the living space, which is, therefore, easy to prepare for visitors.

Aside from kitchen spaces, many Kalymnian homes have some outdoor courtyard area that can be used for processing food—cleaning fish, cutting up potatoes, cleaning lamb entrails for Easter soup. This may be a multifunction area, used to hang sheets and other laundry, as a garden, or as a space to keep animals of various kinds (goats, sheep, chickens, or hunting dogs being the most typical). This outdoor area allows Kalymnian women to process food for cooking while engaged in other activities: socializing with family and neighbors, taking care of other tasks, or keeping an ear open for an itinerant merchant. Such spaces have also been used in recent years for the building of an outdoor oven, a topic that I explore further on.

How much time is spent on cooking activities during the course of the day? Because of the multifunctional and social spaces in which Kalymnians process and cook their food, there is no clear answer to this as there is (implicitly) in typical recipes in the United States that specify time to the minute—fifteen minutes of preparation time, twenty minutes of cooking time, and so on. A typical Kalymnian main meal may begin the night before with planning for the next day and, often enough, the soaking of dry beans overnight for cooking the next day. Preparation of ingredients goes on amid a series of other activities—cleaning, caring for elderly family members, socializing with neighbors, overseeing children's activities, or making a quick trip to the neighborhood church to tend the family graves. Also, because cooking activities may be shared among two or more family members, a woman may run off on an errand, leaving her daughter or granddaughter to tend to the pots, or a man may take fish out into his workroom outside the main house for cleaning before his wife cooks them. Coffee and snacks are also constantly being prepared throughout the day to supplement the main meal (or meals, depending on whether a smaller evening meal is prepared).

I observed that time for food preparation was the most focused when one woman was the primary cook for the household and all preparation was done in an indoor kitchen space. Here one could develop concentration on a particular activity; in such cases, cooking a meal generally took from one to two hours. However, this situation was more the exception in my observations. (I consider one such example in detail in chapter 6, in the section on Popi Galanou.) I observed one family preparing a typical Sunday meal of stewed fish, moussaka, and salad. The meat sauce for the moussaka was prepared the evening before, taking one person just under an hour. The main preparations for the meal involved the activities of a husband, wife, wife's mother, and two daughters in steady, if not constant activity for slightly under three hours (the moussaka was cooked in an outdoor oven, which required considerable preparation and tending). While Sunday is an unusual meal, everyday meals also tend to involve at least several hours of labor time if they are done by a single person. Thus the contrast seems particularly striking, for Kalymnians, between homemade food, and preprepared frozen food, which has recently become available in supermarkets. The latter, most Kalymnians insisted, was simply an unacceptable substitute for the main meal of the day, though it might occasionally be used for a snack or an evening meal.

The significant time invested in cooking (not to mention provisioning, discussed below) enables one to suggest the *value* of cooking to Kalymnians, a theme I will return to. As David Graeber, following Nancy Munn, argues: "Value emerges in action; it is the process by which a person's invisible 'potency'—their capacity to act—is transformed into concrete, perceptible forms. . . . One invests one's energies in those things one considers most important, or most meaningful" (Graeber 2001, 45). It is the shared sense that cooking *matters* to Kalymnian women and men that makes for its value and for the realization of that value in concrete, perceptible forms, in this case the synesthetically pleasing cooked meal.

THE KALYMNIAN MEAL

Kalymnian main dishes are made up of beans or meat or fish and vegetables cooked in a "red" sauce of tomatoes, garlic, onions, and parsley or celery. These dishes are supplemented with fish prepared as a soup, fried, or grilled. These meals will always be cooked in generous amounts of olive oil and served with fresh bread (typically bought daily) to soak up the oil and sauce. Little had changed in this regard since my field-work in the 1990s (see Sutton 1997, 2001). Sunday is when special meals are typically prepared, and the most typical Sunday meal remains grape leaves, stuffed with rice and ground beef and covered with an egg-lemon sauce. These stuffed grape leaves—called *filla*—are common throughout Greece, but their centrality in the Kalymnian diet has led people to refer to them as the "Kalymnian national dish." Sunday is also a day when one might make a dish that takes more time, such as mous-saka or pastitsio (pasta and meat with a béchamel sauce). This might also be the time to make a spinach, mushroom, cheese, or other filled "pie" (*pita*), something that was more of a rarity twenty years earlier but that had increasingly become part of the regular repertoire of Kalymnian cooks in the 2000s.

Other common meals typically found in the weekly cycle include pasta with tomato sauce (with or without meat) and various cuts of meat and sausages. This main meal of the day, taken in the early after-noon, is supplemented during the course of the day by all kinds of snacks, often based on a special find of greens from a local vendor, a catch of fish, or a snail-hunting expedition.[6] The evening meal some-times involves leftovers, but otherwise would be something quick to prepare like fried eggs and potatoes or an omelet. Cheese, olives, and seasonal fruit are almost always consumed throughout the day as part of meals or snacks. The Kalymnian meal would be recognizable to most non-Kalymnian Greeks as typical "Greek food," with some variations, of course. While the first decade of the 2000s hadn't brought any radical changes to this diet, there were a number of interesting shifts, which I discuss in the course of the book. However, as I argued in my earlier work, there remains the sense of a recognizable, shared Kalymnian cui-sine against which variations can be evaluated and judged.

SHOPPING AND PROVISIONING

An essay included in the application to UNESCO in support of the nomination of the "Mediterranean diet" as part of the World Intangible Cultural Heritage—submitted by communities in Greece, Italy, Spain, and Morocco—states, "In Chefchaouen, Cilento, Koroni or Soria, the market—where sales are sometimes less important than bargaining—

represents a special place for socialization and for the recreation and transmission of the Mediterranean Diet. The market is also an essential cultural space of conviviality between the landscape and cuisine, which combines commercial, leisure and cultural activities and contributes to the exchanges and the daily rebuilding of identity."[7] Kalymnos certainly has none of the sense of the bazaar, filled with all manner of foods, entertainers, and other delights, that is suggested in this somewhat stereotypical description of a "Mediterranean" marketplace. But the basic insight of this paragraph, that shopping is deeply embedded in social relations, holds true on Kalymnos.

Yet it also needs to be unpacked if it is to move beyond the stereotypes of the Western imagination or the potential self-exoticization of the preceding statement. What does it mean to say that shopping is "social" on Kalymnos? Perhaps both more and less than is captured in the quotation above (about which more is said in the next section). So, how do people shop on Kalymnos and, more broadly, how do they provision themselves to prepare meals?

In my earlier research I was struck by what I called the "agonistic" nature of shopping on Kalymnos, in which Kalymnians used their knowledge of prices to get the best deal and to avoid being taken advantage of. I showed that despite the importance of shrewdness, Kalymnians were not the maximizing rational actors of economics textbooks, as the fruits of good bargaining were often turned into openhanded generosity toward neighbors and strangers, and Kalymnians were horrified at the idea that someone would try to make a profit off someone they knew (Sutton 2001, 21ff.). I remember this lesson being brought home to me one day after I had been living on Kalymnos for more than a year (in 1993) when I went to the village of Vathi, which I had visited only infrequently as it was on the other side of the island. There I found a store selling rugs and decided to buy a number of them as gifts for friends back home. After exercising my growing bargaining skills to negotiate with the store owner what I felt to be a fair price, I paid him. But as I was waiting for the bus to go back to the main town, we fell to chatting. At some point he asked about what I was doing on Kalymnos, and I told him that I had lived here with my family for more than a year and that I had made many trips to the island since my first visit as a study-abroad student. On hearing this he visibly blanched. He ran to his cash register and reached in; grabbing out a couple a small notes, he shoved them into my hand, telling me that it was so I wouldn't think that he was trying to profit off someone "from the island." Then he insisted that while I wait for the bus I share a coffee with him, to make sure I had no question about his good character.

While there are a number of aspects of this exchange that could be explored, the key thing I want to stress here is that shopping is very much considered to be a *moral* act on Kalymnos. David Graeber has argued to good effect that in most societies, even advanced capitalist ones, only a portion of people's transactions of goods should be considered "exchange," in the sense of an equivalent transaction in which each side "gives as good as it gets" and the relationship can be ended at any time. Many of our transactions partake of an "everyday communism" in which ongoing relations are assumed and no strict account is kept (families are typically "communistic" in this sense; see Graeber 2011, 94–105).

The moral aspects of shopping have become in some ways more obvious on Kalymnos in the first decade of the twenty-first century with the growth of multinational supermarkets on the island, the implications of which are fiercely debated. Prior to the early 2000s there were small, neighborhood grocery stores, along with specialty stores for fruits and vegetables, meat, and fish, as well as itinerant sellers of fruits and vegetables, bread, and other items. Finally, there were many opportunities for special purchases of bulk items like smuggled olive oil from Turkey, cheese produced on other islands, or fish caught by friends and neighbors, as well as shopping excursions to neighboring islands to pick grape leaves, for example. There were small supermarkets that might carry multiple types of products, but these were also locally owned, and many were in fact not substantially larger than, nor necessarily different in pricing from, most of the neighborhood shops. While this shopping landscape had its own complexities, a new dimension was added to shopping after 2000 by the opening of more than a dozen large supermarkets—some locally owned, but others either owned by non-Kalymnian Greeks or locally owned franchises. These businesses use circulars and other promotional devices to advertise their prices and sale items.

Let's take a look at some of the competing pushes and pulls of Kalymnian shopping, first through a discussion that I had about the opening of these new stores with Dionysios, a Kalymnian man in his early eighties, and his niece Nina (his wife's sister's daughter and the subject of chapter 3). Dionysios lived in the United States for roughly thirty years, working as a shoemaker in the Kalymnian community in Campbell, Ohio. With his wife and two daughters he traveled back and forth, spending time on Kalymnos in the late 1970s and then living in Athens, where his daughters were working, for much of the 1980s. At the end of that decade he returned for good to Kalymnos, where he continued to work out of his house as a shoemaker until he retired in the late 1990s. We began with a discussion of different techniques for preparing octopus stew, in which he was comparing the benefits of removing the sea water from the octopus and adding salt, versus cooking it in the salty sea water. I asked Dionysios whether he participated in the cooking and shopping in his household, and this led into a discussion of his shopping preferences and his feeling that the new stores needed to be rejected. But what started as a monologue quickly turned into a debate as Nina jumped in to dispute his claims.

> *Dionysios:* The big supermarkets, because they have a lot of money, put their prices a dime [*mia dhekara*] lower. They collect all the people's money that they get and they take it off the island—to Switzerland, who knows where—and force the little Kalymnian-owned stores to close. I have a friend—
>
> *Nina:* You're looking out for your friend, but it's not benefiting your wallet.
>
> *Dionysios:* Hold on a second. I have a friend. You have a friend too who has a grocery store—
>
> *Nina:* He's not my friend.
>
> *Dionysios:* —and for the ten cents that I will lose, should my friend close his shop and be destroyed? We need to support him, because the money that he will get [from people shopping] or that your friend will get will circulate here, they'll buy a house, they'll build something, they'll do something.
>
> *Nina* [*switching to English*]: Your friend doesn't even pay rent and he's still more expensive.
>
> *Dionysios:* I can't watch my friend destroyed to gain a dime. Let me give up my dime to support my friend and my countryman [*getting heated*] and so that the money remains here, so it doesn't go to Germany and who knows where and people go hungry here.
>
> *Nina:* Yeah, yeah.
>
> *Dionysios:* This is my philosophy, I don't know what you think [*in English*]: I don't care for ten cents. . . . Better to support my friend and to lose each week, what do you call them? One euro.
>
> *Nina:* You don't lose one euro.
>
> *Dionysios* [*waving his hand*]: Two euros.
>
> *Nina:* Higher.
>
> *Dionysios* [*waving his hand*]: Three euros.
>
> *Nina:* Are you willing to lose ten?

Dionysios: Yeah, even forty.

Nina [mixing Greek and English]: He's expensive. One example, from the neighborhood—

Dionysios: I don't care. I'm supporting my fellow countryman and—

Nina: What do you mean? I'm not going to foreigners, I'm going to locals. To the Source [a Kalymnian-owned supermarket].

Dionysios: The Source is cheaper?

Nina: A thousand times cheaper. Your friend is the most expensive in Kalymnos.

Dionysios: You're wrong.

They argued about the prices of different items at different stores on Kalymnos, with Nina insisting that her uncle's friend's shop was "on fire" with its high prices, even more expensive than the small neighborhood stores (which are expected to have higher prices than the supermarkets). Nina gave the example of a can of milk being ten cents higher, and Dionysios said again, It's only a dime. Nina insisted that you buy milk twice a week, so it adds up.

Dionysios: In any case, my friendship and my honor, I'm not selling it for a better price.

Nina: But he owns the building, and he doesn't even have to pay employees since he and his wife work in the shop. At least he could have things the same price as the *neighborhood* grocery stores.

Here they had a heated exchange questioning who had the prices right, with both insisting that they'd carefully compared. Nina pointed out that her aunt—Dionysios's wife—shops at the non-Kalymnian supermarket, because it's much cheaper than the one he goes to. Dionysios said, "How would she know, since she doesn't shop at my friend's?" Nina replied, "Well, she sees the prices of the things you bring home."

Dionysios: My wife shops at Vidali [a supermarket owned by a non-Kalymnian Greek from Tinos]. But she tells me she goes there because it's big and it allows her to get a break from the everyday routine. She thinks that she's back in America. The big stores. She feels better—

David: It reminds her of America?

Dionysios [laughing]: Such are people's idiosyncrasies.

What I initially took as a (to me) familiar discourse on the importance of buying locally reveals itself to be more complex. It is not simply that Dionysios wants to support local merchants over transnational corporations, a kind of anti–Wal-Mart action, while Nina wants to get the best price. Rather, Dionysios wants to support his friend who is a member of his community, and whose children will continue to contribute to the life of the island. So we are talking about cultural reproduction here at a fundamental level. Later Dionysios told me that he and his friend have the same "profession" or "hobby"—he used both words—that of cantor in the neighborhood church, so he is supporting someone who, for him, is completely integrated into local life. This kind of particular knowledge was very prevalent in people's explanations of how they spread their grocery custom around. Some of the reasons for patronizing the different neighborhood grocery stores that different people told me included

1. The husband recently died, so we should support the family by shopping there.
2. The family are known communists, so some people don't shop there. I feel like I should help them out to make up for this.
3. I shop from the people at the grocery store up the street who are struggling to make a life for their family [*viopalestes*], whereas the one closer by is rich, he has bought property in Athens with all the money he has made off his customers. He is also a Greek from Turkey [Boudroumianos]. Those people are smart, but they also are always putting making money first.
4. I shop at the store where the owner was a fellow student with my aunt [who lived with her], because I always felt a connection to her.
5. There is a common practice on Kalymnos now of shopping from supermarkets for some items, but hiding the bags as you walk through the neighborhood so that the local grocery-store owner will not see that you have shopped somewhere else.

These examples all stress connections of different kinds, and highlight the fact that shopping on Kalymnos, as I learned with the rug merchant, is not exclusively or perhaps even primarily about getting the best deal. Indeed, as Nina insists in her argument with Dionysios, it's not that she's trying to get the best price without considering other issues, it's that she feels that the store he shops at *takes advantage of* Kalymnians by putting the store's profits before the community. The important thing is to engage in socially embedded shopping, as is the case with all of these examples, while also not feeling that you are being taken advantage of. As always, this may be a matter of interpretation. One woman told me about how she wasn't intending to buy a lamb for Easter because her husband had died and she was only one person, but the butcher had called and said that he had a lamb with her husband's name on it (as they always bought from this butcher), so she had said, "Yes, I'll take it." It appeared to me that he was taking advantage of the widowed woman, but this was not how she seemed to interpret it; rather, she took the call as the butcher recognizing a good memory of the past Easters with her husband. It no doubt made a difference that since her husband had died, the butcher had often called to offer little favors to her, delivering not only his own products to her door (all butchers do this as a way of competing against the supermarkets), but also drinking water and whatever else she might need delivered.

Such negotiations also play out in the practice of rounding down measurements in favor of the customer, which is particularly done with the nondigital scales used by smaller stores and itinerant merchants. A fruit merchant selling to a regular customer, whose daughter was close friends with the seller's mother-in-law, rounded down the price of any item that was under 50 cents (and added in the price if it was over 50 cents).[8] He also passed on at no cost a number of fruits that were overripe, and when the final tally came to slightly over 41 euros he rounded it down to 40. Buyers expect to pay slightly more for the convenience of having the merchant come to their doorstep, but at the same time this woman expected that higher price to be balanced by special treatment, considering their ongoing familial relationship.

The same attitude—what I'm calling "socially embedded shopping"—is shared by the merchants themselves. For example, many of the smaller stores are in the habit of offering credit to known customers. The foreign-owned supermarkets do not do this, but some of the locally owned supermarkets do, partly because they know their customers so well. Credit is also offered by the itinerant fruit and vegetable sellers.

The word for credit—*verese*—evokes an old-fashioned practice associated with the days of sponge-diving on Kalymnos, when sponge divers would be gone for six to eight months out of the year and would be paid in one lump sum. In 2011 a number of people mentioned the "return" of *verese;* although it was never completely abandoned, this sense of return reflected the more dire circumstances of the economic crisis. Some store owners said that they offered it, but you had to be careful whom you offered it to. One local grocery store owner stopped carrying international phone cards because, he said, too many people were buying them on credit; he stopped carrying them rather than refuse people credit. An itinerant fruit and vegetable seller said that he would always give food to a hungry person, but he complained about giving credit to some people only to have them choose his best produce and then never buy from him again. "Kalymnians are generous, but they don't want to be taken advantage of," he noted, reflecting a sentiment shared among buyers and sellers. A neighborhood grocery store owner admitted that she was embarrassed about telling people the prices of items after the recent rounds of new taxes imposed by the Greek government. She was very aware that people were comparing prices with those at some of the big supermarkets, including ones from outside Greece, which could buy particularly cheaply because of their monopolies, and she was disturbed not that she would lose all her customers, as there were always people coming for some small purchase that they had forgotten, but *that her neighbors might think she was trying to make a profit off them.* She admitted that she could survive partly because she uses her house as her store space and doesn't pay employees, but this merely allows her to get by. "We used to live well, now we are the store of last resort," she said, speaking to the plight of many of the neighborhood groceries.

Dionysios's comment about his wife shopping at some of the big, foreign-owned supermarkets because she wanted to get a break from her day-to-day routine (and because it reminded her of America) was a not uncommon sentiment on Kalymnos. Particularly for older, married women, shopping was one of the few activities, aside from going to the church, that legitimately took them out of the home space, and so it was a way of taking a break from home stresses (*stenohories*).[9] Thus, women might go to a number of different stores for grocery shopping in order simultaneously to comparison-shop for bargains, fulfill obligations to different store owners, and let off steam or unwind.

The point, then, is that shopping is a multifaceted activity, only one piece of which involves any abstract calculation of value for money. This was true even in the face of the economic crisis in Greece in 2011. When I asked people about how they were responding to the crisis in terms of their shopping habits, some suggested a return to more beans in the diet (as opposed to meat), while others argued that the foreign supermarkets had opened up the possibility of getting many different cuts of meat, so that rather than reduce meat, families might buy cheaper, imported cuts. People noted that there were hazards to this as well, as you had to worry about the provenience and freshness of the meat sold at the foreign supermarkets. But they also commented that people were not as embarrassed about asking for a lower-quality product as they might have been in the past.

Others still suggested that there was something shameful about worrying too much about prices: rather like Dionysios, one older woman replied with a dismissive "pa, pa, pa" when I asked if she shopped at the big supermarkets in order to save money. In the practice of buying cheaper foreign meat we also see some of the conflicting values that might come into play in food choices: both the notion that local, Greek-produced food is superior (see below) and the idea that men have grown accustomed to eating meat and cannot go without—"It's a male thing, feed him some meat, and make it bloody!" (*agori prama einai vale na faei kreataki kai na ehei kai ligo aima*). One woman casually mentioned needing to add meat to a dish of green beans and potatoes she was making since the men would be home for lunch, and they would expect meat. As another woman put it to me simply, "My son-in-law would die without meat." On the other hand, eating too much meat is known to be unhealthy and is talked about in terms of some of the unhealthy changes from more "traditional" eating habits.[10] It is balancing such competing imperatives that makes shopping a constant topic of conversation, and sometimes of conflict, as we saw with Dionysios and Nina.

But there is another aspect of food shopping that I only half recognized in my earlier work. While I wrote about the ways that Kalymnians would try to get good deals in order to have more to share (with visitors, strangers, and sometimes neighbors), I didn't take in the extent to which shopping was only one piece of a more general system that, for many Kalymnians, involves constant multiple lines of "exchange"—though once again I'm using this word not to imply the kind of "equivalent exchange" of economics textbooks, but rather a sense of flows of debt and obligation.

Let me give one example of such flows: Angeliki (about whom more is said in chapter 6) is a widowed woman in her early seventies. Children of friends pass by her house on a regular basis and offer to carry anything heavy that she needs. She always keeps sweets of some kind on hand to offer to them. She makes twice-weekly trips to the cemetery in the center of the island to care for her family gravesites. A nephew fixes the headstone and refuses payment; she tells him to come for coffee whenever. She has a taxi driver whom she has known for a long time who insists that she call him to take her where she needs to go for a lower price. Angeliki often brings a beer or whatever else is at hand to give to him. She prefers this taxi driver because he has children to feed, while many others are single. When she is done she hitches a ride back on the main road. When cars pass without acknowledging her she shakes her head, laughing at the perceived slight. Within five minutes she is invariably picked up by someone—a priest, a family friend, the daughter of a woman who worked as a servant to her family, who had her stop at her house to give her a plant cutting that she had been wanting to pass on to her. Sometimes she takes the bus, noting that one particular bus driver will refuse to take a ticket from her because of the help her husband offered him when he worked in the mayor's office. She brings him cookies. Angeliki's daughter sends 50 euros a month for her to buy things for one of the local monasteries of Saint Katerina, where she often goes for different ceremonies, and where she knows many of the nuns. When they have too much of anything they redistribute it to another monastery, and there is also the "meal of love" that the church offers daily for poor and disabled Kalymnians. Angeliki holds the memorial ceremony for her husband at this monastery, and they never charge her for this service. Her neighbor who fixes appliances went to the monastery at her instigation to fix their refrigerator when it wasn't working, so when he held a memorial for his father there, they, of course, again refused to take any payment.

These were some of the exchanges that I recorded over an ordinary two-week period. At one point I asked Angeliki to keep track of all of the exchanges, but she was too embarrassed, saying that these are not things that you write down. I was trying to objectify and quantify these flows when the point was that no strict accounting should be kept—just as with the gesture of the rug-shop owner who didn't count the "discount" he offered me. I felt at that moment like anthropologist Richard Lee, who when trying to keep track of exchanges among his !Kung informants was finally told clearly, "You see, we don't trade with things, we trade with people" (cited in Cronk 1997, 160). As Graeber (2011, 386) notes, "The difference between owing someone a favor, and owing someone a debt, is that the amount of a debt can be precisely calculated."

This is not to say that there aren't many occasions for misunderstandings to arise that may strain or break relationships, and the theme of "ingratitude" or "betrayal" is never far from people's minds and lips.[11] But that doesn't keep people from continuing to build such relationships, which are, in fact, the very fabric of Kalymnian society. These types of acts are seen as a human ideal that all should strive to approach, coming as close as one can to the ideal of the gift of Christ.

Purely commercial relations are seen as lying at the opposite end of the spectrum, a turning of social relations into profit.[12] This contrast was brought home to me when a woman noticed a Gypsy trader eyeing the watermelon that she was serving to her family on a hot day. She told the trader that if she wanted to come join them, she should forget about her wares and come share their food and keep them company. It is in the context of this ethos of sharing and trust that people can speak of their choice to buy at the local grocery store as an "act of charity" (*elaiamosyni*).

FOOD VALUES

The preceding discussion of provisioning suggests how deeply embedded food is within systems of value. Scholars studying food and cooking "choices" have been interested in exploring the values that these choices express. Some have suggested schemes of key values, often in tension with each other, such as care versus convenience, economy versus extravagance, and novelty versus tradition (Warde 1997), or cost, convenience, health, and taste (Trubek n.d.). Others have suggested more general values expressed in food and cooking choices, such as love (Adapon 2008, 18ff.; Abarca 2006; Harper and Faccioli 2010) or family (Kaufmann 2010, 85), and within them more diverse expressions of values such as autonomy and intimacy versus tradition and discipline (Kaufmann 2010, 91). Kaufmann more broadly suggests overarching values such as a "passion" for cooking as an outgrowth of and response to "the deadly chill of reflexive modernity" (168). Kaufmann also usefully argues that values are never determinate because they are always deployed in relation to habits, desires, and (often unconscious) traditions.[13]

I am in strong agreement with the idea that values must be studied in relation to practices, rather than in the abstract, which is one of the reasons that I argue for a cooking ethnography that goes into kitchens to observe everyday cooking. With these provisos in mind, however, let's explore some of the key values that Kalymnians express in relation to food as a way of framing some of the issues we'll be looking at in greater detail in later chapters.

As already mentioned, in the autumn of 2010 the community of Koroni in mainland Greece, along with communities in three other countries, had their application to the UNESCO World Intangible Heritage Commission accepted for the "Mediterranean diet." In letters from some of the local organizations supporting the application we find the following statements:

1. We know that, in our times, globalization and the pace of life are such that other, more harmful foodstuffs dominate eating habits. The shift towards healthier eating habits and ways of life has become no longer a luxury but a necessity.

2. It is important to mention that the eating habits of our region and the associated habits, techniques and knowledge which our grandfathers and grandmothers handed down to us and which we possess, are not simply some fad diet or an isolated recipe for preparing food. They are a multitude of other things that reflect the relationship our land and its people have with the natural environment such as the sea, trees, herbs, vegetables and flowers; in other words, the actual landscape which surrounds us. In addition, it is important to mention that all of this is also reflected in our songs, in our oral traditions and in our collective memory.[14]

These statements capture ideas found on Kalymnos and throughout Greece that eating is a total social fact, incorporating health, taste, tradition, and a strong sense of local place, a Greek version of the French concept of *terroir*. Eating well—in the sense of both health and taste—means eating food that has been produced in the traditional fashion, with traditional recipes and without "modern" fertilizers and pesticides (note that the Greek word for organic translates literally as "biological"). Authentic food is local food, locally grown in the particular conditions of climate, soil, and sun of different regions or even villages of Greece, with different knowledge of particular local ingredients, herbs, and spices, and with different local traditions, customs, festivals, and particular regional and local histories. There is also a sense that authenticity always belongs more to the past, only fragments of which can still be accessed today. And it is, of course, a rural phenomenon, which urban Greeks romanticize as part of their village origins.

In some ways this could be seen as part of a "self-exoticization" through cookbooks, cooking shows, and other forms of culinary tourism that celebrate the local as well as, recently, the cuisine of Greek minorities for the benefit of a largely urban, middle-class audience, and may even serve as a form of social capital and "distinction" in Bourdieu's sense.[15] However, as I explore further later on, this discourse of *terroir* pulls on longstanding issues in Greek society about the meaning of locality. Eric Ball, for example, suggests the significance of place, environment, and landscape in Greek literary discourse in the twentieth century. He notes the significance of naming plants and other features of the landscape as part of an "ecological awareness" that is seen as tied to a cultural identity: "Authors regularly invoke even scientific taxonomies in ways that blur or intertwine social and ecological boundaries, cultural identities and the facts of natural science" (Ball 2005, 8). C. Nadia Seremetakis's discussion of the implications of EU regulations on Greek agricultural products (1994) both analyzes and partakes of a common perspective in Greece that ties social reproduction to particular, local and embodied sensory, medicinal, and skilled knowledge of food and other material objects.[16] The notion that this knowledge would serve as a buffer against the negative aspects of modernity is implicit or explicit in such views, as is clear in the first statement from the Mediterranean diet letters quoted above.

But it is not *just* because "The shift towards healthier eating habits and ways of life has become no longer a luxury but a necessity." Rather, it is because in keeping some aspects of "modernity" at bay, it is not only health and local landscapes but also cultural identities that are being preserved and revalued, through a conscious embrace of traditional cooking and eating practices, while what are seen as the positive aspects of modern life are simultaneously embraced. This is what I refer to as "existential memory work" (Sutton 2008)—that is, on Kalymnos, the issue of how to live in the present remains a question of what to remember and what to forget, or how to place oneself and others in time in a way that both recognizes continuity and acknowledges change.

When I would ask Kalymnians what "good food" and "healthy food" meant to them, I would get answers that stressed personal, local knowledge: "Healthy food is fresh food, food produced on Kalymnos, where you know whether they've used a lot of chemicals or not." People would tell me, for example, that they got their fish from relatives, so that they could be sure they were wild-caught. While they would also talk about cholesterol, salt, iodine, fiber, and other perceived "good" and "bad" elements in food, they insisted on the overall health of "traditional" food, which also meant "simple" food, without a lot of unusual or unknown ingredients, not pretentious or prepared in a fancy way. As one man put it, "For me, bread, tomatoes, and olive oil is good food." Some did suggest that in the past food was "heavier," with more fat that they now feel obliged to avoid, at the cost of a loss of taste. For example, Polykseni told me that they used to make moussaka on Kalymnos with two layers of everything, potatoes, meat, eggplant, and béchamel sauce, and "It was much tastier. But over time the nutritional habits change and we said, Let's eat it, but not quite so heavy." (For a fuller discussion of Polykseni and ideas about health and tradition, see chapter 6.)

Such complexity was at work also in some of the Kalymnian restaurants that were featuring "local" or "Mediterranean" cuisine. I spoke with Evdokia Passa and her mother, Aleka, who had owned the restaurant named, after Aleka's deceased husband, Harry's Paradise. Their restaurant and rooms for rent, in the small village of Emborios, featured a stunning flower garden out front. In the back they kept a small vegetable garden to stock their kitchen, but otherwise they bought much of their produce from an organic farmer who lived in the village. The restaurant had developed over time from a traditional Greek restaurant with noted specialties such as *papoutsakia* (eggplants stuffed with a meat sauce), reflecting Aleka's upbringing in mainland Greece, to a more recent focus on local sourcing and "Mediterranean cuisine."

Mediterranean cuisine was defined by Evdokia as based in the way of life that she had learned growing up on Kalymnos. She said it was something "natural," but something that much of the world had moved away from because of the influence of fast food. Evdokia had trained at a hotel school in Rhodes, but she noted that she learned only minimal cooking skills there, as the focus in cooking classes was on French theory rather than on practice. She had been excited to participate in a seminar on local cuisine that took place in 2008, noting that Kalymnos needed more visiting chefs to help the island's restaurateurs learn how they could incorporate local products into their menus. The AegeanCuisine Association had indeed produced a cookbook based on what were considered local recipes from many of the Dodecanese islands.[17] Evdokia told me that every so often she made a "tour of the Aegean" menu, drawing on recipes from this book. Evdokia had indeed been working since then on creative ways to incorporate local ingredients into her cooking, such as Kalymnian mountain tea (*alisfakia*), which she uses in making risotto as well as in a sauce for rabbit. She said that her customers want Greek food but have gotten bored with the usual stuff and were looking for different flavors. I asked whether any of her Kalymnian customers asked for recipes for her dishes, and she said that most requests came from foreigners; only a few of the younger Kalymnians were interested in incorporating new ideas into their home cooking.[18]

Cost plays into food values, as noted above, though as we'll see, the stress on "simple" food also means that many Kalymnians dismiss expensive food as "putting on airs" and in fact not tasty or worth the money. Convenience plays into people's values in more subtle ways: the issue of time pressure and time management was raised as significant by

FIGURE 1. Aleka and Evdokia Passa cooking lentils in their home kitchen (2014). Photo by Dimitris Roditis.

some Kalymnian cooks (cf. Silva 2010). Convenience might also account for the choice of whether to cook a meal in the mother's or the daughter's kitchen, but it is not one of the core values associated with preparation of food, which is supposed to deserve and demand effort (effort, of course, which is largely the responsibility of women). Indeed, the rise of fast food of various kinds on Kalymnos is seen as one of the aspects of modernity that is putting health and cooking under threat for the younger generation. In 2008, before the economic crisis had hit Greece, I heard much outrage expressed by middle-aged and older Kalymnians that younger women spend more money on clothes than on food; this is seen as a particular attack on tradition, because clothes are considered foreign (most are not made in Greece), while food is, as noted, ideally Greek. Clothes also represent a concern with appearance, while food is internalized, making fast food seem even more of a threat, not just to health but to identity in general.

It should be noted, though, that different kinds of fast food have different meanings, from the hamburgers and other Americanized fast food associated with a Greek chain like Goody's to the more "traditional" fast food on Kalymnos, souvlaki, and to partially prepared food, now increasingly available in supermarkets. Many Kalymnian women insisted to me that they would never consider buying prerolled phyllo dough at the store, much less prepared frozen spinach pie, though a few did note that the latter could be useful if guests dropped by unexpectedly. One woman, a nursery school teacher, noted that fast food hadn't really inundated Kalymnos because there was no Goody's or McDonald's like they have on neighboring Kos, but that when Kalymnian students go to Athens, they go crazy for fast food and since their bodies aren't used to it, it affects them more.

If there is a "key" food value on Kalymnos that encompasses all the others, it is surely taste. Taste is the touchstone in assessing food, and it encompasses other values in the sense that "traditional" and "simple" food is also tasty food. Taste is constantly referred to in assessing prepared food, and Kalymnians take pleasure in their ability to distinguish small variations in dishes, as well as to assess the quality of different ingredients.[19] And it is the taste of food that, as I argue in my earlier work, is key to unlocking memories of all sorts, personal, familial, local, and national.

Abarca (2006) and Adapon (2008) argue that taste—*sazón*—is central to discourses about Mexican cooking and forms a "sensory epistemology" guided by memories, personal histories, embodied knowledge (Abarca 2006, 54), and "precisely that inexplicable quality that sets some cooks apart from others" (Adapon 2008, 22). On Kalymnos, taste is seen as individual but within a range of known quantities. People may debate the taste benefits of cutting versus grating tomatoes for a stew, or of peeling them versus leaving the skin on, and the amount and varieties of ways to salt a meal. Some Kalymnians do talk about the importance of "love" to proper cooking, and others about the little "tricks" that create flavorful foods.

But with a rare exception or two—those who might say "I'm easy about food"—Kalymnians assert the importance of good, tasty food in their lives. As Manolis, a fisherman and seasonal migrant to the United States, asserts: "Good food means a good life. Because we work to eat well. And if the food is crappy [*halia*], life is crappy!" In exploring the value of weaving in a South India community, Soumhya Venkatesan draws an analogy with the value of cooking: "Mainly undertaken by women, cooking is a necessary chore, although care is taken in preparing a meal. But there are times, on feast days or special events, when people delight in cooking fine and special dishes. On such occasions both men and women plan and cook the meal and there is much discussion about what to make, how it will be prepared, and by whom" (2010, 159).

On Kalymnos it is perhaps not an exaggeration to say that every day has that quality of a special event when it comes to cooking. Even though dishes are standardized and repeated according to a common pattern, there is nothing taken for granted or purely chorelike for most Kalymnians in the daily decisions and preparations of meals. And cooking is not devalued as "women's work," but seen as essential knowledge in producing high-quality meals and publicly recognized value.

In an American context the phrase "we work to eat well" seems strange and perhaps sounds too much like "will work for food," an act of desperation rather than a philosophy of life. But in fact, it brings me back to my comments about the significance of "authenticity," which is not simply a characteristic of certain foods; to eat with authenticity is a characteristic of being human, and the opposite of authentic food is "plastic" food: something nonbiological, essentially nonhuman. Food fit for human consumption is food fundamentally in agreement with a dignified human existence—what people at the local level recognize as the correct or right way of existing as human beings.

The same is true of shopping, sharing, and provisioning. Too often anthropological analysis has embraced the idea of "cultural capital," that people's consumption choices are about status and "distinction," as Pierre Bourdieu famously argues. I don't want to deny that considerations of status play into such actions, but I also have wanted to stress their existential quality as well, that they are really addressing questions of what kind of person we want to be and what kind of society we want to live in. This is why I argue that the important thing on Kalymnos is not only to engage in socially embedded shopping but also to not feel taken advantage of. This is what the Kalymnians are saying when they refuse to keep track of favors and turn them into debt. Doing so would cancel out the way the system is supposed to work, which is really why you should also not feel you have been taken advantage of. Being taken advantage of means that you feel the other member of the exchange has tried to make profit out of a relationship that is part of a system in which profit is allowed only at specific times, under specific conditions, and only in moderate amounts. The refusal to turn favors into debt and "keep track" while also making sure they are not being taken advantage of is the way locals reflect, and reflect *on,* their choices of how to organize their social world. The quotes from the UNESCO application illustrate these points in that they state that these dietary concerns are not "isolated recipes for preparing food," they are addressing the question of "how" we reproduce this moral system of socially embedded shopping, cooking, and eating.

CHAPTER 2

Tools and Their Users

The tasks you do depend on who you are, and in a sense the performance of certain tasks *makes* you who you are.

—(Ingold 2000, 325)

When I began filming people's everyday cooking practices, it was not on Kalymnos but rather in southern Illinois, where my student and collaborator Michael Hernandez and I worked with about half a dozen volunteers as we developed through trial and error our methodological approaches and battery of questions, trying to get at some of the different ways that cooking shapes the texture of people's daily lives.[1] At the time Michael, a keen observer of his friends, noted what he felt was a predictive correlation: the more fancy tools and gadgets a person has, the more expensive the cookware, the fancier the kitchen, the less that person actually cooks. This observation reminded me of something that Katina—a Kalymnian woman in her thirties at the time—had told me: that the point of buying new kitchen gadgets was to be able to carry them ostentatiously past your neighbors' doorsteps to make them jealous, a sentiment they would hide with the formulaic phrase "May you have good luck with it!"[2]

Perhaps these observations play too easily into the popular prejudice that *real* cooking is done by hand. Perhaps this is a generalized version of the "deskilling" hypothesis, which in various forms laments the loss of human skill and its replacement by black-box, push-button machines that strip life of its humanity—the technophobia that seems to be part and parcel of modern society's technophilia. Such views tend to lead to all kinds of ironies, as performer and social critic Mike Daisey points out in his one-man play about the labor conditions in Chinese factories that produce Apple electronics, *The Agony and the Ecstasy of Steve Jobs*. Daisey argues that we have never had more handmade products in the history of the human race, but "handmade" can in fact be its own nightmare when the price of human labor has been reduced to almost zero.

Of course, if we start from dichotomies like this, such as "traditional" and "modern," "authentic" and "ersatz," we won't get very far except to say that it's more complicated. Instead, here I simply follow some of the tools, technologies, and appliances that make up the kitchen environment on Kalymnos, and see where they lead. In this chapter I focus on a few specific items—knives, rolling pins, can openers, outdoor ovens, and the layout of kitchens. I also suggest ways that we can think of the body itself as a cooking tool, and what that might mean for our understanding of skill and deskilling. In considering these diverse topoi of kitchen engagement, I am somewhat eclectic in my approaches and inspirations, but at the same time attempt to argue that careful ethnographic exploration and observation of daily practice can yield important and often unexpected insights. While historians and sociologists have treated kitchen tools and especially kitchen appliances as texts to be read to reveal their often-gendered "scripts,"[3] my interest here is in tools-in-use and what they can tell us about how the everydayness of cooking is negotiated. At the same time I suggest that the everydayness of cooking in fact opens up much larger issues of memory and identity, agency and embodiment.

OF KNIVES AND CUTTING SURFACES AND THEIR ABSENCE: WHAT I LEARNED FROM KALYMNIAN WOMEN CUTTING VEGETABLES

Let's start by considering a brief extract of some of the first videos I shot on Kalymnos, titled "Cutting Medley" (video example 1), which compiles footage of Katerina Kardoulia cutting potatoes for a stew, Nina Papamihail cutting an onion for a salad, and Katerina's granddaughter, known as Little Katerina, cutting zucchini for an omelet.[4] While it had caught my attention that Kalymnians were cutting all kinds of things in their hands rather than on a hard surface, it made even more of an impression on me when I showed these videos to colleagues in food studies, some of whom had had professional training in cooking, and they were *horrified*. How could people cut in such an awkward fashion? They assumed that they were viewing experienced cooks, and while no doubt these cooks had many recipes and perhaps preparation techniques particular to Greece, my colleagues wondered why anyone would use such an inefficient method of cutting. Their queries brought me up short and really got me to take a closer look at Kalymnian cutting practices. It also got me to think about what we might mean by words like *awkward* and *efficient*.

On closer examination, I found that there is a style, a *skill* to Kalymnian cutting. In the case of the potato, notice how it is cradled in one hand and scored all the way across in two or three passes, and then with a wrist motion the knife is drawn toward the thumbs, which serve as a guide and balance. Effectively, the thumbs serve in the role of cutting board; only the thumb of the hand cupping the potato is used when the potato is large, while both thumbs are employed for smaller potatoes or once a larger potato has been partially cut. In the case of onions, one hand typically again serves as a cradle, while the loose wrist of the other hand is brought up and down in a repetitive motion to score a pattern of shallow cuts on the surface of the onion. Then the thumb is once again used as a guide to draw the knife across the onion while the cradling hand rotates the onion. It is not just vegetables that are approached in this way. In the case of loaves of bread, the bread is held against the chest and the knife is used in a sawing motion to score cuts in the bread that can later be fully separated by hand. I must admit that the first few times I was witness to this technique, it was rather frightening! It seemed to go against everything I had learned as a child about how to avoid injuring oneself with a knife. But in fact while motorcycle accidents are extremely common on Kalymnos, and danger seems to be courted in the ritual throwing of dynamite bombs at Easter and other important events throughout the year, I have never heard of people accidentally cutting themselves across the jugular.[5]

So there is method in this technique. One of the issues that made my food studies colleagues wince was that this approach to cutting seemed to preclude ending up with small, evenly shaped pieces. The use of a surface (cutting board or other hard surface) allows for greater balance, and in the case of bread, for example, one can use the surface as a guide for evenness of cut. In terms of vegetables being used for cooking, presumably evenness of shapes and sizes leads to more even overall cooking. (This is not such an issue for Kalymnian salads, in which uneven shapes seem fairly normative. And for stews, vegetables undergo lengthy cooking; Kalymnian vegetables are not cooked al dente, so once again the irregularities might not make so much of a difference).

However, to say that this technique is "not so bad," or that it doesn't make that much of a difference, is not to grasp its logic, why it has been passed down from one generation to the next in Kalymnian (and Greek) kitchens more generally. One issue, of course, is whether counter space is even available. Calling for a cutting board assumes that there is counter space to put it on, at the right height to facilitate such activity. Yet the prototypical "mother's" kitchen consists of a space no more than five feet square, primarily with room for storage and a bottled-gas, two-burner stove. These kitchen spaces were not designed with counter space for cutting in mind.

The more recent "daughter's kitchen," by contrast, does have counter space, built of marble or other materials, as well as a standard oven, often missing in the mother's kitchen. However, as noted previously, the daughter's kitchen often opens on to a living-entertaining space, so in many cases it is not seen as the place for heavy processing or cooking of foods that have strong smells, and is more typically used for baking and preparing snacks. However, even when this kitchen space is used to prepare food (in the absence of a mother's kitchen or simply out of some daily exigency), the counters are rarely used for chopping or other heavy food processing.

A further issue might have to do with the height of counters. I asked Katina Miha why she preferred to assemble food, roll dough for *pitas,* and undertake other processing activities at the kitchen table rather than on her counter surfaces, which seemed largely decorative. She responded that the counters were "off," and weren't "making me comfortable."[6] Many kitchen counters are built in with prefab cabinets bought from major furniture retailers, which come in standard sizes, though some women ordered lower cabinets to accommodate their height. I found that most counters were 90 centimeters (about 35 inches) in height. Built for Americans or northern Europeans, these counters create a challenge for Greek women of smaller stature, the kind of standardization of kitchen spaces that has long ignored the perspective of the female user, as documented by feminist historians of technology (Wajcman 2010).

I was struck by a story told to me by Neni Panourgia, an anthropologist of Greek descent, about her father building a kitchen in their summer home in the early 1970s. A trained engineer, her father had built everything to his own specifications (at the time prefab kitchens were much less common). When he had put in the counters, he asked his daughter what she thought of them, obviously quite proud of his handiwork. Neni responded, "They look great, but they're too high." He replied, "What do you mean, they're too high? Counters should come up to the waist of an average-size person." Neni asked, "An average-size *male* person, or an average-size *female* person?" This left him speechless.[7]

These reflections on counters are still based on the premise of an "ideal" transcultural working space. The universalism of such a view has its own particular history, as those readers familiar with the efficiency studies of Christina Fredericks, the "Frankfurt Kitchen," and other twentieth-century attempts to bring the principles of "modernization" into kitchen spaces are no doubt aware.[8] Perhaps there are other, more proximate reasons that Kalymnian women avoid using their counters for cutting. As I was thinking about these issues, I was also reading the work of Patricia Greenfield and her colleagues on Maya weavers. In developing the skills to become weavers, Maya girls' bodies are trained in a number of ways, such as kneeling for extended periods with upper-body balance and stillness.[9] While cutting in the hand is in no way as elaborate as weaving on the backstrap loom, it does involve a process of bodily training leading to proficiency in this technique (a few women noted that they always found it difficult, but I will discuss their cases later). Indeed, my colleague Neni Panourgia insisted that her mother, along with many other Greek women, could with practice use this technique to produce the kind of small, even-size results desired by my food studies colleagues. Consider, for example, the speed with which Polykseni Miha dispatches eggplants into even slices in the video "Polykseni Cutting Eggplant" (video example 2). It seems that the skill developed with other vegetables pays off when doing the kind of cutting for which a counter might provide no clear benefit. Instead, she glides the knife through the eggplant with a slight sawing motion, gently rocking her body forward to allow the slices to fall into a colander, and even pulling the last two slices through the knife while holding the already cut end.

Tim Ingold's description of sawing a piece of wood provides additional insight into the skill of cutting in the hand. Ingold notes, "Although a confident, regular movement ensures an even cut, no two strokes are ever precisely the same. With each stroke I have to adjust my posture ever so slightly to allow for the advancing groove, and for possible irregularities in the grain of the wood" (2011, 52). He summarizes: "Cutting wood . . . is an effect not of the saw alone but of the entire system of forces and relations set up by the intimate engagement of the saw, the trestle, the workpiece and my own body" (56). In the same way, cutting Kalymnian style effectively replaces the solid balance of a cutting surface with the intimacy and control of the hand and object. Each cut is felt—not just by the hand that is holding the knife, but by the hand that holds the object to be cut—and allows for adjustments to be made as the hand rotates the object.

It became clear to me that cutting in the hand was a skilled practice, but what about its supposed "inefficiency"? As I thought more about this question, I realized that there were times when I might cut food in my hand—for example, if it was a particularly small item like a clove of garlic that I could hold over a pan, allowing the cut pieces to drop directly into the pan. Indeed, in the case of Katerina cutting potatoes in the "Cutting Medley" video, we see that she uses a bowl in a similar fashion, as a receptacle to catch the pieces of potato as they fall from her hand. By the same token, Kalymnians do use surfaces when they are cutting something very large: a sheep carcass or a large whole fish would certainly not be attempted "in the hand," but rather on a table in the yard or on a counter in a daughter's kitchen. So it is not that these techniques represent absolute differences, simply that they are the norm, the habitual, the everyday.

Other colleagues mentioned cooking traditions in other countries in which food processing might be done largely in a kneeling position. Perhaps what threw me off at first was that the first example I saw of this technique was Nina cutting an onion while standing over a counter, where it seemed to offer no advantage to hold the onion in her hand rather than lay it on a surface. When I saw Katerina sitting in a chair, facing me, cutting potatoes with a bowl cradled in her lap, things started to make more sense. I recalled Marcel Mauss's notion of "techniques of the body." He defined technique as an act "that is traditional and efficacious. It has to be traditional and effective. There is no technique and no transmission if there is no tradition" (cited in Narvaez 2006, 60). Efficiency, in other words, is defined not by some absolute standard, but through experiences within a particular social order, what Ingold calls a "taskscape" (Ingold 2000, 194ff.).

So, how does this cutting technique fit into the larger Kalymnian taskscape? As noted earlier, much of the processing of ingredients does not necessarily take place within the confines of the mother's small kitchen itself. Rather, it might take place in the courtyard directly outside the kitchen area. Like Katerina, women often prepare ingredients while seated, potentially avoiding the back pain associated with standing for long periods. Cutting in the hand also allows them to socialize with family or neighbors while the ingredients are being processed. It is a technique for multitasking: processing ingredients doesn't in this case necessitate turning one's back on the environment around oneself. One can oversee other activities going on in the household, watch for passing friends or neighbors, even make processing food an occasion for sitting in a circle and sharing news and stories. This social aspect is also reflected in the tendency of family members to check in constantly with one another as a dish is being prepared, tasting and consulting on processes that they have enacted many times in the past.

It might be tempting here to draw a contrast between "social" Greek cooking and "asocial" American cooking. Surely, trends in kitchen design suggest a greater desire among Americans to make cooking a social activity that happens in the shared, public space of the home, rather than as hidden labor. Indeed, a Kalymnian might reverse the comment of my food studies colleagues, and marvel at the "inefficiency" of American cooking, which makes people turn away and bend down while trying to remain actively involved in the social surroundings!

However, for some cooks in the United States or western Europe, asocial cooking may actually be seen as a distinct advantage. To quote a scholar of taste reflecting on her own experience of cutting and cooking alone: "'I took up cooking at a very early age out of need but I never liked it. Now, cooking is my stress buster. I meditate as I chop vegetables, each piece as perfectly cut as possible.'"[10] As with any everyday activity, cooking serves multiple purposes, conscious and unconscious, explicit and implicit.

Richard Sennett has advocated viewing skill as a holistic process of negotiating a particular task, rather than something that can be analytically divided: "Rather than the combined result of discrete, separate, individualized activities, coordination works much better if the two hands work together from the start" (Sennett 2008, 164–65). One of his key examples of such hand coordination is the use of a cleaver in Chinese cooking to develop the skill to "cleave a grain of rice" (168). I would simply add that a holistic view of bodily techniques would draw on Mauss's notion of the "traditional and efficacious" to understand how something that from a technical point of view may seem inefficient makes considerable sense in a larger social context.

ROLLING THE DOUGH: THE BODY AS TOOL

Growing up in New York City, I spent a lot of time at the pizza joint in my Washington Heights neighborhood. Owned by a Greek and run by a Dominican, this place taught me early not to expect "authenticity" to come in national stripes. I always enjoyed watching the tossing of the pizza crust and the ability of the pizza chef to achieve the desired thinness using simply rhythm and bare hands. Although I wouldn't have phrased it in this way at the time, the pizza maker's art seemed the epitome of "embodied skill," exactly the kind of practice that can't be learned by following a set of written instructions, only through a process of guided apprenticeship involving the slow discovery of the interactions of materials, tools, and one's own body in the presence of a skilled master. It also suggests an interweaving of the senses in evaluating one's progress, what Heather Paxson has dubbed "synaesthetic reason" (2011) to capture the combination of sensory and discursive knowledge that a craftsperson develops. In this section I extend my discussion of embodied techniques to understanding the sensory relationships among bodies, tools, and the material ingredients of cooking—in this case, dough.

As a youth watching pizza dough being made, I was not aware of Greek phyllo dough, or how much thinner that dough can, in fact, be made. Phyllo dough, however, is "opened" (as they say in Greece) not with bare hands, but with a rolling pin. On Kalymnos, rolling pins come in three varieties: two seem similar in size to rolling pins I have used in the United States, but they do not have separate handles with ball bearings or a metal rod to run on. Instead they are tapered, either into the form of a handle or simply so that the ends are slightly thinner than the middle. The other type of rolling pin represents more of a thin, long dowel, all one length with no tapering, and only about an inch in diameter.

When Polykseni and I sat down to make mushroom pies (*manitaropites*), she brought out both a long, thin one and a tapered one with a handle. As we were making filled pockets rather than a "pie," we were breaking off small pieces of dough and rolling them out to about one-third-inch thickness. Polykseni, a nursery school teacher who lives in her dowry house on the hillside overlooking the church, cemetery, and upper neighborhood of Ayios Mammas, had told me rather proudly that she always rolls her own dough. But she quickly qualified this: "Well, not for *galactoburico* and other 'pan sweets' [*glika tou tapsiou*] like *kopeckhi*; then, of course, I use store-bought phyllo. But certainly for all the pies that I make ... [she lists five or six different kinds of pies].[11] And each time I make a different dough; I have four different recipes that I use."

I realized that most Kalymnians I had observed making pies or pockets of various sorts would do it in two layers, a layer of dough for the bottom, some filling in the middle, and another layer on top. *Galactoburico* and other such pastries call for the multiple layers that require the extremely thin dough that you can buy factory-made and frozen in packages, which you must layer on very quickly and cover immediately with butter so that they don't dry out. I've also seen Kalymnian women use this type of ultrathin factory-made phyllo dough as separate sheets to roll around cheese and mint in the shape of tubes. So when I was working on the mushroom pockets with Polykseni, it was simply an average thickness that we were going for. Indeed, Polykseni encouraged me not to roll the dough too thin, and to leave some dough around the edges when I folded it around the mushroom mixture, as she liked the taste of a little extra dough.

When I asked her whether she knew how to make the thinner phyllo, she said, "Of course," illustrating quickly with the dough in front of her, "I can make it as thin as you want. If you put some flour on top, you can roll it even thinner." She noted after rolling out the dough to about an eighth of an inch thick that you couldn't get it much thinner than that "because it would tear on you." This illustration was done using the thick rolling pin and a small piece of dough, which she then rolled back up into a ball, noting that she likes to have the doughy taste that results from rolling it out less. But as she encouraged me to try my hand at it, she also pushed the thin rolling pin in my direction, saying that she felt more comfortable with the thick one.

When it comes to rolling out phyllo (see video example 3, "Polykseni Making Mushroom Pies"), Polykseni and I use somewhat different techniques. Polykseni uses eight to twelve firm and distinct strokes for each piece, lifting the rolling pin between strokes. She opens the dough in one direction and then rotates it once before opening it in the other direction. While she makes several rotations on the first piece of dough, after that she simply curves off to the side with her rolling pin to keep it roughly rectangular. She doesn't, for the most part, use the tapered handles, but grasps the rolling pin by the thicker part.

By contrast, my first tries are hesitant as I attempt to get a feel for the process, especially after being told by Polykseni, "Like anything else, there is a craft to opening [rolling] phyllo."[12] Instead of grabbing the pin firmly (more difficult to do with the thinner one), I put the pin on top of the dough and then attempt to extrude the dough by rolling the middle of my fingers over the pin with a rapid back-and-forth motion. The first one takes an excruciatingly long time; at one point Polykseni suggests that I haven't rolled it long and thin enough, and that perhaps I should try with the thicker pin. But I continue on, turning the dough five or six times till I finally get it thin enough. Polykseni gives me careful directions and constant encouragement for how to fold the dough over the filling, noting that I have to make sure my folds go in far enough that the filling doesn't escape out of the side. On the second try I haven't made it long enough in one direction, so Polykseni first tells me to open it further; then when I do it more hesitantly, she puts her hand on the middle of the pin and rolls it out firmly. In part the different style of rolling is explained by my own lack of knowledge, in part by what seemed to be afforded by the thinner rolling pin, which didn't seem—at least in my attempts—to lend itself to the kind of short, distinct strokes of the thicker one. However, much depends on what one is trying to achieve as well.

I observed Evdokia, in the kitchen of her small restaurant in the village of Emborios at a remote end of Kalymnos, opening phyllo using the thicker rolling pin as well. (See video example 4, "Evdokia Rolling Dough." The noise in the background is from construction work going on nearby.) In this case, however, she is making not pockets but a larger piece of dough for a leek pie. It should also be noted that although she has had professional training at a restaurant and hotel program in Rhodes, when I asked if she had learned her techniques there, she insisted that she had learned from her mother, who is not Kalymnian but from mainland Greece.[13]

In this case she begins the process by using her hands to achieve a first opening up of the dough, stretching it with her hands at first slowly, and then faster and more rhythmically until it forms a basic round shape before she employs the rolling pin. Because she is standing over the dough rather than sitting down, she can put her whole body into the rolling process, using shorter back-and-forth motions that resemble a more practiced and confident version of what I was trying to do with the thinner pin, as opposed to Polykseni's distinct strokes.[14] As she opens it up a bit, she begins folding over pieces of the dough and then rolling them again. This, she says, is a method called *sfoliata*—layered like puff pastry—which makes the phyllo crunchier in the end.[15] Each rolling involves the introduction of a bit more flour to increase the elasticity of the dough and make sure it doesn't start to stick to the rolling pin. At certain points, in order to open up the far edges of the dough, Evdokia uses one hand on the rolling pin and the other hand for leverage on the countertop. In the end, the phyllo does take on a distinct round or rectangular shape, but Evdokia folds it on top of the leek filling, making something that more resembles a strudel than a traditional pie.

When her restaurant and pension is open in the summer months, Evdokia typically makes one or two such pies per day. I ask her whether making them so regularly makes the rolling of the dough automatic, or whether there is still a craft to it. She doesn't respond directly, but notes that she has added a little too much yogurt to the batter for the dough, which is why the final phyllo has a few tears in it.[16] She uses some extra dough to patch these tears, calling it a "trick" (*patenta*). Once again, the knowledge that Evdokia deploys can be compared to Paxson's description of cheese makers, who engage in a "reflexive, anticipatory practice, guided by a synaesthetic evaluation of how the materials . . . are behaving and developing in a particular instance, as understood in light of past experience" (2011, 119). As Harry West, also studying cheese makers, describes it, "They engaged with the curd by *making* it, *touching* it, *feeling* it, *pressing* it in the form, and what is more by perceiving how *it* felt, how *it* behaved in their hands, and how *it* stitched together and aged into a cheese" (West 2013, 331).

I still wondered about the use of the thinner rolling pin. When I press Polykseni about her choice of the thicker one, she says that the thin one doesn't suit her, but doesn't elaborate. But my question does push her to mention northern Greek women, who are known to use the thinner rolling pin, "and they open their phyllos until they're as big as this whole table! How do they manage it?" Indeed, the first time I had a pie (a leek pie) made by Georgia Vourneli, who was visiting the United States from the northern city of Thessaloniki, I noticed immediately the difference between her pies, for which she used four sheets of phyllo on the bottom and four on top, and the Kalymnian variety, which typically have only one or two. My graduate student Michael Hernandez and I did a series of interviews with Georgia about her cooking, and then filmed her making the leek pie. Georgia was staying in Carbondale, Illinois, at the apartment of her son (my student, Leonidas Vournelis), so when she saw that he had only a thick rolling pin she eyed his broom, asking if he could cut off the handle and use that to open her phyllo. He refused, so she settled for the thicker pin.[17] This is how we described the process of rolling out the phyllo dough:

> Using the palms of her hands, she began to roll the pin over the dough. The first few times, she rolled the pin quickly and in short strokes directly in front and away from her. Then she rolled the pin forward and to the right and the strokes became slower and longer. The dough was flattened to about three times the circumference of the original palm size. Once it reached this size, she rotated the flat dough a quarter-turn to the left. This was repeated until the dough was twelve to eighteen inches in diameter.

Thus far, the process was similar to what I observed with Evdokia, and, on a smaller scale, with Polykseni. But then began the second phase of rolling the dough:

In this phase, Georgia took the dough edge closest to her and folded it forward over the rolling pin. She then rolled the pin away from her, drawing the phyllo over itself as she pressed down. The forward motion flattened the dough and kept it in place on the roller. By this time, the top edge of the dough was on the rolling pin face up. Georgia flipped the rolling pin quickly forward and the top edge of the phyllo was flicked forward and then unrolled. This flicking motion allows the phyllo to move away from its original position to accommodate its increase in size. She then rotated the dough a quarter-turn to the left and repeated the steps until the dough was thin.[18]

Video example 5 shows Georgia rolling dough. One striking aspect of her method is that because the dough is rolled up against itself on the rolling pin, the rolling process allows the entire dough to be opened evenly. In this case, the dough itself becomes a tool, working in tandem with human hands and the rolling pin to stretch as thinly as possible.[19] This is where Georgia complains in particular that "this [thicker] rolling pin isn't helping me," so she has to correct with her hands. This is because it is hard to get the dough over the lip of the rolling pin, and it can't be wound around the pin as many times as with the thinner one, so it takes more repetitions of this technique to open the phyllo to the desired thinness. Note that she uses her hands to smooth out wrinkles, but also to stretch the dough a bit farther. If this is done with a thin rolling pin, the pressure of one's hands on the pin is distributed more evenly and effectively to the dough that has been wrapped around itself multiple times.[20]

When Georgia described the difference between her technique and her mother Dimitra's, another dimension of the relation of tools to the rolling process was revealed. While Georgia typically opened her phyllo on a table or counter, her mother used a special legless table—a *sofra*—which she cradled in her lap while sitting on the floor of her kitchen.[21] While the *sofra* was a circle of the perfect size for rolling the dough, it also offered the advantage that I discussed before in relation to Kalymnian cutting techniques: Georgia's mother could roll her dough while socializing with others, telling her daughters what other things to prepare, and monitoring the activity of the rest of the family as they moved through her kitchen domain.

In examining cutting and rolling techniques, I have been interested in getting at the unspoken, embodied habits that make them effective in the varied situations and demands presented by cooking. In relation to rolling dough, I have considered the sensory engagement with materials and tools that Paxson has described as a kind of "synaesthetic reason."

FIGURE 2. Dimitra Kampouri rolling dough on a *sofra* (2007). Photo by Hercules Vournelis.

In the following sections I continue to look at technique in considering other tools of the Kalymnian kitchenspace. However, the focus shifts to more particular choices about using one type of object over another, and the narratives that these choices are embedded in, as they open up interesting perspectives on the role of kitchen tools in the negotiation of identities and memories.

TOOLS, IDENTITIES, ENVIRONMENTS: KATERINA AND THE CAN OPENER

The video camera is an invaluable tool for this kind of ethnographic research because it can often take your observations in completely unexpected directions. Granted, the video camera is not some transparent window onto reality, and one must always be aware of its effects on any situation. But I was fortunate in working with Katerina Kardoulia, who became so used to my daily presence with the camera that she went about her everyday activities barely paying it any attention.[22] So one day I was sitting in the kitchen filming Katerina preparing fish in a tomato sauce that she seasoned with herbs she kept frozen. My question about her keeping the herbs frozen leads Katerina to talk about her own forethought in preserving herbs in the freezer to have available for use year-round, including local herbs (one called *maskalies*) that she has foraged, and how impressed her neighbor had been at her forethought.

As she is talking, she begins opening a can of tomato paste with a knife-style can opener. Working the can opener around the can, she is creating a series of jagged spikes on the side of the can; but this process also provokes an internal discourse, which I analyze below. This was a moment in my research when I was reminded forcefully of the idea of the kitchen as similar to a tool shop. Janet Dixon Keller had suggested this analogy to me when I was presenting some of my ideas about food and memory at a seminar at the University of Illinois, before I began to analyze cooking itself. After the seminar she wrote to me in an e-mail, describing the work she had done on blacksmithing with her husband and collaborator, Charles Keller, "Your move to study smells and tastes as cultural mnemonics reminds me of our treatment of visible storage. The latter is simply the observation that artist blacksmiths store their tools in clear sight on the walls surrounding their work space. . . . This open storage provides constant visual access to tools, which can then evoke memories of past circumstances in which they were employed."[23] At the time I noted the parallel to Kalymnian kitchens, in which tools are hung from walls and all available visible spaces are filled, much as Dixon Keller describes the blacksmith's shop. Over the past ten years I have begun to notice the same practice in fancy kitchens in the United States, in the form of pot racks that hang from the ceiling. This parallel of kitchen and tool shop, however, was brought home to me even more in Katerina's kitchen than in any other Kalymnian kitchen that I observed.

Video example 6 shows Katerina opening a can. You can see the problem of the jagged spikes created by the can opener and how Katerina deftly solves it. Within arm's reach in a kitchen drawer Katerina has a mallet, an all-purpose solution for problems of this sort. This specific tool had had another life as part of the leather-tanning shop that she and her husband had run for many years in their backyard, collecting the skins of the lambs killed at Eastertime on Kalymnos and turning them into leather bags of various kinds, wallets, even traditional musical instruments (mainly the *sandouri*). So there was a constant sense of potential flow between the kitchen and the tool shack that sat twenty feet away in the backyard. I had seen things flow in the other direction as well: Katerina's son-in-law poking his head into the kitchen to find some oil to work on his motorcycle, for example. Taken together, Katerina's kitchen fitted very well with Dixon Keller's description of the blacksmith's workshop, where the setting provides stimulation and easy access for "problem resolutions and strategic approaches to current production tasks" (Sutton 2001, 129).

Donald Norman notes that the complexity or simplicity of a particular tool is inherent not in the tool itself, but rather in the organization of a system of which the task at hand forms a part (2011, 41ff.). This provides a way to think about Katerina's choice of the knife can opener, which fits within the larger set of tools that she deploys in her kitchen space and "simplifies" her life. Douglas Harper suggests that "making and fixing form part of a continuum" (1987, 21). This also speaks to Katerina's practices. Even though he was talking about processes involved in "heavy" machinery, his description of the skilled practitioner as a problem-solver with a "'live intelligence fallibly attuned to the actual circumstances' of life" is very much in line with Katerina's approach.

However, one might feel once again, in terms of "efficiency," that Katerina's method seems a bit odd. Here's where a careful unpacking of what she says, and in particular the internal dialogue that she has while opening the can, is revealing. It took me a long time to follow accurately and translate everything that Katerina says in this video. Interpreting this section of the video was difficult not only because certain parts are muffled, but primarily because Katerina is moving back and forth between her own internal reflections and the voicing of both her daughter Katina's view of the can opener and her own. Let me present the translation, along with some annotations, before commenting further.[24]

> Katerina says, "Now we'll see Katina's [Katerina's daughter's] way of opening."
> She says this while she has started opening the can in her own way, but when she realizes this she changes the pitch and tone of her voice to indicate that she is speaking as Katina, saying, "Since we have the tool, grab it so that our hands are not ruined."
> Katerina continues to open the can, and then says, "So that I don't slow myself down, I open it . . ."
> She is looking for an adverb here and I suggest "correctly," though I believe that she perhaps wanted to say "in my own way." [Indeed, she copies my tone of voice, suggesting that she is simply repeating what I have said]. She then mutters something barely distinguishable about putting the can, with its jagged spikes, in the refrigerator, once again suggesting that she is taking her daughter's point of view. Then she reflects on her critique of her

daughter again, noting, "Yes, well, we have said all this before, she is ours, whatever we do with her, it can't be helped." She means that Katina is family, she loves her, and whatever issues Katina has, they don't change that fact.

She then focuses on the can opener she is using and says, once again switching back to her daughter's point of view, "You can eat your hands with this thing."[25]

I ask for clarification and she repeats this phrase, nodding at the sharp edges of the opened can. Fully into Katina's point of view again she notes, "Take a minute with the proper opener."

Not having understood this back-and-forth flow between her own and her daughter's points of view at this point, I ask, "Why don't you get the newer kind?"

She responds to this question, taking it in stride, "I have one, Vangelia [her friend] gave it to me, I have it. I am not made comfortable by it. I am traditional [*laughing*]. A real traditionalist. What to say?"

Here the choice of a particular set of tools for a particular set of problems comes to represent an existential attitude. In these brief comments Katerina presents what is an ongoing debate between herself and her daughter, Katina. She recognizes the validity of Katina's approach while at the same time complaining about her insistence, dismissing it as part of her character by noting that she is "ours" and can't be changed. At the same time, the "rationality" of her daughter's view that she is creating a hazard ("You can cut your hands on that") is acknowledged by Katerina's insistence that the newfangled can opener simply doesn't suit her, and that a certain series of gestures, those that would mark her daughter as "modern," are ones she's not willing to adopt in light of her view of herself as a "traditionalist." Interestingly, she uses the word *epidekseuomai* to describe this. *Epideksios* is an adjective meaning "skillful." There is no corresponding verb in either standard Greek or, to my knowledge, Kalymnian. Katerina has turned this adjective into a verb in the medial-passive voice, meaning that it is a verb that usually does not take an object. Thus, the word here might be translated as "When I am with the new can opener I am not a skillful person." This suggests a recognition of distributed agency: neither she nor the can opener is responsible for this, but both together.[26]

In other words, the same action—opening a can—lends itself to interpretation and analysis at the level of both gesture and representation. It is an embodied skill, yes. Surely it is what is implied when Bourdieu suggests that skill is "not something that one has, like knowledge that can be brandished, but something that one is."[27] In this case, however, it is also clearly not an unconscious habit, as typically described by Bourdieu,[28] but one that in this case has generated a discourse of old and young, traditional and modern, in the kitchen as *approaches toward life*. No doubt it should be noted that these are not static categories, and in other ways or in other kitchen situations Katina might label herself as "traditional," while Katerina might wish to make claims for being up-to-date. Still, it should be noted that the can opener is not an isolated instance. Mother and daughter have had disputes in the past over whether to throw away old pots or continue to use them.[29] Katina told me on a number of occasions how she enjoyed shopping for new kitchen gadgets, especially ones for baking. Even so, Katina would still make fun of what she classified as the wasteful spending of neighbors and those who are "show-offs" (*oi faneromenoi*), buying useless new kitchen gadgets. But she also expressed a sense of embarrassment at Katerina's unwillingness to throw away at least some of the old, beaten-up pots and pans. Kitchen choices are existential choices. We will see this on a much larger scale in the next section, in which I consider a traditional, yet recent addition to Kalymnian kitchens: the outdoor oven.

BIOGRAPHICAL OBJECTS: THE RETURN OF THE OUTDOOR OVEN

Despite their debate over "old" versus "new" kitchen tools, I never heard Katina, or other Kalymnian women, touting particular *brands* of tools. Katina was content picking up any knife to do her cutting, and, as we'll see in later chapters, this reflects a general attitude of seeing cooking skill in terms of adapting whatever is available to the particular task at hand. For the most part, Kalymnians don't seem to treat kitchen tools as "biographical objects" that "tell the stories of people's lives" (Hoskins 1998). In our U.S.-based cooking research Michael Hernandez and I looked at a number of cases in which specific tools played the role of "inalienable possessions" (Weiner 1992) for their owners, and were accompanied with dense narratives. As Michael and I described these objects, they "are valuable because they have been removed from the stream of commodities and have acquired an almost totemic personal and family history so that they could not be sold, but only passed down from one generation to the next" (Sutton and Hernandez 2007, 75). By contrast, although some of the objects that people on Kalymnos use to decorate their kitchens might have strong associations with the family members who had originally owned them (some examples for Nina Papamihail and Nomiki Tsaggari are discussed in chapters 3 and 6, respectively), or might simply create a generalized mood of "pastness," by and large the cooking tools people use do not seem to be densely textured with stories on Kalymnos. While people might prefer one can opener or rolling pin over another, and these choices might have symbolic significance, I found no cases of favorite knives or pans as in the United States. The only objects that come close to being "biographical" are the clay pots used for preparing Easter lambs and the outdoor ovens in which they are prepared. The pots themselves are kept and passed down in families and, as we'll see, sometimes removed from circulation for preservation. The ovens, on the other hand, tend to be a new feature of Kalymnian kitchenspace, though their existence refers to past times and previous practices. Taken together it is perhaps their association with Easter, the most important ritual occasion in the Greek liturgical calendar, that marks them out as special.

It wasn't until the early to mid 2000s that I became aware of the growing trend of families building outdoor ovens in their yards. While outdoor ovens have always existed on Kalymnos, in recent times they tended to be thought of as a special feature, more likely to be found in homes of relatively wealthy Kalymnians or used by shepherds for cooking when they were spending time on the mountainside. So the demand for building these ovens could be seen in part as reflecting what at the time were rising economic fortunes on the island, and indeed throughout Greece prior to the economic crisis.[30] But considering these ovens in more detail gives me a chance to connect concern with kitchen tools and their use to some of the other themes I've been suggesting throughout this chapter, that everyday (and ritual) kitchen tools are tied to questions of identity and memory. Other kitchen researchers have focused on kitchen remodels as a productive subject for getting at the values that people bring to their cooking environments.[31] While I was not fortunate enough to have my research coincide with a remodeling project, I found that in talking to Kalymnians about the uses of and reasons for building outdoor ovens I was able to raise a similar set of concerns. In some ways, these ovens, like Katerina's can opener, seem to be about existential choices concerning how to integrate the "traditional" into contemporary life on Kalymnos. But they also caught my attention for what they reveal about memory and temporality, and for the way they are often embedded in shifting family, friendship, and neighborly relations.

Outdoor ovens have two key functions on Kalymnos, one of which is a more "everyday" use, for baking dishes like moussaka or stuffed vegetables. Here the outdoor oven is simply an extension of the regular oven: Kalymnians could prepare these dishes in their regular ovens but choose to use an outdoor oven in order to improve the flavor of the dish. Previous to the spread of these ovens, Kalymnians might choose to cook a pot of greens on coals to give them a special, smoky flavor. Ovens make this easier, and allow for extending that smoky flavor into the process of making all kinds of baked foods. The second key use is for cooking Easter lamb. Here the outdoor oven is seen as a replacement for the baker's oven, which is available for rent at most bread shops. Before the spate of new oven construction, most Kalymnians typically would take their lamb to their local bread shop for baking. Once again, taste is a major factor behind the shift, but the cost of using the baker's oven (40 to 50 euros in 2006) is also a consideration.

The preparation of the Easter lamb in an oven is a Kalymnian tradition; in other parts of Greece, lamb is prepared on a spit. To prepare lamb in an oven requires an aluminum container that comes with its own cover, a makeshift aluminum container (a large empty olive oil container, for example), or, the most traditional choice, a clay pot (*mourri*). The pot, and sometimes the makeshift can, is sealed with dough, which is said to help circulate the heat in the container so the lamb cooks evenly. Some Kalymnians were still using these clay pots in 2006 when I collected much of this material. But for many who owned one they had taken on the status of an inalienable possession, and had been removed from use for fear of breakage, especially when out of people's control in the public bakers' ovens.

As one woman in her forties, a shop owner, explained to me,

> *Irini:* I have the clay pot, but I'm trying to preserve it because it's very old, valuable, so I don't use it. I have a new aluminum casserole dish that I use instead. I don't want to break it because it's old, ancient!
>
> *David:* From your mom?
>
> *Irini:* Keep going . . .
>
> *David:* Your grandma?
>
> *Irini:* Keep going . . . three generations, four, or even more.
>
> *David:* Did you grow up in this neighborhood, in this house?
>
> *Irini:* Yes, I grew up here, as did my mother, and my children—a chain [*alisida*].

Irini's comments give a sense of the connection of objects such as these to family and community memory. On Kalymnos, many kitchen objects might have a patina of age—as I describe for Nina's kitchen in chapter 3—but as noted, there is less focus on specific kitchen tools than a general sense of attachment to the past through tools, recipes, and kitchen preparation methods. The exceptions are objects like these clay pots, old flour sifters, or other objects that have been by and large taken out of everyday use, and are now put on display on top of kitchen cupboards as part of a general kitchen ambience.

On the Saturday before Easter 2006, friends and family gathered in the courtyard of Maria's house for the preparation of the oven to cook the lambs, not just for her family but also for several others. Maria's grandsons and granddaughter had cleaned out the courtyard in preparation; Maria had been hard at work cleaning and stuffing their baby lamb, while her daughter Eleni prepared the expected snacks for the guests. The cleaning took place in the middle of the courtyard, as did much processing of ingredients, while in the meantime Eleni and Maria worked together on a stuffing of rice, tomato paste, onion, spices, and parts of the internal organs of the lamb, sautéed in Maria's small kitchen. But it was Eleni's husband, Stavros, who took the lead in getting the oven ready to receive the lambs. He filled the oven with wood and set it to burn. Maria offered advice about the balance of woods to be used, as different woods impart different flavors. Stavros's male friends helped carry various things over to the oven, giving small bits of advice about whether the wood had burned down enough, among other things. When the wood was reduced to coals, all the men participated, but Stavros again took the lead in filling the oven with the roughly ten containers (all metal) of lamb to be cooked. Then came the bricking up. Stavros had extra bricks around the house and had prepared a mortar. Once again, the men gathered around, helping in small ways, but for the most part making comments such as, "Don't miss that corner." Once the bricking was done and no smoke still escaped, we were ready to relax and enjoy the booze, sausages, and other snacks, and listen to the dynamite throwing, which carried on throughout the afternoon in preparation for the big dynamite event that evening.[32]

The fact of Stavros taking charge of the process reflects that this is a typical outdoor ritual and thus coded more male than female. Even if the actual preparation of the lamb—its cleaning and the preparation of the stuffing—was still done by the wife and mother-in-law, the husband took charge in preparing and tending the outdoor fire, conforming to a seemingly universal association of men and barbecue. But during the process he received advice and help from his mother-in-law, Maria, and a few of his friends who were participating in the get-together. The one

FIGURE 3. *Above:* Katerina Kardoulia and Katina Miha stuffing the Easter lamb (2006). Photo by author.

FIGURE 4. *Below:* Nikolas Mihas preparing the outdoor oven (2006). Photo by author.

FIGURE 5. *Above:* Nikolas feeding the oven while his mother-in-law, Katerina, looks on (2006). Photo by author.

FIGURE 6. *Below:* Nikolas bricking up the oven, while his friend gives advice (2006). Photo by author.

unusual gender association in this event was Stavros's sons sweeping and tidying the yard prior to the arrival of the visitors, typically a female task. This could be associated with the nature of the event as a special occasion, so that the boys were pitching in to help while the female members of the family were otherwise occupied (their sister had been assigned to clean the indoor kitchen).

The relaxed nature of the event belied the careful calculations that went into whom to invite and whom to allow to cook a lamb in the oven. By 2006 Stavros and Eleni had had the oven for only a couple of years, and later Eleni recounted to me some of the thinking that went into its construction, and some of the issues that have arisen since they built it. A few extended excerpts of this interview give a sense of the complex social relationships that are encoded in an oven, as well as some of the different temporalities that Eleni invokes in her reflections on it.

> At first we used to go to my brother's. We were happy to be all together like that, family and friends together; we had a steady yearly count of who would come, and we went as if it were a holiday; some would bring cookies, the owner [her brother] would provide the oven, some would bring beer. But we gradually lost patience with each other and animosities developed among people; children would mess up the garden, some relatives would complain, the housewife always had to have the place clean and tidy, always be prepared to serve coffee . . . so it was a tiresome thing to own an oven at your own home. And then they decided to get us to leave—not out of meanness or anything, but they told us that since they had decided not to make lamb anymore, we would have to go the next year. I didn't care. But is it not easy to go to a bakery and use their oven, because although you have to pay fifty euros, the end result is that it does not smell like Easter, like the natural smell of burning wood the food should smell like.

Here Eleni describes a memory in the imperfect tense, a memory repeated over a number of Easter celebrations. Because her parents had built the brother a house on the outskirts of town, they had enough land to include an outdoor oven in the backyard (prior to the recent rage for such ovens). Note that Eleni's memory doesn't actually extend back to the period of twenty years earlier, when they had to use one of the public bakeries for their Easter lamb, but instead to a relatively recent past since the building of the brother's house. Like all memories, memories of food lend themselves to this kind of telescoping, in which the idealized aspects of the past are what are best recalled. It is interesting that Eleni claims that everything was initially harmonious. In doing so, she draws on a discourse about the past as a time of easy sociality and generosity, of closer-knit social relations that have been lost in the present, what I have referred to elsewhere as "memories of *gemeinschaft*" (Sutton 2001, 53ff.). Eleni then shifts to a different memory register, the sensory memories of taste, to talk about why she couldn't imagine going back to using the bakers' ovens. She slightly exaggerates the cost, but stresses the idea that in order to celebrate Easter, you must taste the tastes that have become Easter's familiar, recognizable signature, thus tying the familiar sense-scape of Easter to sociability. These kinds of embodied taste memories are instantly recognizable on Kalymnos, drawing as they do on community discourses that stress the intimate details of the tastes of different foods. It is because of the *value* ascribed to taste, as noted in the previous chapter, that different methods and techniques of preparing dishes are given such significance, a theme that will recur throughout this book.

Eleni continues to describe their decision to build an outdoor oven, elaborating on the importance of her memories of taste:

> And that is why I told my husband to build an oven for us. He did not want to because he knew what was going to happen if he did build it: that is, that the owners would end up being like invited strangers. I insisted, though. Mostly because of the taste. My kids tomorrow they will get married and there's enough money to go around but there won't be any taste if we did not have an oven. And the custom is only once a year and you have to live it in a nice beautiful way, you have to taste it, it is not part of your everyday routine. It is not like you do on any other occasion when you go to some other place and do it there; in everyday life in the old days we would find a bakery and we would bake our foods there when we did not have a regular oven at home, and it would taste good; but there is something special about lamb that requires it to be cooked in a wood-burning oven in order to be tasty.

This is quite a complicated passage, which shows a number of different temporalities at work in Eleni's recollection. She begins with a memory of the decision to build the oven, which she claims was made based on her insistence, motivated by her own taste memories. This leads her to project her family into the future, imagining it with and without the oven and the proper taste of Easter lamb. She follows with a generalizing statement about the importance of ritual observance: "the custom is only once a year . . . you have to taste it," once again bringing together bodies, tastes, and social contexts in a moral economy that is able to transcend temporalities, sometimes functioning in idealistic representations of the past. Finally, in switching between the second person and the first person plural, she also makes a statement that distributes the memory of different ovens among herself, her family, and the wider Kalymnian community. Note also that the building of the oven itself was not based on any manual or suggestions from a local home store. Rather, Eleni's husband, Stavros, drew on his own embodied skill, as well as on the direction of his mother-in-law, Maria, who told me that she explained to him how it should be built, its dimensions, and so on, based on her recollection of her own mother-in-law's now-defunct oven.

In the next section of Eleni's narrative we move from the register of temporality to a statement about the significance of the oven to social relations in the present.

> When we built the oven, at that time the kids were young and they did not have any mothers-in-law [referring to her sons who were not married, and thus still ate at home]. So we told a friend to join in because he was to go away next year. He did come, and he told us that he never wanted to leave. We invited another friend, Pantelis [the son of a neighbor with whom they have been close for a long time], and he said the same thing, too. And then, there is this cousin of ours who is crazy and wild and asked if he could come in. And we told him he could come in until the kids grew up and got married, and then he would have to leave. And we said the same to everyone. But no one would leave, and they would all argue with us. And now as a result I have to always be ready to treat people with coffee and octopus and other things [this year they made sausages], not so much because I have to, but also because I want to because it is the custom to do so. In the old days, in the old ovens, we fasted, baked, and joked, and though we were mad at each other, that is how we spent the time. Now people will get drunk, they expect alcohol and whiskey and beer, and we do provide them with that and we don't even get any respect from them, even though we honor all our customary obligations . . . rather, they become annoying with their demands to bring in other people. We don't have the space for other people. . . . In a couple of years we, the owners, we ended up having no space for our own pot. So this year was an upsetting one for us, but I hope next year won't be the same, because I will let them know the rules in advance, or else we will have a Chicago-style drive-by shooting!

I have elided some of the details here to give a feel for the complex social negotiations that go into deciding who gets to use space in the oven, which can fit eight to ten containers. Eleni, in fact, spends much longer recounting the ins and outs of these negotiations, which are tied not only to decisions about one particular year but, once again, to thoughts of future reconfigurations and claims that people will make on their oven. In deciding whom there is room for, a balancing of different kinds of social relations comes into play. There are some relatives related through men (since women tend to be all included in the immediate family on this matrifocal island). In this case, that group includes Eleni's husband's brother and her father's maternal nephew. There are close neighbors, and there are friends, including those in godparent relationships. All these different demands must be weighed and evaluated, which may put strains on the immediate family as different family members press for the inclusion of their connections. In this recounting we can see Eleni's relation to the wider community of Kalymnos spread out against a landscape of past and future Easter preparations.

There is an interesting blurring of temporalities here. Aside from the nostalgia for more harmonious times past, Eleni is simultaneously looking back to her intentions when building the oven and forward to a future in which her sons are married. Thus she says, "When we built the oven, at that time the kids were young and they did not have any mothers-in-law," which would indicate to an uninformed listener that they are now married; but at the time of the interview they were not even engaged. Thus past, present, and future temporalities are projected onto the locus of the oven. A second blurring of lines is that between people and the containers they bring to put in the oven. At various points she refers to the people entering or leaving the oven, rather than their pots. She also refers to the "landlord" of the oven, as if the oven itself were a home that was being invaded by outsiders. All of this metonymical switching is suggestive, giving the oven a kind of personhood, or agency, what some might call fetishism, but which I would argue is the simple recognition that the oven is a key site for reconnecting with the past and projecting into the future. In other words, the oven stands for both good tastes and good social relations, which may be always imagined as better in the past, but which Kalymnians might be able to reclaim through proper action in the present and future.[33]

CONCLUDING THOUGHTS: TOOLS AND THEIR USERS

Peter Dormer writes about the knowledge involved in craft, "To possess it in any form is to see the world in an enriched way compared with someone who does not possess it" (1994, 95).[34] I have been arguing that an approach that follows the tools and their users can reveal aspects of this enriched world that one might otherwise miss, from the importance of preparation methods that orient the body toward the surrounding social environment to the significance of tool and kitchen design choices in the play of Kalymnian ideas about the traditional, the modern, and the role of prospective memory in orienting people temporally in relation to their cooking practices. "Skillfulness" and "authenticity" are, of course, relative to a total environment in which cutting in the hand makes sense, while using a thick rather than thin rolling pin may not be as authentic as the practices of the pie makers of northern Greece. But this doesn't reduce what Polykseni called the "art" of opening phyllo on Kalymnos to the particular requirements of Kalymnian tastes. Of course, even working with premade phyllo dough, though some Kalymnians might look down on it, requires considerable skill and embodied knowledge, a point brought home to me as I was writing this chapter when I noticed an article in the *New York Times* on working with phyllo (Landis 2012). I was excited to read it and see how a professional food columnist would write about the issues I had been thinking about. Alas, I had assumed it would be about rolling phyllo dough, but found that it was instead about how to use frozen, prerolled phyllo dough without letting it dry out!

My ethnographic subjects themselves are clearly aware of the significance of tools, as reflected in the distributed agency between humans and objects suggested in many of these interactions, including Georgia's claim that the rolling pin "is not helping me"; Neni Panourgia's insistence that women, not abstract "people," use kitchen counters; Katerina's phrasing that she and the new can opener together are not skillful; and Eleni's subject-object reversals regarding her outdoor oven. Indeed, there is a sense in which tools are not thought of apart from the context of their uses, in the manner that one might say this is the ideal knife for chopping. When I asked Georgia and her mother (by phone) whether there were differences in using a thin or a thick rolling pin, they responded that the thin one *and the dough rolled around it* are good for making thin phyllo, while the thick one *and the dough rolled under it* are good for making thick phyllo. Tools, ingredients, and bodily skills and gestures are all of a piece, part of a larger potentiality of tools-in-use in the kitchenspace.[35]

My subjects are, nevertheless, also attentive to the risk of tool use in the kitchen, even if they don't imagine the same sources of risk as I might: indeed, some of my informants had cut their hands while using a knife, but remembered more examples of this happening when they *did* use a counter or cutting board. So just as cooking involves skill and creativity, it also involves risk and danger: the risk of the failure of a dish and the danger of injury. Indeed, this is a reflection of the open-ended character that makes cooking *cooking*. For now it's important to note that just as there are male activities of risk and value on Kalymnos, the most obvious examples being sponge diving and dynamite throwing, the kitchenspace holds similar dimensions for women.[36] That is one of the reasons why, when Georgia talks of her mother's phyllo dough, she lowers her voice in respect: "It's so thin, you can see through it"; and why Katerina embraces her choice of can opener as part of her identity: it holds rewards as well as risks.

Cooking is a way of understanding the world, as Dormer said about craft, and Kalymnians are also aware of the significance of "knowledge" for cooking practice. But what is cooking knowledge, and how is it deployed in the process of cooking? What role do recipes and cookbooks or other media play in storing and disseminating this knowledge? How is cooking learned, and how is cooking knowledge transferred from one person to another? These are some of the questions to consider as we proceed to the next course.

CHAPTER 3

Nina and Irini

Passing the Torch?

Kitchenspace is always one woman's territory, regardless of
the number of women working there. . . . In a society where
women's power is rooted in their role as mothers and
nurturers, it should be no surprise that older women are
reticent to give up their territory in the kitchen, or their sons
for that matter, to another woman.

—Christie 2008, 245–46

"MY MOTHER HATES MY COOKING!"

"My mother hates my cooking! Every day she tells me how much she
hates my cooking." This was the first time I had filmed Nina Papamihail,
as one of the first subjects of my new cooking project, in 2005.[1] I had
known Nina; her mother, Irini; and her husband, Manolis, since the
early 1990s, so Nina's claim was striking to me, applied as it was to her
mother, who seemed mild-mannered to me. Nina stood out in the neighborhood of Ayios Mammas, one of Kalymnos's more "traditional"
working-class neighborhoods. She spoke Greek with a strong New York
accent, reflecting her birth and upbringing in the town of Seneca Falls in
Upstate New York. Her father, a cook, had retired in the late 1960s, and
by 1971 he had wanted to move back to Kalymnos, or at least to his
memory of what Kalymnos had been when he left it as a boy of sixteen.
Her mother was more ambivalent. As Nina remembers, "She missed her
friends when she left. And she missed all the conveniences of the United
States. In 1971 Kalymnos was not like it is now; there was *nothing* in
the way of conveniences." While Kalymnos had no conveniences, Seneca
Falls had no Greeks. The lack of Greeks, much less Kalymnians, in

Seneca Falls led her parents to want to return to the island so Nina could have a "proper" marriage. Nina remembers a very difficult first year on Kalymnos, when on many occasions she thought about moving back to the States on her own: "Kalymnos in 1970 didn't have everything you take for granted in the States: bubble bath, perfumes, shopping—everyday things that are really not that important to your life, but they are when you're twenty-two. But eventually I decided I had to be a good girl and not disappoint my parents, so I stayed." By 2005, when I began this project, Nina had never been back to the United States, even for a visit.

I have to admit that during my initial fieldwork in 1992 I had avoided Nina, as her penchant for speaking English and her knowledge of the United States went against what at the time I believed fieldwork to be about. This was before an interest in transnational migration and lives lived across borders had become a staple of anthropology. But the fact that Nina's circle of friends included a number of non-Greek women who had married on the island, and the fact that Nina seemed to have both an insider's and an outsider's perspective on island life, began to intrigue me. More significant, perhaps, as an English speaker Nina befriended my wife, and their reciprocal get-togethers for coffee pulled me along with them.

While I soon found that Nina cast a critical eye on Kalymnian life, and retained what to me seemed a rather idealized picture of life in the United States based on her childhood memories, she never spoke over-critically of her mother. I thought Nina and her mother got along quite well most of the time. This admission of conflict in the kitchen, therefore, took me a little by surprise. By 2005, unfortunately, Irini was in her mid-eighties and in physical decline, so I was never able to see her in action in the kitchen. But as I explored cooking with Nina, I became intrigued by questions of control and transmission of cooking knowledge, and how this knowledge and skill might develop and change quite late in life. In 2005 Nina was in her mid-fifties. A few things were immediately striking: Nina had still not cooked "on her own," but only under her mother's guidance. Nina and Irini were a bit unusual in that they shared a kitchen. Thanks to the combined wealth from Nina's father's work in the United States and Irini's inheritance (her father had been a well-off merchant), they had built a large kitchen rather early by Kalymnian standards, and didn't have the dual kitchen setup of many other households in the neighborhood of Ayios Mammas. When Nina married Manolis Papamihail, a fisherman and later a seasonal migrant to

FIGURE 7. Manolis Papamihail eating garlic bread in the kitchen of his downtown home (2013). Photo by Nina Papamihail.

the United States, when she was in her mid-thirties, he moved in with them, following the matrilocal pattern of the island. They also had a house—part of Irini's dowry—on the other side of the island that they used in summer. Nina recalled Manolis commenting on his good fortune—this was his second marriage—at meeting such a good woman with two such beautiful houses.

In 2005 Nina was extremely hesitant in the kitchen, telling me repeatedly that she was not a good cook, that she often didn't know what she was doing. Irini had clearly been in charge in the kitchen throughout Nina's life. But by 2005 Irini's health had become precarious. While she might occasionally show the fire in her eyes that I remember from my earlier fieldwork, she more commonly would sit half asleep in a corner of the kitchen. Irini died, after an extended period spent bedridden, in 2008. By 2011 Nina was saying, "You know what, I *can* cook." I was curious to learn how this transformation had been effected, and what it implied for Nina.

To understand the significance of Nina's metamorphosis, let's start with 2005 and the first cooking video I made with her (see video example 7, "Nina Making Octopus Stew"). Nina is cooking octopus stew in the large kitchen of her summer house. Her mother is there, but dozing. Nina's friend Julia Koullia, an American woman married to a Kalymnian man, is also there, accompanied by her daughter Marianthi. This video shows Nina processing the ingredients and putting together the stew while I ask her a series of questions. What follows is a transcript of a few key moments in the video, interspersed with a few scene-setting descriptions.

Nina is cleaning and rinsing the octopus and preparing to cut it over the sink into a bowl. She cuts the tentacles by holding each in one hand between thumb and forefinger, sawing the knife upward through the tentacle to cut off one inch, and then feeding another inch between thumb and forefinger.

> *David:* When did you take over the cooking from your mother? Did you take over from her at a certain point, or did you do it together?
>
> *Nina:* Well, my mother has stopped cooking since May.
>
> *David:* Really? She was still cooking—
>
> *Nina:* She would still cook basically. But I would help her, I would do some foods, it all depends. Like I would clean the fish. She hasn't cleaned fish in years, I don't know when. . . . I would clean the octopus, I would cut up the meat. For years. But if you brought all the tomatoes, all the stuff to her, and it's all ready . . . she could carry on from there. But now she can't.
>
> *David:* And she liked to do that?
>
> *Nina:* Oh, yeah! She says I'm a terrible cook. She hates my cooking. Every day! She *hates* my cooking [*Julia laughing in the background*].
>
> *David:* What's different about it?
>
> *Julia:* It's not hers.
>
> *Nina:* It's not hers, "It tastes terrible," she tells me. Terrible, she hates it.
>
> *David:* And when your husband is here, does she also always do the cooking?
>
> *Nina:* Not now.
>
> *David:* I mean, did she?
>
> *Nina* [offhand]: *Nai* [yes]. Now she doesn't cook. She can't stand because of her hip. My mother used to be a pretty good cook. But now she's aged, she's not as good as she used to be, if I'm honest. But she's still good.
>
> *David:* Do you make things that she didn't make before, or do you make the same things?

Nina: Oh, I make a little bit different. I like it hotter [spicier]. I like spaghetti with . . . I don't use cream, I'll use milk, but she doesn't like that kind of food that much 'cause she's not used to it. Nor Manoli [Nina's husband]—Manoli is like a traditional Kalymnian. They like all the traditional Kalymnian foods. So when he's here I'll do it [spaghetti with cream sauce] once and they'll eat it. You know, blue cheese and things like that. Carbonara I like, but no one else seems to like it.

David: Where did you get the recipe? [*Pause*] . . . From friends?

Nina [offhand]:   Yeah, friends.

Later I ask her about cooking recipes she has seen on cooking shows, and she mentions a meat pie that her mother "of course didn't like. . . . I bought ground pork, and I put in a whole bunch of spices. It was quite good! . . . But my mother is a traditional Kalymnian, she doesn't like all that stuff." She begins washing tomatoes.

Nina: I'm going to grate them. Now, other people put them in the blender [processor]. You know, a little mini-blender. But I don't do that, I have done that, my mother does not like them in the blender.

David: Because it's a machine?

Nina: No, because it mushes everything up. Now, I leave the skin on. Do you want the skin on? [*She begins to cut the tomatoes into a plastic bowl, holding them in one hand over the bowl.*]

David: I don't care.

Nina: Okay. 'Cause other people do not like it with the skin. She likes it with the skin. Other people—[*turning to Julia and Marianthi*]. Do you like it with the skin on?

Marianthi: It doesn't matter.

David: You cut it rather than grate it?

Nina: Oh, I could grate it.

David: What do you normally do?

Nina: I do both. I got the grater out, you see? Should I grate it?

Julia: Do what you normally do.

Nina: I'll ask my mother [*smiling, turning to her mother and speaking in Greek*]: Ma, should I grate 'em or cut 'em?

Mother: Cut 'em up really small [*kopse tis mikra-mikra*].

Nina: She likes 'em cut.

Julia: She wants texture.
[*Nina continues to cut as she had been.*]

Julia [noticing the large pieces]:   Now, remember, she said really small, "*mikra-mikra.*"

This was the first video session I had done with Nina. I had done only two or three others with Kalymnians at this point. Right away it raised for me a number of interesting issues. One was the way that community norms shape even the most subtle of practices and choices: whether to cut or to grate, whether to peel the skin off tomatoes, even issues of how to store rice (in jars or in the woven bags that Nina's mother had made many years earlier but that were still in use). Such questions were adjudicated based on a notion of what the wider community does and finds acceptable. Indeed, Nina told me that her mother complained about her cooking not just in terms of flavor, but because, for example, Nina would knock a wooden spoon against the pot while she was stirring something. "Why do you do that? I don't know anyone who does that" was her mother's exasperated comment. Nina's cooking alerted me to questions of tool use as well: I had assumed that perhaps the older generation would prefer hand tools to machine technology, and this did seem to be the case for some. But kitchen technologies like a small food processor or blender were also embraced by older Kalymnian women. As Nina told me, many elder Kalymnian women do use blenders and other motor-operated kitchen devices because these tools allow them to continue to exert control over the processing of ingredients even when their bodies begin to fail them.

Notice how Irini struggles to retain her power through her control over the kitchen environment and such micro-decisions as whether to cut or grate the tomatoes. As Nina notes, her mother is simply too old to carry on cooking, and in a sense her criticism is her only source of continued relevance in the kitchen. Clearly at stake are Irini's power and her reputation. The fact that the larger community values such sensory distinctions gives them the importance to justify Nina's mother's demand for compliance. Hence, Irini still exerts her power in telling Nina *how* to prepare dishes and process ingredients. *Cooking*, here, is defined as the actual assembly of the ingredients and their transformation by heat, as distinct from the "processing" that Irini has already increasingly delegated to her daughter. Irini's ability to distinguish between her own cooking and her daughter's "terrible" cooking is based on her sensory evaluation of different qualities of cooked food.

Despite these constraints, Nina was already tentatively experimenting from the time that she took over primary responsibility for daily cooking. She had experimented with flavor through adding hot sauce as a condiment to already cooked dishes. She had a particular penchant for Barbadian hot sauce, a combination of mustard, vinegar, and habanero chiles that one of her friends, a British woman who had been living on Kalymnos for a number of years, had brought her. She noted that her friend used the sauce on Kalymnian stuffed grape leaves, *filla,* and that she couldn't really imagine doing so because *filla* is a "traditional dish" that she "wouldn't want to screw up." Thus the category of "traditional" puts a brake on some experimentation.

Before my visits to the island, Nina would request that I bring unusual spices, different colors of peppercorns and the like. She had also begun to try recipes she saw on food programs on TV, or a spaghetti carbonara (which a number of Kalymnians had been making during the past decade), but because of her mother's and husband's preferences for what Nina clearly defined as "traditional Kalymnian dishes," and because of her sense at this point in time that she wasn't a "good cook," these were rare events. I also sensed some of the improvisational aspects of cooking when Nina discussed making a meat pie that she had seen on TV. When she mentioned one of the ingredients, leeks, she said, "Oh, I have some of those—wild leeks from the field outside that I froze. I'll put them in the octopus stew for today. Normally I wouldn't because my mother is traditional and doesn't like things like that in the food." Using the leeks, however, was also a way of connecting with her husband who, though he shared her mother's "traditional" tastes, did enjoy wild leeks. Indeed, in the middle of the filming Manolis called from New York, and she told him that she was using leeks in the octopus stew, so he would have enjoyed it.

It was clear that the category of "traditional" had significance for Nina in that it meant being stuck in the past, not willing to try new things. "Traditional" served as a foil against which Nina was establishing her own tastes. In noting that she didn't like as much olive oil in food as her mother, she commented, "I'll add more today to make it more traditional—because I know you like it and my mother likes it and everybody likes it, so I figure, you know, so not everybody complains that I'm not a good cook." But the pejorative connotations she associated with "traditional" cooking were complicated by the attachment she felt for individual kitchen objects she used to decorate her kitchen spaces. So in other ways, as we see in the next section, the kitchen was also clearly a space of continuity for Nina.

NINA'S KITCHENS

When I began this research in the United States, I found that people seem to develop a strong attachment to certain cooking tools: a cast-iron pan, a steel knife, a bread board. In an article with my student Michael Hernandez, we wrote about these tools as "biographical objects" that people use to tell the stories of their lives. On Kalymnos it seems that there is less of a focus on particular objects, and more a style of kitchen decoration and display that emphasizes meaningful objects that connect people to the past. This was certainly the case in Nina's kitchens. Nina gave me a tour of her kitchen in her main home, emphasizing each knife, pot, serving plate, and other object that was "old." The cabinets themselves were new wooden cabinets brought from the United States by Manolis for $800 in 2005 to replace the original Formica cabinets that had been put in when Nina and Irini had returned to the island in 1971. But every available space on and in these cabinets was littered with objects that represented "old times." Some of these objects were clearly for display purposes: the china figurines and china canisters that were part of her mother's dowry on shelves above the sink; a set of glassware of various kinds sitting on insert shelves or on top of cabinets—wine decanters, vases, water pitchers, and glasses. Nina said she would be tempted to use some of these, but was afraid they would break. As for the brass mortar and coffee mill, copper pots, oil lamps, ceramic oil dispenser, and copper coffee grinder, "These are like over one hundred years old, they're ancient," Nina commented. They were inherited about 1973 when her father's unmarried sister had died and the family members who remained on Kalymnos—Nina's family and the son of another of her father's sisters—had divided up the house and furnishings. While many objects belonged to a generalized past of "my mother's dowry," some were specific, like a ceramic pot with the face of a little girl, which, Nina noted, Irini had bought "as a gift to herself" before they returned from the United States.

At a certain point in her review of the past of these objects, Nina encountered several sets of china plates of Italian manufacture, purchased most likely by Irini's parents during the Italian occupation of Kalymnos. It seemed as if she hadn't thought about these sets for a while. Nina suggested, "Maybe we could use old dishes for lunch." She looked in a cabinet. "What do I have here? . . . David, these are old dishes, my mother's. We will use these today," adding in reference to my video camera, "Aren't they nice? Show them in America." But quickly she changed her mind, noting that the bowls were too small, and thus not practical for serving fish soup.

Under the sink Nina kept various arrays of pots and pans, including many aluminum pots from before World War II. She was aware of the health risks associated with aluminum, but said simply that she liked them, that they were "heavy-duty," and for certain things they worked especially well—fish stew, casseroles in the oven, "Kalymnians use them for stuffed grape leaves because they taste better in aluminum." One aluminum pot had a special lid with holes at the top, which Nina said was especially for making herbal tea from local mountain herbs. The holes made it so that you could boil the herbs in the pot and it didn't boil over.

One drawer in the summer-house kitchen was exclusively filled with bone-handled forks and steel knives that had been Nina's father's, from his work as a chef. She pulled out one knife with a curved blade, noting, "I use this one, but mostly I keep them here for sentimental reasons. . . . Why shouldn't my father be present in the kitchen? He's always present anyway." Here we get a hint of biographical objects, like the Easter ovens discussed in the previous chapter, although for Nina it was not any one particular object that seemed to be the focus of her memories, but rather how all of these objects combined to create a milieu of pastness in her kitchen.

It should be noted that Nina was being somewhat metaphorical in her claim that her father was "always present anyway." Despite his job as a chef, Nina's father rarely cooked in their kitchen, in either Seneca Falls or Kalymnos, although he might do more typically male-gendered food preparation such as grilling fish outdoors or helping to prepare lamb or other festive meals. In Seneca Falls his work took him away from home six days a week for long hours. On his one day off, typically Wednesday, he requested that his wife prepare traditional Kalymnian bean soup (*fasolada*), not, Nina insisted, because Wednesday was a religious fasting day, but because he would grow tired of all the meat and non-Greek food he consumed at work during the rest of the week. After he retired to Kalymnos, his days would be filled with taking care of their fields (often with Nina's help), harvesting olives, or going downtown for business or socializing. So even in this case of a husband who was a professional cook, gendered cooking space determined that the kitchenspace be the domain and responsibility of Nina's mother, who, Nina insisted, had a lifelong penchant for cooking. Nina never remembered observing or learning cooking techniques from her father.

One object that Nina focused on was the white bag that her mother had sewn more than thirty years earlier for storing rice. She noted that bags like these were practical; they didn't take up much room in her pantry. As a type of object, Nina spoke of these bags as being much older than the thirty years since Irini had made them, because the technique of storing rice in bags went back to "before the war." Nina added, "I don't know where other people store their rice, maybe in glass jars, but I'm still doing it this way because that's how my mother did it and that's how I was brought up."[2]

As previously mentioned, while Nina and Irini did have a small kitchen in an outdoor shack, used for frying fish and other intensive food processing, they did not follow the typical pattern of a mother's kitchen and a daughter's kitchen. From the time they moved back from the States to Kalymnos, kitchenspace was shared between mother and daughter (and occasionally the daughter's husband, when Manolis cooked). In part this reflects the fact that Nina and Manolis had never had children together,[3] so they did not create a "separate" family, but continued by and large to share meals with Irini (Nina's father was dead by the time they married). Although in many cases there is a putative separation of mother's and daughter's kitchen (and shopping), there are other cases in which this separation does not hold up in practice, as mother and daughter often jointly negotiate the cooking of meals for both the mother's husband and the daughter's husband and children. Another explanation for this lack of spatial division might be that Irini had grown accustomed to an American-style kitchen, and thus did not want to return to the Kalymnian pattern of using a two-burner stove in a limited space with visible storage of cooking tools. This American influence was also reflected in Irini's penchant for baking pies and making other oven-cooked meals such as roast chicken, going against what was until recently the typical Kalymnian pattern.[4]

But when I discussed their kitchen setup with Nina (in 2011), she pointed out that her aunt Katerina, who had also lived for many years in the States, returned to Kalymnos and *did* adopt a Kalymnian-style kitchen. Nina noted that her aunt's commitment to not using an indoor kitchen for most cooking was part of the Kalymnian pattern of keeping the indoor kitchenspace clean and free of odors, one that she and her mother rejected out of habit. Part of this might then be personal differences, but it also reflected the unusual circumstance that Nina's father was a professional cook, and accordingly it was not only the women who wanted a large kitchen when they moved back to Kalymnos in the early 1970s.[5] The lack of division between mother's and daughter's kitchen might also have contributed, to some extent, to Irini's control over Nina's cooking, since she didn't have her own separate space to cook in (although as noted, daughter's kitchens are usually not used for cooking the main daily meals anyway). But if a lack of kitchen autonomy was a downside, this arrangement also gave Nina greater freedom in relation to other household work. Nina said it was a relief at the time not having to cook because it was such a time-consuming activity, "and my mother never liked my cooking anyway." So as part of their division of labor after their return from the States, Irini controlled the kitchen while Nina worked in the gardens and did other physical labor.

No doubt the fact that Nina and Manolis never had children influenced her relationship with her mother, and perhaps her mother's control over her in the kitchen. When I asked Nina about this, she replied, "It's hard to know, but probably having someone else in the kitchen would have changed our relationship." This suggests that if Nina had had a daughter who was learning kitchen tasks, the dynamics between her and her mother might have shifted. I also thought that perhaps if Nina had had children for whom she was doing some cooking (even though grandmothers often take primary responsibility for feeding grandchildren), it might have given her more confidence in relation to her mother's judgments. However, when I suggested this to her, she once again replied, "It's hard to know. Some grandmothers aren't domineering in the kitchen, but they are domineering about other things, demanding constant attention, or things like that."

When Nina and Manolis renovated their summer house in the early 2000s, they also built it with a large kitchen inside the house with all the amenities and a small outdoor kitchen and oven (once again, cabinets were brought back from the United States from one of Manolis's seasonal work trips). Nina recalls that when she was renovating the kitchen a neighbor told her, " 'Don't make your kitchen so nice you're not going to use it.' I said, 'Of course I am. If I have a nice kitchen, why not use it?' " Nina noted that her outdoor kitchen is on a lower level, down some stairs leading to the garden, a few minutes' walk from her main kitchen. If she has work down there, she might use the outdoor kitchen for cooking, but she certainly wasn't going to walk up and down the stairs from the house to the garden to do her daily cooking.

COOKING CONNECTIONS

In 2006 Irini was no longer cooking at all, but she continued to dominate the kitchen through her presence and her commentary. And Nina still considered herself to be incompetent in the kitchen: "My mother will tell you I have two left feet for hands." During an interview with

FIGURE 8. Irini Psaromati and Manolis Papamihail in the kitchen of their summer home with family friends (2004). Photo by Nina Papamihail.

Nina and Manolis, Nina remarked, "I'm not a good cook, am I, Manolis?" Manolis insisted that she was "good." But Nina responded, "And my mother?" "She's better," he begrudgingly remarked. Nina laughed, suggesting to me that this exchange was not simply a statement of opinion, but part of an ongoing joking relationship among wife, husband, and mother-in-law. There were other jokes of this kind, such as Manolis's frequent suggestion to his mother-in-law that he was going to "find you a boyfriend," a comment that she would always dismiss with annoyance. Similar comments could have a loaded edge to them. In other families I would hear comments—with perhaps a small undercurrent of sexuality—about whether a son-in-law preferred his wife's or his mother's cooking; these seem to be part of the interesting dynamics of matrilocality on Kalymnos.

In the case of Nina, Manolis, and Irini, there was an interesting ongoing balance within what was, in many ways, a very warm and loving family relationship. Manolis would sometimes get annoyed at Nina because of her deference to Irini on everyday decisions. As Nina voiced Manolis: "You're so-and-so years old, and you're still asking your mother?" Nina admitted that she leans on her mother for such daily cooking decisions: "I'll even carry the pot over to her and say, 'Look, Ma, did I add enough water? What should I do next?'" But Nina also seemed to recognize the more complicated constitution of intrafamily relations of love and of power. As she noted, her mother always "ran the household" and "made the daily decisions," but at the same time would lean on her father, "see him as the boss," and expect him to make the "major" decisions like whether to stay in the United States or move back to Kalymnos, in large part because those were the expected gender roles at the time. Since her father's passing, Irini would increasingly lean on Nina for those major decisions while at the same time continuing to dominate the kitchen space. Nina struggled to capture the ambiguities of their relationship: "Really [my mother] is the child, even way back then. And I was always the mother but I'm also dependent on her. Do you know I can't even make a decision sometimes . . . because all my life she has told me what to do." This unpunctuated stream of thought captures, I think, some of the difficulty of making any clear statements about "power" or "dominance" within a relationship that Nina characterizes as "still basically good."

Some of the positive aspects of Nina and Irini's relationship also came through in discussions about food. Nina's fondest memories are of some of the foods that her mother used to cook in the United States. When I mentioned the rhubarb growing in my garden, Nina had a Proustian moment, remembering a particular rhubarb pie that her mother had made. She recounted an image of her mother, describing in detail the housecoat she was wearing (saying first that it must have been summer, and then that maybe not, because the houses were so warm you didn't change dress for the season the same way you do here). She said she was carrying a small rhubarb pie, taking it to the neighbor's as a gift, and she could taste the tart flavor of the rhubarb. Nina spoke many times of the delicious pie crusts her mother made, which she had learned by observing her father as he worked in the restaurant in Seneca Falls.[6] "I'm her daughter, but anybody who tasted her pies . . . they were great!" Nina's conversations about cooking over the years are sprinkled with flavors of her mother's kitchen. Irini's pies are a constant touchstone in these conversations. "When my mother used to make pies in America, she used Crisco. What do they use now? Do you think that's why her pies were so flaky?" would be a typical interjection, brought on by a discussion of different kinds of cooking fat.

At another moment Nina reflected on her hybrid food upbringing in the United States and what food culture was like when she was growing up in the 1950s and 1960s, as well as some of the changes in Kalymnian eating patterns:

When I left America I never had a McDonald's. There was no Mexican food [no Mexicans or Puerto Ricans in Seneca Falls], there was none of this *other* kind of food. There were TV dinners. My mother cooked. I don't remember any neighbors making shrimp in those days. The only fish that I ever ate was fish sticks at school and at home and tuna fish in the can. And fried haddock and scallops. My mother used to fry them or make them in a *pilafi* with tomatoes. I had octopus only once, when someone from Greece came and brought a dried octopus and my mother cooked it. I never had fresh fish or fish soup. My mother used to make pizza and *ftasimo, kourambiedes, koulourakia* [baked goods], she used to make good pies, excellent crust, mine is crap. She used to make meat loaf, which I consider an American food, now they make it here. She would make grilled [i.e., roasted] chicken in the oven with lemon and savory. Once I had Chinese food, but in Syracuse. A nice restaurant, not take-out. I lived a very sheltered life. She used to make macaroni salads and potato salads, she made *revithia* [chickpeas] and *fakes* [lentils]—they're in the grocery store. I had grilled lobster out, with butter. My aunt would catch sunfish and my mother would fry them. My mother would go with another woman and cut wild greens, and she would boil spinach. When we came here forty years ago, there were vegetables only in season. I'm still stuck in this time capsule; I still only buy vegetables in season. You had to buy onions in the summer to have all year around, the same with garlic. Oranges only in the winter. Then I tasted fish soup, which I liked. My mother used to make clam chowder in America. My father must have taught her. I don't know if I ate that. My mother would make lamb chops; I had more lamb in America than I have here, it tasted better too, or maybe it's just that I think it did. When I first came to Kalymnos, there were no *spanakopites, tiropites* [spinach or cheese pies], my mother said they make them *pano stin ellada* [in mainland Greece]. But when we came forty years ago, nobody was making this type of food.

Nina also recalled a tuna noodle casserole that she had learned to make in home economics class. Nina had liked it so much that she had gotten her mother to reproduce it at home, and it became a staple in their household during the winter months. Now, in 2006, Nina says that she herself makes it every year, even though Manolis hates it, referring to tuna as a fish to eat fresh, and only if the tuna are small ("up to ten kilos"). For Manolis, canned tuna is something "to feed the cats." Nina and her mother would eat it, Nina noting, "since it reminds me of my childhood, and it was different from the foods we had at home [i.e., Kalymnian foods]." These small connections were part of a relationship of caring that characterized many aspects of Nina and Irini's daily interactions and that had given me the initial impression that they were "close." All of this led to my surprise the first time Nina told me about her mother's control over and deprecation of her cooking.

TRANSITIONS: 2008

By the spring of 2008 Irini was much worse, and confined to bed much of the time. Nina was anxiously fretting about the lack of her mother's daily participation in the household. She noted the feeling of security she got from having her mother telling her what to do (even if she often didn't do what her mother said). She was particularly concerned while I was visiting because Manolis was on the cusp of leaving for his seasonal migration to the States, so she felt that she would really be on her own with "no one to lean on," and worried about something happening to her mother while he was gone. When she told Irini that Manolis would be leaving soon, Irini responded, "Who will protect us?" but then added, "We'll be okay, Mary [the Virgin] will protect us."

At the same time, Nina was growing increasingly confident in her own abilities. When she made octopus stew this time, there was no deferring to her mother, simply some casual coordination with Manolis: she got him to cut up the octopus before she started cooking it, and asked him to throw the water out in the backyard "to save her the trouble." There was still very much a sense of kitchen practices being done in relation to a larger community: adding a little tomato paste to the base of tomatoes and onions, she noted, "My neighbor only uses tomato paste, because they like it really red"; even the gesture of throwing the water out in the backyard (to add its nutrients to the soil) was noted by Nina as part of her "traditionalness," as opposed to other Kalymnians who might now simply dump the water down the sink. She consulted with Manolis about whether to use well water or tap water in boiling the octopus. Here it struck me that such back-and-forth was not simply about the small differences that make a difference for Kalymnians in creating proper flavor, it also served the role of a recipe—as a memory jog for all the procedures involved in creating even a familiar, well-tried dish.[7] There was a sense that I had seen in many Kalymnian kitchens of a kind of distributed cognition (Hutchins 1995) in Kalymnian cooking.

Nina was taking pleasure in using more spices, including a variety of different peppercorns that I had brought her from the United States. While making the octopus stew, she added some whole pink peppercorns and crushed some of them up with a spoon. Earlier she had asked me for a recipe that explained what to do with pink peppercorns, and I had found one on the Internet and printed it out for her. Apparently the recipe had said to crush the peppercorns with a spoon. Nina was still hesitant: "I don't know if it goes in here or not, but since you brought it

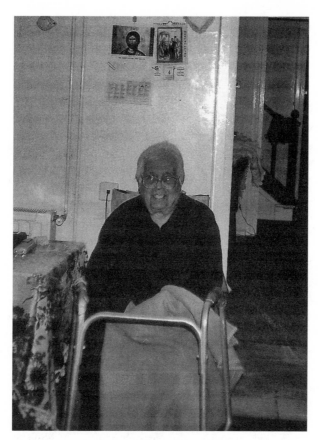

FIGURE 9. Irini in her favorite spot (2005). Photo by author.

I'll put it in." She added while crushing the peppercorns, "I don't know if I'm doing it right, but, you know, I like it." The sense that her own preference might outweigh the "proper" way was a new aspect of Nina's cooking that emerged as her mother's control receded.

But there was still a very strong sense of Irini's presence, both in terms of memories evoked—Nina remembering the use of Crisco in her mother's pie crust—and in terms of everyday practice. "I asked my mother recently how to do the pie crust, but she was out of it, she didn't say anything." The pie crust was still a touchstone: "Well, at least I can't make a pie crust good like my mother used to, that's comforting." Here, her own lesser competence is seen as a positive thing, as if this indicates that Irini had not been superseded and thus still had a place in the kitchen.[8]

One sign of Nina's newfound confidence in the kitchen in 2008 was her eagerness to cook *veryioi,* a type of wild field onion that is now difficult to find on Kalymnos, though it was more common in the past. This is the kind of food that is associated with Kalymnian tradition, and the mere mention of it can make people express nostalgia. Nina had run into a neighbor whose cooking I was also observing, and who was carrying a bag full of *veryioi.* When Nina asked her how she was preparing them, the neighbor was dismissive, saying, "To be a good cook and cook *veryioi* so they aren't bitter, you have to have toughness." Indeed, it requires several days of soaking and processing to remove the bitterness from *veryioi.* Nina took this as a challenge; she asked two other neighbors how to prepare the *veryioi,* and bought them (at some expense, they were 5 euros a kilo at that time). Because of my project, I happened to taste the neighbor's *veryioi.* Nina was extremely pleased when I admitted that her neighbor's *veryioi* had still tasted somewhat bitter to me, while Nina insisted that her *veryioi* had come out sweet.

By the fall of 2008, Irini was in serious decline. Nina recalled one day at her bedside when Irini hadn't spoken for a month. Nina was feeding her and suddenly she knocked the spoon away, saying, "Stop!" Nina asked what was wrong, and Irini said, "My brother-in-law [*kouniados*] is trying to come to greet me." Nina asked, "Which brother-in-law?" and Irini replied, "Mihalis." "Did he come?" "No . . . he didn't," said Irini, before lapsing again into silence. Sightings of Mihalis by those close to death are interpreted by Kalymnians as the presence of the archangel Michael, preparing the person for heaven. Nina also talked about how beautiful her mom looked on her last few days—no wrinkles, beautiful color in her face. Irini died on November 17, 2008.

"My mother went out in glory," Nina recalled, speaking of Irini's memorial service (*kollivo*). The archbishop was having coffee with the priest who was going to perform her *kollivo,* so he came along to it, even though he didn't know her personally. "So she had the archbishop of Kalymnos attending her memorial!" The memorial was held at the neighborhood church of Ayios Mammas, where Irini hadn't been in the ten years prior to her death, and now she is buried in the church cemetery. Now when Nina goes to tend to Irini's grave, she tells her that she can enjoy all those liturgies she used to miss. On the nine-day anniversary of her death—one of the days that one marks with a memorial ceremony—a bird appeared at Irini's grave, an "eighteen" bird (named after the call it makes, which sounds like the Greek word for eighteen). Nina had a stranger experience six months after her mother died, on what would have been Irini's ninety-first birthday. A peacock had been visiting their summer house for several weeks, coming in the evening and spending the night there. On that particular evening, "When I was going out of the kitchen, I look up and there is the peacock on the small kitchen roof looking at me. We looked at each other for a few minutes and it flew away. I was surprised it could fly so far, though not high." When Nina told her family and neighbors about this, they told her it was her mother's soul paying a visit. At the time she wrote in a letter to me, "I *do* think it was my mother's spirit." Looking back two years later, Nina noted, "It's all how you interpret it."

NEW EXPLORATIONS, 2009–2011

I visited Nina and Manolis a little over six months after Irini's death during a short trip to the island (accompanied by my wife and two sons for the first time since 1998). Because it had been a long time since they had seen my family, Nina and Manolis took pleasure in making a huge meal for us. This meal included octopus stew, two kinds of fish, baked chickpeas, fava beans, boiled zucchini, and a salad. As Nina looked over the table, she expressed amazement that she could put on such a spread without her mother's direction. As we sat around after lunch my son Sam filmed us as Nina and I talked about some of the changes over the past year. Nina immediately underlined the fact that without her mother to cook for, she was "experimenting more," trying different ingredients and spices in dishes. She noted that she was aware of adding certain ingredients to the cooking "because Mom's not going to eat it." This felt like a license for experimentation: "I put a lot of cloves in the food; I put quince [*kidoni*] in a beef, zucchini, and potato dish, and it turned out good, wasn't it good, Manoli?" The idea for using quince, normally used only to make preserved spoon sweets, was something Nina had picked up from watching *Boukia kai Sihorio* (*Forgiveness with Every Bite*), one of the popular Greek cooking shows, hosted by celebrity chef Elias Mamalakis.[9] Nina noted, "He made it with pork. I saw the quince at Smalios (one of the supermarkets near her summer house). I had been to go shopping and I saw it there and so I bought it. I thought I'd make it with pork, but I didn't get around to it, I didn't have any pork, so I made it with beef." In this short description I got a sense that Nina was developing a more improvisational approach to cooking, sparked by new inputs beyond the neighborhood and her mother as judges of what is proper and what goes with what. While in past times quince might be a discovery to be consumed fresh or preserved, and variations in a recipe for beef and potatoes might have included whatever vegetable came to hand, it was only because of the wider circulation of food recipes and knowledges introduced on cooking shows, and the coincidence for Nina that it was being made available by supermarkets stocking it more regularly, that this new combination became part of Nina's kitchen experiments.

At the same time, Nina admitted that she still felt "used to [Irini] telling me, 'Do this, do that, go here, go there.' I even ask Manoli *odigise me* [guide me], tell me what I should do. You know, like it could be simple things like should I put this in the refrigerator now or should I put it in later. She would tell me 'all right, Nina, it's time that that goes in the refrigerator.' I'm used to somebody telling me even little things. I might not do it, but I'm still used to her telling me." Nina admitted that this was a pattern that she felt "conditioned" to expect "after sixty years, even though I might get mad, or I might not do it." I asked Nina, "Do you think that as time goes on, this will change?" "I don't know, David, I don't know." This referring of small decisions to her mother or to Manolis did not simply reflect Nina's insecurity. It can be seen as part of the "outward orientation" of Kalymnian cooking that I discussed in relation to the technique of cutting in the hand. Part of cooking was exactly these kinds of social interactions about the small details of preparation, which might, or might not, reflect unequal power relations.

Despite this awareness of a desire for things to continue the same way as before, Nina also noted the incredible freedom she felt to do things in the house that she had never done because her mother had not wanted them. She gives the example of putting a canopy on the bed that her mother had been using, which she had long thought about doing, "and now I'm going to do it."

"And that feels okay?"

"It feels okay, because *den eimai ego i nikokira?* [Aren't I the head of the house now?] I've always been the *nikokyra*, but she always ruled, but now I am the *nikokyra*, aren't I?" Later she added that her mother had always sat at the dining table at the seat closest to the stove "because she was always the head of the household sitting closest to the kitchen [i.e., the stove], but now I sit next to the stove."

Here, as elsewhere, Nina seems to recognize the subtle balances of power that go into family relations, relations in which on the one hand her mother may have "ruled" in the daily household activities (against which Nina could sometimes chafe and rebel), but in which on the other,

FIGURE 10. Nina Papamihail enjoying a cup of coffee at her kitchen table (2014). Photo by author.

Nina had long been accustomed to playing the role of her father, someone to lean on for major decisions. Food preparation is, of course, among the most mundane of daily household activities. Yet considering the value that Kalymnians ascribe to good food and good flavor, sitting next to the stove stands as a kind of symbol for household power, or *nikokyra*, a word that represents the good household management that is often central to an evolving sense of self and identity.[10]

During late 2010 and early 2011, Nina kept a food diary of her daily meals. While she had recorded this for me in the past over short periods (see Sutton 2001, 105–7), this diary stretched for three months from the beginning of December through early March. I then followed up by discussing the diary with her when I visited for several weeks in May. One of the issues on Nina's mind during this entire period was health concerns. While she had earlier talked about avoiding excessive salt in cooking, she had become increasingly concerned about cholesterol. Then over the winter Nina had to have several biopsies and finally a tumor removed from her breast. It took until late June for her doctor to determine that she didn't need additional therapy for it. Over this period Nina was thinking about food as both a source of pleasure and a source of stress. As she joked to me at one point, "Isn't it funny, I'm more depressed about cutting back on sweets [because of cholesterol] than about having cancer?"

Despite this backdrop, what struck me most in Nina's diary were her comments next to different meals—"good," "really good," "tasty," and "I'm becoming good" with exclamation points littered throughout. These comments all reflected Nina's new balance in her sense of herself in the kitchen, a confidence that extended to other areas as she bragged to her husband's cousin about taking the Metro (subway) all over Athens and often by herself, while she was there for her operations, an idea that her husband's cousin found outlandish. Just as in 2005 cooking was very much seen in relation to what other people in the community do or like, by 2011 the "community" had broadened increasingly to include practices in Athens or on the increasingly ubiquitous cooking shows. This wider circle was apparent when I asked Nina about the "good!" that she had put next to her meal of split-pea soup (*fava*) on February 1. Nina exclaimed, "We always have *fava*, it's nothing special. But my cousin in Athens orders it from restaurants [*tavernes*], for twelve to sixteen euros a plate. I said, 'You're shittin' me.' I couldn't believe that people order this because it's so common here, but in Athens they don't make it anymore. On some TV show when I was in Athens in late March for my operation, they showed how to make *fava* with beef broth. My cousin Popi said, '*dhen einai nistisimo*' [it's not appropriate for fasting days]. But I just couldn't believe that they were showing fava on TV." Nina's tone was ironic, because she felt that her *fava* was as good as anything they could make in a restaurant. She was distrustful of what she saw as fancy, status foods, just as she ridiculed me when I told her what I had spent for an espresso maker. As she told me in an earlier interview: "Good food should be tasty. I'm not the fancy type that wants everything to look pretty. . . . Just as long as it tastes good and it satisfies me and I get full, I'm happy."

The clearest influence on Nina's cooking over this period was Jamie Oliver, the British celebrity chef whose cooking show had been playing in Greece for the previous several years. While Nina had drawn from some of the Greek cooking shows in the past, she had become a devoted fan of Jamie Oliver's show, which turns up in her diary. During the winter and spring of 2011, Nina made four meals based on his recipes. In each case, however, it is notable that Oliver provided the inspiration, but Nina made significant changes (as she did in substituting beef for pork above). When I use the word *inspiration*, what is implied? Not, for the most part, that Nina followed a menu, or even a particular recipe presented on the TV show. Rather, the show seemed to provoke ideas of possibilities, or it acted as a memory jog. For example, Nina made a salad and added fresh mint and basil leaves from her garden because she had seen Oliver use these ingredients in a salad (basil is not typically used as food in Greece). Or Oliver made grilled zucchini brushed with olive oil and that reminded Nina of how her mom had done it in the past, so she made it; or she noted that Oliver was using fennel in a cooked dish, while she had only used it raw in salads (it grows in her garden). So without reproducing the recipe, Nina got the idea of using fennel as one of the ingredients to make a meatless (*pseftiko*) pastitsio. She put vegetables on the bottom, followed by a layer of mushrooms, and béchamel with cheese on top. For all of these dishes Nina was very pleased with the results, commenting, "I'm getting really adventurous," "I outdid myself," "It was quite good," and, with her sardonic humor, "Nobody died!"

The fact that Jamie Oliver was such an influence on Nina also reflects her hybrid-outsider identity—that is, she was often looking for justifications for practices that might lie outside the community of Kalymnos, to keep her in touch with her non-Kalymnian identity. She often took pleasure in noting when something was superior in the United States as opposed to Kalymnos. This, too, carried an overtone of potential rebellion against her mother and her "traditional" ways, even if Irini had adopted a number of American practices in the kitchen as well. For example, Nina noticed that Jamie Oliver uses enamel bowls to mix things in the kitchen, which she also does. Here, she is taking from Oliver not the idea but the justification, as she noted that on Kalymnos most people consider enamel bowls to be old-fashioned, using plastic bowls instead. She also remarked on his plates, which are "old and nice," once again implicitly comparing this to her kitchen practice.

Another source of cooking explorations and adventures came from ideas taken from neighbors or friends, which seemed to work as a kind of horizontal source of knowledge. For example, on December 3, Nina made a bean soup with sun-dried tomatoes, which she had started making in 2010. She had been talking with a store owner near her summer house who had mentioned that she sun-dried her extra tomatoes, so Nina asked her how and decided to try it, noting the fun she had adding different spices to the jar to create different flavors.[11]

At other times, the availability of certain ingredients would guide the meal. They might get fish or goat milk as a gift from a neighbor and make it the main course or part of a meal (the goat milk, made into a kind of yogurt, accompanied a meat and orzo dish). They were also making more egg dishes, from fried eggs to eggs cooked with tomatoes (*avgozoumi*), because their chickens were producing lots of eggs during this period. By contrast, Nina might create a change by using a special ingredient like alcohol in cooking. She noted, "I don't usually cook with wine because I don't have it, it's too expensive, we're economizing. But maybe I find a cheap brand and why not change, cook gourmet? Sometimes I cook octopus with ouzo—I'm becoming good!"

Another factor is a balance of desire and boredom. For example, on January 16 she made cabbage with rice because they were "tired of meat." On March 1 she made meatballs with rice and potato soup because she "missed it, haven't had it all winter." On March 2 she noted that Manolis had wanted this food for months: rice in a tomato sauce with fresh tomatoes. Manolis said, "Delicious." On January 27 Manolis made pizza with homemade pizza dough as a "supper" snack, something that "Manolis always does better than me."[12] When I asked her about this, Nina said that they had probably been talking for a few days about having a pizza, a dish that her mother used to make for them, and had finally decided to do it. The same goes for pies: Nina made a lemon pie on January 16, which she noted she does every winter, as in the summer they eat more fruit for dessert. However, on February 10 Nina made a "beautiful coconut cream pie," which she noted that she "thought about and made it." Like the rhubarb pie, this dish was strongly identified with her childhood in America and with Irini, and her mention of it led to a flood of reminiscences about food and childhood experiences in the United States. Here the thought of particular foods both project into a near future of their making and consumption, and index a past not of habit, as in the dishes that are commonly eaten every week, but of more distant memories and connections.

But pie also is projected into the future through Nina's concerns about health and cholesterol, as Nina complained that she couldn't control her appetite, unlike her mother who, she recalled, could fry a dish of chickpea "meatballs" and not eat a single one, "whereas if I'm frying something I'll have filled up before I get it to the table." Nina also noticed how worries about her biopsy had affected her cooking, telling me about making stuffed grape leaves and forgetting to put the rice in. So she ended up making the rice on the side; "It turned out okay," she conceded. A month later, after getting good results from the doctors, she noted that her grape leaves had been very good, and she had made them

FIGURE 11. Nina cooking "American-style" baked beans with
sausages (2013). Photo by Manolis Papamihail.

along with some delicious grilled green chiles. "I bought them from the
woman from Kos who sells down by the customs office. I asked her,
'Why are these peppers over here, not with the other ones?' It turns out
they're hot, really hot! I'm going to put them in beef stew tomorrow
along with potatoes from the garden. I'll only use one pepper so it's not
too hot for Manolis. I'll add hot sauce if I need to for me." Thus, Nina
was striking a balance between her tastes and Manolis's, while continuing to explore different possibilities. However, it was clear that "health,"
with its nebulous ties of present eating to future states, had become one
of the key values around which cooking had to be negotiated at the
same time as Nina was becoming increasingly confident over her ability

to control "taste" and to be in control in the kitchen, to be "the head of household" in her mother's absence.

CONCLUSION: HYBRID MEMORIES

Like many Kalymnians who have lived through a migration experience, both Nina and Irini were deeply shaped by their divided experience living in the United States and on Kalymnos, and this shows in their kitchen practices. In some ways Nina reversed Irini's experience of girlhood in Kalymnos and mature adulthood in the United States, and it was clearly Nina's youthful experience that shaped many of her food preferences and desire for "difference" in spicing up Kalymnian food. While in my earlier work on food and memory (2001) I was interested in the imprint of local foods on Kalymnian memories, especially for Kalymnians who were living abroad and were desperate for a "taste of home," I did not take in how deeply shaped some Kalymnians might be by their childhood experiences outside of Greece. Nina's strongest memories were of some of the "American" foods that her mother made—the pie crusts that she despairs of reproducing, or a summer salad with coconut, pineapple, and rice, the kind of concoctions straight out of 1950s Americana (see Shapiro 2004). It is these foods that connect Nina and Irini in a positive sense, as it is these memories of her mother's cooking that she cherishes. Nina does have some strong Kalymnos-based food memories, though even these are not for typical Greek dishes. When she was complaining about limiting the fat in her diet because of concerns about cholesterol, she recounted a particularly vivid memory: the first time she saw her grandmother dunk cheese—the Greek hard cheese, *kaseiri*—into her coffee (this was when they had recently moved back to the island). She told me that the fat from the cheese goes into the coffee, and then the cheese gets soft and delicious, forming at the bottom of the cup. Watching her grandmother do it for the first time, Nina remembered thinking it was disgusting, but then she tried it and thought it was incredible. This anecdote united a family memory with a rich sensory feeling of longing for the kind of food of which she was currently depriving herself.

Nina certainly adapted to many Kalymnian foods after her move to the island, and she is extremely aware of community tastes and standards; yet she also has a strong awareness of her *difference* from standard Kalymnian views and "traditional" Kalymnian tastes. This brings up a more general point that every dish on Kalymnos is fraught with myriad decisions as a cook negotiates a path between her own tastes, the tastes of other family members, and a sense of how the larger Kalymnian community has determined standards of taste. Therein, I think, lay Nina's attraction to a figure like Jamie Oliver, who represented a source of authority outside the local community with whom she could identify.

Nina's preferences had often been muted by Irini's control of the kitchen, which produced a sense of insecurity for Nina in her cooking competence, noted in such practices as asking her mother whether to cut or grate tomatoes, or in her tendency to check the food constantly while it is cooking: "My mother asked me why I always check the food; she didn't need to check so much." Irini's voice continues to echo in the kitchen and to shape her, even as she grows increasingly confident in her abilities. During the same discussion in May 2011 she proudly bragged to me about producing the best Easter cookies in the neighborhood (because of her willingness to use good butter) but also said she was still using Manolis as a crutch for her uncertainties in daily tasks: "I'll still ask *ela na deis, einai etoimo to fai, ti nomizeis?* [come look, is the food ready, what do you think?]; maybe not all the time, but I still ask. It's comforting. And then [*laughing*] it's his [Manolis's] fault if it doesn't turn out good [*pause*]. But I'm not as bad as I used to be." Here she recognizes the comfort of sometimes subsuming one's agency to the projects of others, while at the same time making some claim for her own desire for creativity. This is a tension that was clearly constantly in negotiation and expressed to different degrees in Nina's relationship with Irini, and now with Manolis. It makes a mockery of the notion that cooking knowledge or skill "passes from mother to daughter" in any smooth, uninterrupted sense.

Nina remarks on her difference from her neighbors, as well, in the more limited role she allows for ritual prescriptions in mourning her mother's death. Unlike some of her neighbors, Nina notes, she stopped wearing black about a year after Irini's death, and now does not shun bright colors. She chides other neighbors—some young or middle-aged women—who carry on wearing black for the death of a parent because "it's easier, they don't have to worry about what to wear, but they're too young to be wearing black all the time." Similarly, Nina kept a light constantly at her mother's grave for forty days, but does not follow her neighbors in paying someone to keep it lit beyond that point. Nina once again sees a certain practicality in her approach to Kalymnian traditions. Nina's memories of her mother are less activated by these ritual actions than by the objects with which she surrounds herself: Irini's chair, sitting in the corner offering advice and criticism, and the myriad kitchen objects, the "inalienable possessions" that seem to store memories through their ubiquity. To give Nina the last word: "When I die, they're going to have truckloads to throw away. And I feel bad, because I appreciate these things. . . . Nobody appreciates this crap like I do. . . . I wish I had more room to display these things. . . . These things are old and they're my mother's. And they're old, they're nice. I like them. They don't make things like this anymore."

CHAPTER 4

Mothers, Daughters, and Others

Learning, Transmission, Negotiation

A post on the bulletin board of the Association for the Study of Food and Society relates the following story: "There was a woman in a small town in Ohio; evidently, she made a great potato salad. Members of her community badgered her, repeatedly, for the recipe. Her response, 'Over my dead body.' When the woman passed away it was revealed in her will enough money to have her potato [salad] recipe chiseled on her tombstone."[1]

Such anecdotes have the familiar tone of descriptions of "colorful, backward" rural communities. However, they took on a different resonance for me as I pursued my study of daily cooking on Kalymnos. To me such stories point to cooking as a medium that interweaves relationships of knowledge, skill, and power. These relationships beg for ethnographic exploration. How is cooking knowledge transmitted, or not transmitted, within families and communities? Does it lead to the simple reproduction, or the transformation, of food tastes and practices? And is "transmission" really the right way to think about how cooking is taken up by a younger generation?

When I began to explore how cooking was learned on Kalymnos (Sutton 2001, chap. 5), I was met with the pat phrase, "It passes from mother to daughter," a maxim that seemed to require no further comment. Cooking skill, in this view, is imagined as an objectified body of knowledge that can be passed down like cooking equipment, land, houses, and other more obviously "material" property. Undiscouraged, beginning in 2005 I undertook interviews and videos in Kalymnian kitchens. And I immediately began to question whether the course of cooking knowledge indeed ran smoothly, and to look for other ways of understanding the relationship of knowledge, skill, and transmission.

Traditional anthropological approaches to the relationship of knowledge and power in small-scale societies have been particularly focused on questions of the control of knowledge and its dissemination and blockage—in other words, secrecy—within society.[2] In his groundbreaking ethnography, *Knowledge and Power in the South Pacific*, Lamont Lindstrom, for example, writes, "Access to cultural knowledge and to its use is rarely equal or open to all. . . . Conversational practice establishes individual cultural incompetence as well as competence. Discursive procedures regulate who may speak and who may not—who is conversationally qualified, and who is disqualified" (1990, 19).[3] Furthermore, the control and flow of knowledge are central to the authority of the older generation. As Lindstrom notes, "Throughout Melanesia, there is . . . a pervasive suspicion that the wise take care never to exchange what they know in its entirety" (1990, 121). As Fredrik Barth has argued in his study of ritual transmission of knowledge: "The value of information seemed to be regarded as inversely proportional to how many share it" (1975, 217).[4]

Much of this work, useful as it is, tends to focus on discursive and conversational knowledge and not on the kind of skill that tends to be learned in less discrete ways. Fortunately, there is a substantial literature on apprenticeship, particularly in the learning of various types of crafts, to help us fill the gap. The anthropology of apprenticeship focuses on learning that takes place typically in formal master-apprentice relationships. It may seem strange to apply this master-apprenticeship rubric to the learning of cooking, which typically takes place in the context of the home.[5] Like the anthropology of ritual knowledge, this literature has, with a few exceptions, concerned itself with male apprenticeship, almost always in extradomestic contexts.[6] But Jean Lave has recently demonstrated that the notion of apprenticeship might be applied more broadly to different kinds of learning (2011). I find such a perspective particularly useful in bringing together a notion of social skills and technical skills, which are acquired through legitimate peripheral participation in "communities of practice" (Lave and Wenger 1991). Recently, researchers have been attentive to the complex and power-laden dynamics that exist between "masters" and "apprentices" in different cultural contexts, as well as the way that learning specific technical skills is intimately tied to learning to be *the type of person* who can master such skills (see Bryant 2005). Indeed, a number of writers have analyzed apprenticeship more as a power relation than as a process of knowledge transmission.[7] I believe that knowledge transmission is equally interesting, especially insofar as this literature also stresses the different implications for learning that takes place through sensory engagement, play frames, observation (often surreptitious), or embodied habits as opposed to traditional Western models of explicit, school-based learning.[8]

One of the few in-depth studies of female transmission of knowledge is the work of Patricia Greenfield and her collaborators on Maya weavers. Ashley Maynard, Greenfield, and Carla Childs use Marcel Mauss's notion of *bodily techniques* (*techniques du corps*) to show how Maya girls' bodies are prepared from birth to have the capacity to weave using the backstrap loom, which requires that "a woman's body becomes an essential part of the loom. Weaving is not possible if there is not a body serving as a part of the loom frame. The warp or frame threads are stretched between a post and the weaver's body" (1999, 381). They argue that Maya girls' bodies are shaped "culturally and biologically" in such capacities as "low motor activity," maintaining a kneeling position for extended periods,[9] developing balance through tasks such as carrying wood on their heads, and acute visual perceptive abilities that fit the local model of "learning through observation" rather than learning by doing (1999, 384–85). Another study of female apprenticeship is Jacquetta Hill and David Plath's on Japanese abalone divers, the majority of whom are women. They note that mothers never trained their own daughters, as they were not eager to have a potential competitor tagging along to "steal their moneyed knowledge." As one daughter put it: "My mother! She drove me away! I tried to follow her to the bottom to watch, but she shoved me back. When we were on the surface again, she practically screamed at me to move OFF and find my danged abalone BY MYSELF" (2006, 212). Instead, Hill and Plath describe a process of learning among peers that occurs in relation to the environment in which the diver "must train herself to seize each new 'learning experience' when it appears . . . much as she must train herself to pounce upon a live abalone when she detects it" (215). The experience of these women has interesting echoes in Michael Herzfeld's work with male masters and apprentices on Crete. Cretan master potters are not in a situation of intrafamily competition; indeed, one cannot take an apprentice who is a relative. Yet there is still a deep concern on the part of masters not to part easily with their knowledge. As Herzfeld argues, "apprentices often learn despite the fact that their masters, far from teaching them, often seem to discourage them from learning anything at all. . . . The apprentice was supposed to watch and observe 'So that he will learn how to steal the work, and it will stay in his brain'" (2003, 51, 101; see also Patel 2008, 133).

All of the aforementioned cases suggest that skill and knowledge don't simply "pass" from master to apprentice. This ability must be actively appropriated. The approaches of Maynard et al., Hill and Plath, and Herzfeld also suggest, in their different ways, the importance of observation as opposed to direct teaching or verbal instruction in the learning of skills, a finding confirmed by much research on bodily skills in general (see, e.g., Ingold 2000; Sennett 2008). The term *observation*, however, may be limiting in its ocular-centrism. Learning skills certainly does involve the eyes, but on Kalymnos it also clearly involves all the senses, immersed in a landscape where common phrases such as "listen to see" index the synesthetic orientation of much of Kalymnian daily practice and ritual experience (see Sutton 2001, chap. 3).

On Kalymnos there is no formalized learning of cooking, and therefore there are no particular periods of the life course in which women (and a few men) learn to cook. Thus, in investigating the transmission of cooking, I took the Kalymnian injunction "it passes from mother to daughter" seriously, even while questioning whether this was in any sense a simple or natural process. I looked at mother-daughter relations (as well as grandmother-granddaughter, aunt-niece, etc.) at different stages of the life course to see what kinds of learning, what kinds of influence, and what kinds of negotiations were taking place. In the following descriptions I ethnographically explore some of these negotiations, while bringing questions of skill, knowledge, and power to the fore.

MOTHERS, DAUGHTERS, AND FAMILY HIERARCHIES

In the rest of this chapter I outline what I believe to be crucial for understanding cooking knowledge. Cooking knowledge on Kalymnos is embedded in gender roles, female hierarchies, architectural space, and a sense of the "proper," "traditional," and "healthy" ways of food preparation. I begin with some examples of different kinds of mother-daughter relations as seen through struggles over the actual doing, and control over the understanding, of cooking. These examples include discursive struggles over the meaning of tradition and the role of change in Kalymnian women's lives.

In the previous chapter I examined how Irini's control of the kitchen precluded Nina's learning to cook until later in life. While this may be an unusual case, the theme of control was constantly present in mother-daughter negotiations in one form or another. For example, I filmed a daughter about age twenty, visiting home from college outside of Greece, as she prepared a Sunday dish of moussaka. I was interested in the preparation of this meal because the tasks had been divided among the mother, maternal grandmother, father, and daughter, with the daughter preparing the meat and tomato sauce portions of the dish. I specifically wanted to get the daughter to describe the making of the dish so that I could apprehend how she conceptualized the process. This led to the following exchange:

David [to the daughter]:   Can you tell me what's in the ground meat?

Mother: Ah. David wants to know the ingredients in the ground meat.

Daughter: I sautéed [*tsigarisa*] the meat, so that the liquid would evaporate. Then I added butter, to sauté with it.

Mother [sotto voce]: To "cook."

Daughter: To cook. Then I added cinnamon, pepper, onion, garlic.

Mother: Bay leaf . . .

Daughter: Bay leaf.

Mother [reaching into the pan and pulling out a bay leaf]:   I'm using my hand, it doesn't matter, cooking requires hands. Bay leaf.

Daughter: A little red wine . . .

Mother: A little red wine.

Daughter [hesitating slightly]:   Tomato sauce.

Mother: Fresh, grated tomatoes. And tomato paste on top. [*Daughter gestures agreement.*]

Mother: And a lot of stirring. Each ingredient, they don't go in all together. One by one in its turn. There is an order to sauté—to cooking generally. You'll put in the cinnamon, then after a bit the pepper, the salt, the bay leaf, one by one.

Daughter: So that each ingredient gives off its scent—

Mother: So that you can hear the smell of each ingredient.

Even this relatively benign interaction shows the tendency of Kalymnian mothers to refuse to cede control to their daughters, here not just in the cooking process itself (where, indeed, the family seemed to work together well), but also in the process of explaining and disseminating knowledge, with the mother offering embellishments. These descriptive interruptions and corrections worked so that ultimately, the daughter turned over the task of explaining to her. Some of the details are interesting as well, as the mother stresses the orderly but synesthetic aspects of cooking in grabbing the bay leaf out of the pan so that I could see it, and in employing the common Kalymnian expression "listen to the smell" (see Sutton 2001). These kinds of claims about "order" are a typical part of what Kalymnians often describe as important cooking knowledge. For example, one Kalymnian woman, while making a bean stew with herbs and vegetables in the oven, noted the importance of adding the herbs and vegetables (parsley, dill, leeks, carrots, onions) after putting the boiled beans and tomatoes in the oven. She used the lively phrase "This will give the dish life in the oven," noting, when I asked for clarification, that it is only by adding these ingredients at the last stage of cooking that the flavorfulness (*nostimia*) comes out. Interestingly, this knowledge is also about flexibility: the same woman noted that while dill really adds to the flavor, if you don't have dill, use what you have and it will come out fine.

So this relatively minor example shows not so much the control of mothers over the cooking process as the authority of the older generation in explaining cooking processes. In this case the explanation was directed explicitly toward an outsider—myself—but also, perhaps, served as a reminder for her daughter who was partaking in an education of sensory attention that is central to Kalymnian daily experience. It was a reminder again of how Kalymnians cast the sensory aspects of cooking as deeply important: not only must one choose the proper seasonings, but one must employ them with the proper technique and sequence so that the cooked dish fully takes on the desired odor.

Other examples revealed that teaching daughters to cook, or even simply standing aside, was often a challenge for Kalymnian mothers. This was not simply a matter of mothers hoarding knowledge, as the case of Nina and Irini seemed to suggest. Vakina Roditi, a woman in her forties at the time of our interview, who had moved away from Kalymnos in her late teens, told me that she never learned to cook while she lived at home because "I couldn't steal cooking from my mother; it was too important to her." She went on to explain: "I never cooked before I left home because my mom was not working and she was a housewife and a mother and food was important to her; and she always cooked with love, cooking was an indication of love for her; what we were eating was cooked by her; and she was always a great cook. So I never had to think I needed to change something in the kitchen because I liked the way it was."

While in this case the daughter did go on to learn to cook, the learning process began only once she had established her separate existence living outside of Kalymnos (and Greece). She drew, she revealed, from her memories of the tastes of her mother's kitchen (*I yevseis tis mamas mou*) and from years of having observed her mother in the kitchen. Vakina was a fascinating hybrid: she worked in the fashion industry, scandalizing the older generation with her revealing clothing, while at the same time she insisted on the importance of Greek tradition in the kitchen. "I never measure anything, always using my hands or my eye. I trust my instinct," she stressed. While Vakina has prepared many "traditional" Kalymnian dishes in Italy, especially the various bean stews that are standard fare, she insisted that she liked to combine things and be creative, rather than plan out a recipe in advance:

> Often I am gone till late, so I always have some basic materials and I put them together and see what I can do with them. I combine them and it always comes out good. I am not blowing my own horn or anything but Maximos [her husband] still remembers this pasta recipe that was not planned, it was accidental. At home I only had one slice of feta; some peppers, red, yellow, and green; some pasta and olive oil, which I always have at home; pasta, olive oil, tomatoes—those things are basics and I always have them at home. So I cooked the pasta this way: I sautéed lightly the peppers, but so as not to be heavy with the pasta I did not sauté them with oil; I just put them in the frying pan by themselves and then at the end I added the olive oil and then I added some balsamic vinegar; . . . then in the end I added some fresh tomatoes, boiled the pasta, and put everything together and melted some feta. And it came out very beautiful, and it was all I had at home.

Vakina also echoed Nina's mother in eschewing blenders because they mush ingredients up so that you can't tell them apart. This was part of a health discourse that was in the background of Vakina's discussion: "If I cannot tell the various ingredients in a dish, then that is suspicious, or that means the dish is extremely complicated and thus not healthy." Vakina's mother, Angeliki, often referred to her daughter's talents in the kitchen, and would talk especially about her ability to whip something up at a moment's notice, even for visitors. Her daughter was a constant reference point. When I asked her why she used boxed tomatoes rather than canned tomatoes in her lentil stew, she responded, laughing, "My daughter tells me cans are unhealthy." Similarly, when I asked why she made her mayonnaise by hand instead of using a small mixer, she replied, "My daughter is an ecologist, she doesn't want any electrical appliances." She admitted that using a mixer was easier, but insisted that she preferred it made by hand as well. This is the one case I found in which the mother actually claimed that her daughter was, at least for some things, a better cook than she was. As Angeliki put it, "She makes everything tastier than I do." This unusual claim, however, needs to be taken in the context of the fact that Vakina has left the island and is living a nontraditional lifestyle in Italy with no children. I believe Angeliki talks about her daughter's cooking and housekeeping skills as a way of legitimizing her daughter's maverick choices.

Note that even in this case of a relatively positive mother-daughter relationship, there was almost no direct vertical transmission (aside from Vakina's observations and taste memories). On the contrary, as noted above, Vakina said she couldn't "steal" cooking from her mother. Now that they are both older, however, casual knowledge sharing might occur during their frequent phone conversations. I observed Angeliki talking to her daughter about some okra that she had prepared, and Vakina said that she had found fresh okra at the market and wondered how to cook it. Angeliki described making a familiar "red sauce," which prompted Vakina to ask, "Do you put tomatoes in at the end?"[10] "No, at the beginning, so that they wilt; I don't sauté [*tsigarizo*, literally, "to sizzle"] them too much." They went back and forth about herbs and spices, with Vakina querying whether she should use parsley, celery, or cinnamon and Angeliki insisting that dill was all that was needed, and only if she had a little fresh. This kind of recipe exchange among family members living apart was a frequent occurrence, and part of the general practice of discussing food as a way of making sure that those living away from Kalymnos were eating well and thus doing all right.[11]

Vakina's hybrid consumption and lifestyle also provide an interesting contrast to Stephen Steinberg's discussion of cooking transmission and identity in the loss of knowledge of how to make his bubbie's (grandmother's) challah.[12] He describes a situation in which despite the grandchildren's love for their grandmother and her "culinary magic," none of them wanted to take on the social identity that went with cooking knowledge: "How, after all, did my grandmother acquire her culinary magic? It required an elder not just willing but determined to share her powers with a neophyte. And it required an upstart who craved to follow the path treaded by forebears. Is it possible that as much as my grandmother's eighteen progeny revered her, that none of them wanted to be her?" (Steinberg 1998, 296). By contrast, there is no contradiction for Vakina between "being modern" and "learning cooking"; the conflict comes within the context of Kalymnian matrilocal practices, with mother and daughter typically at home, potentially sharing the same, or an interconnected, kitchen. This is a reminder that such issues must constantly be placed within a larger context of culture and history. In the case of the 1960s U.S. ethnically marked culture, cooking stood for "tradition" in a way that precluded "modernity." For a turn-of-the-twenty-first-century Kalymnian living in Italy, however, these contrasts were not felt in the same way.

One other important consideration here is the growing importance of education for daughters during the second half of the twentieth century. As Kalymnian families saw the possibility for economic mobility not just for sons, but also for daughters, through education, mothers had another reason to not allow their daughters to involve themselves with cooking: their time was seen to be better employed in study. As Polykseni Miha noted, "My mother was very able, and she liked to do all the household chores by herself. She had a great love for my sisters and me to learn letters [i.e., education]. And it gave her joy for us to be reading while she was doing her housework. . . . So I never learned cooking while I was living at home." In her telling, Polykseni made it clear that her mother wanted her daughters to have the opportunity to study that she never had herself. But Polykseni also left ambiguous the extent to which her mother used their education as a reason to do what she would have done anyway. Regardless of whether this is the case, it is clear that Kalymnian girls are not expected to master cooking at a young age, and the growth of female education and of jobs that employed educated women on Kalymnos has fed into this historical trend.

In the next section I explore in depth a three-generational family that has followed the Kalymnian pattern of mother and daughter sharing the same living complex—though with separate kitchens. I want to look at how issues of knowledge and learning are constantly negotiated on a daily basis among grandmothers, mothers, and daughters. The actors involved are Katerina Kardoulia and Katina Miha (introduced in chapter 2, in the section on the can opener), as well as Katina's daughter, known as Little Katerina.[13] I look at issues of negotiation of cooking and its associated knowledges through a series of vignettes taken from videos, alongside more general observations from my fieldnotes.

"WE HAVE A MUTUAL AGREEMENT": SHARING KITCHEN SPACE

Video example 8, "Kitchen Choreography," shows Katerina and her daughter, Katina, preparing several dishes for a Lenten meal while negotiating the limited space of Katerina's kitchen. My description follows.

In Katerina's tiny kitchen, "fasting food" is being prepared (it is Easter week).[14] Katerina has a pot of *veryious* boiling on the large burner, while on the small burner a pot of orzo and tomato sauce is simmering. Katina and Katerina enter, Katina saying that the shrimp need to be cleaned to add to the orzo and stirring the pot, commenting that it is already quite cooked. Katina goes out, while Katerina begins peeling the shrimp using her hands, occasionally yelling at the lamb, constantly baying in the yard outside, to shut up. Katerina is called out of the kitchen to attend to someone passing by; Katina comes in and begins peeling the shrimp with a knife, while talking to her son and husband about plans for the week and whether the priest has stopped by yet to give her father (who is ill and confined to bed) communion. Katerina returns and starts to prepare a shredded wheat for her husband, complaining to Katina that Yiorgos, her father, has been up since five in the morning demanding that he be fed or he's going to die, and that he has been demanding food all morning. Katerina moves the *veryious* to a table to cook more later, while beginning to boil milk.

When Katina notices that she's boiling milk, she says, "Don't make the shredded wheat with milk, my child" (a diminutive).

Katerina says, "Well, how then? With cheese?"

Katina, talking fast and increasingly loudly, replies, "My child, we're going to have problems again. His insides will burn. Don't be—"

Katerina asks, "Do you know what shape I'm in at this point?"

"Yes," says Katina, "but you're going to create problems with your tricky plans."

Katerina takes the pot of milk off the stove, putting it aside, and grabs another pot, filling it with water. As they continue to discuss him and his problems, Katina's husband comes in and reaches over Katerina to get the cooking oil to use on one of his tools. Katerina goes out to tend to Little Katerina, while Katina finishes cleaning the shrimp, adds it to the orzo, tastes the orzo, and adds a bowlful of water to the pot, noting to Katerina as she comes back that it needs to be softer for Yiorgos. Katerina is called in by Yiorgos and comes back, noting to Katina that he actually does want the shredded wheat with milk. Katina demurs, and is called out of the kitchen to talk with her son.

Katerina puts the milk back on to boil and starts clearing dishes. Little Katerina comes into the kitchen and exchanges words with her grandmother about why the lamb is baying so much, Katerina noting, "It wants its mother." Little Katerina is called out by her mother for some chores. While Katerina is doing the dishes, the milk, which is on the large burner, boils over. Katerina pulls it off, wipes the pot, and puts it back on, attempting to lower the flame, but while opening the package of shredded wheat (*fide*) it boils over a second time. So she pulls it off and this time takes out the pan underneath the burners to wash that off. Katina returns, still talking about her father and whether he can eat before he takes communion. She stirs the orzo, tasting it and adding a pinch of salt. This time Katerina switches the orzo to the large burner and puts the milk on the small burner. Further boiling, and the kitchen fills with steam. As Katina leaves to begin doing laundry, Katerina continues to clean up and begins preparing a bean stew while, stimulated by my presence, starting to reflect on religious themes relevant to Easter.

This vignette is meant to show both mutual trust and some of the sources of conflict that go into sharing a kitchen space. Here there is less of a direct sense of hierarchy than in the case of Nina and Irini. However, because cooking involves constant adjustments and use of the senses to judge its progress, as well as adjustments for the many things that can alter the quality of even a commonly prepared meal, there are many points at which mother and daughter trust each other, but also some at which they come into conflict. Cooking is just one of a number of daily activities, and it is constantly being interrupted as Katerina and Katina address the concerns and demands of spouses and children, and go about organizing not only the daily meal, but also the family relationship with the wider community. Within the kitchen itself there is a constant negotiation of space and of mutual control over cooked food, which shows up when you watch the video in the maneuvering of bodies around each other in this small space. In writing about work in bakeries, Krina Patel refers to this negotiation as a somatic intersubjectivity, which she describes as follows: "I interpret this in baking work to mean the awareness of moving in the workspace in relation to whoever and whatever else is in that space. The bodily or somatic mode of attention to others' bodies and other objects including tools is essential for successful task implementation" (2008, 141). Negotiating the kitchen space and the small two-burner stove involves constant judgments and adjustments, both of a "social" and of a "practical" or "technical" or even sensory nature. In this example we see the negotiation of diets and ingredients in relation to Katerina's husband, but we also see the negotiation of the kitchen equipment itself, as Katerina moves pots back and forth to deal with the milk that has boiled over. These kinds of adjustments are a constant part of daily cooking, and Katerina refers to her responses to them as "tricks" or "swindles" (*kombines, patentes*), making them part of what I discussed in chapter 2 as the "risks" of everyday cooking. Other examples of such "tricks" in Katerina's kitchen included

FIGURE 12. Katina Miha preparing coffee in her kitchen (2014).
Photo by Katerina Miha.

heating a plate of water for dishes on top of another pot of cooking food (thus saving on heating water), and warming up a piece of Parmesan cheese on top of the grater set on top of a pot of water (being boiled for something else). Sometimes Katerina mentioned "tricks" that arose out of her response to social situations. When she suggested to me that lately Katina's cooking had been hurried and offhand, she recalled a lentil soup that Katina had made while Katerina was downtown at the Social Security office. She noted that her daughter had forgotten to add the bay leaf. So Katerina added it at the end when the stew was mostly cooked, saying that at least it would give it a little scent (*mirodia*). She referred to this as one of her little "tricks" as well.

Mothers and daughters, of course, cook not only in negotiation with each other, but *in relation to* other family members, particularly fathers and husbands. We see this above in the tension created by the fussiness of Katerina's husband (Katina's father). Another interesting aspect of mother-daughter relationships in Kalymnian kitchens is the "joking relationship" that exists between mothers and their daughter's husbands over whether they prefer their wife's or their mother-in-law's cooking, discussed in the previous chapter as well. To give one example, Katina's husband and I were eating some fresh fish in red sauce when Katina came in and asked, seemingly rhetorically, "Who made the fish?" The flat-footed ethnographer was about to respond "Katina" when her husband winked at me and said, "Katerina made it!" Katina responded with a half-serious tone, "She didn't cook it, I did, it was my recipe." This kind of joking relationship seemed quite common in my observations of other Kalymnian households. Without delving into the murky waters of Freudianism, I may perhaps suggest that the structure of Kalymnian matrifocality might encourage the expression of mother-daughter competition through such joking relationships.

In the case of Katerina and Katina this sort of humor seems to index the by-and-large positive cooking relationship. There is also the potential for carving out personal domains: unlike Nina and Irini, when Katina got married, she had her own house and her own kitchen built; even if only thirty feet from her mother's, it allowed for a certain independence. In 2006, when the video described above was made, Katina did most of the baking and preparing of sweets, and for these she used her own, much larger kitchen (her kitchen includes a four-burner stove and an oven). Katina would also use her kitchen to prepare more elaborate dishes, such as moussaka (which requires an oven). And there was always the possibility to make separate meals if the daily routine seemed suited for that. Katina could impose her own style on her kitchen, buying newer equipment, for example, than her mother's battered aluminum pots. Katina also liked shopping at the kitchen chain store associated with cooking-show host Vefa Alexiadou (see chapter 5), which she would visit to shop for various baking and cake-decorating implements, as well as things like oil decanters, decorative salt shakers, and an oregano shaker for pizza. Katerina, on the other hand, saw keeping the old pots not simply as an economic measure, but rather, much like the can opener discussed in chapter 2, as part of her "traditional" identity and the wealth of practical knowledge that went along with it. Despite such minor conflicts, Katerina pointed out, cooking and feeding was for the most part still shared between mother and daughter, and this took mutual understanding, which also required work.[15]

Multiple occasions arose not only for the negotiation of kitchenspace, but also for the exchange of knowledge between Katerina and Katina. Some of these were simple and practical: Katerina showing Katina where she had stored frozen herbs in the freezer. Others seemingly had a mnemonic function, as when they watched cooking shows on TV they might repeat ingredients back and forth, both as a way of confirming that the recipe was recognizable, and thus made sense, and to emphasize any unusual elements in the recipe for future reference. For example, Katerina told Katina about a Turkish recipe she had seen earlier in the day with ground meat, eggs, and strained yogurt in a layer on top, noting that it had recognizable ingredients, but was a preparation she was unfamiliar with. In these small, everyday ways, mother and daughter exchanged knowledge, just as they negotiated tasks and movements in the kitchen. In general when mothers and daughters cooked together I often noticed that they might consult on a variety of decisions—how many eggs to add to a béchamel sauce, whether a dish was too thick and needed water, or simply whether there was enough salt in a dish. I sometimes wondered about this because it seemed that mothers and daughters might consult even on dishes they had made hundreds of times in the past. I asked Evdokia Passa about this as she and her mother were preparing an elaborate meal in their restaurant kitchen. She had just asked her mother what to add to the béchamel sauce that she was making, and when her mother mentioned eggs, she asked how many, and whether to add them after it had cooled a bit. At first I assumed that her mother usually made it, and that was why she was asking her. But Evdokia said that sometimes she makes it and sometimes her mother does. But, she explained, "Even though I pretty much know, I prefer to ask, so I can say if it doesn't turn out right 'you told me' [laughing]." In this and similar cases, mothers and daughters use each other both as memory jogs and, as Evdokia suggests, to assert a kind of collective responsibility for the meal, like what we saw with Nina and her mother in the previous chapter.

Whether mother and daughter have a relatively equal relationship, as in the case of Katerina and Katina, or a more hierarchical one, cooking knowledge does not simply "pass" from mother to daughter, but is more a part of the daily environment of Kalymnian interactions. I'll explore this idea further below, but first I take a look at how the granddaughter of Katerina and the daughter of Katina took some of her first tentative steps in the kitchen, and what her experience might suggest about the processes of learning cooking.

LEARNING COOKING: LITTLE KATERINA

Little Katerina was thirteen and a half when I filmed her in the kitchen. The previous summer I had asked her what she knew how to cook, and she had said, "Coffee." Now she was making grilled cheese regularly, and occasionally coffee. She noted that she likes to cook, but her mother and grandmother don't let her because they want to get it done quickly. Her grandmother insisted that she would learn in time, but she was more concerned that Little Katerina focus on her studies, and that she had been an "A" student up till now. Like all Kalymnian children, male and female, she was surrounded by information and sensory commentaries about proper food, which she absorbed and reacted to. Like her mother and grandmother, she watched the cooking shows on TV. One morning we were watching Vefa Alexiadou's show, and she was featuring a chef and hotelier from Santorini preparing shrimp and fried tomato balls. Little Katerina commented that Vefa was always advertising stoves for the German brand Miehle, but the visiting chef was using a traditional gas-bottle stove like theirs and things seemed to come out fine—a rather sophisticated comment about commodification for a thirteen-year-old, I wrote in my notes at the time. Despite her critical eye, Vefa's show was also influencing Little Katerina, as I came to understand when I filmed her cooking in her mother's kitchen for the first time (see video example 9, "Little Katerina Learning Cooking").

I had asked if she wanted to cook something for the camera, and, becoming excited, she planned in consultation with her mother, Katina, to make a zucchini omelet. Katerina displayed considerable self-consciousness about being filmed. While Katina talked her through setting up to present the recipe and the details of how she would make the omelet, Little Katerina insisted that I should turn off my camera. There was a strong sense that she was mimicking cooking shows, just as her mother and grandmother at certain times would say that they were "playing Vefa" when they explained a recipe to me. Here, despite the fact that the family allowed me to observe the normally private intimacies of kitchen preparation, they also recognized the performative aspects of cooking in front of a nonfamily member.

In the video, Little Katerina and her mother discuss and argue about how to arrange ingredients on the table as Vefa would. Katina also wants her to explain the recipe clearly at the beginning, and gets upset when she breaks out laughing the first time through. Katina remains off-camera, whispering corrections and instructions to her, with particular concern for her to speak in a way that would introduce the dishes clearly. But Little Katerina is not simply passive in relation to her mother's instructions. When she disagrees with the way her mother wants her to arrange the ingredients to be prepared, she says insistently, "It's my show!"

Since this was her first experience of making a dish from start to finish, what of the more embodied aspects of cooking? Her mother had told her to cut the zucchini lengthwise in four pieces before slicing crosswise to create the "mince." Doing this in her hands proves a considerable challenge for Little Katerina, as you can see from the video. First off, she uses a butter knife, so she is unable to cut it into pieces that she feels are small enough. "Offstage," her mother continually whispers to her to make the pieces smaller. "If they're too big, cut them again." Katina also tells Little Katerina not to cut the zucchini lengthwise all the way to the bottom, because that way it will "get away from you" (*tha sou xefigi*). Instead, she tells her to cut the top half and, when done with that, cut the rest. Further, at a certain point Katina notices that Little Katerina is cutting the zucchini in round slices because she hasn't made proper lengthwise cuts. When she tells her this is no good, Katerina responds, "But Mom, that's how it came out" (*etsi mou vyike*). "Ssst!" is her mother's corrective response, along with educational scolding telling her in essence to try harder. She does offer positive encouragement as well, saying "Bravo" a few times when Little Katerina manages to make the pieces the proper size.

One interesting moment comes early on when Katerina is struggling to cut the zucchini. She marks this by saying, "It didn't turn out [for us]" (*den mas petihe*). Her mother responds, "Don't say stupid things," before coaching her on how to cut the zucchini smaller. This phrase does not simply reflect her mother's attempt to deflect her sense of failure. What Katerina said literally makes no sense because the verb *petihaino* ("to turn out, to come out, to succeed") is supposed to refer to a finished dish. One doesn't say "It didn't turn out" in reference to one small process in the overall cooking procedure. Note that Little Katerina's education is a linguistic one, as well as a process of learning bodily skills.[16]

Also, just as we saw in earlier examples in this chapter, there is a certain amount of motherly hovering, so that when I try to direct questions to Little Katerina, her mother offers the answers first. And at one point when Katerina is struggling to cut the zucchini, her mother offers to do it for her, in order to show her how to cut it properly, once again stressing learning through observation. Later, Katina wants to cut the zucchini further, "off-camera," while Katerina is heating up the oil for frying. But Katerina insists that it is her dish to make and refuses to cede ground to her mother.[17]

Little Katerina notes to me that it takes a long time to fry if the zucchini is not cut small, and it doesn't get that nice brown color all over.[18] In pointing this out to me, she seems to be confirming it experientially for herself as well. Thus, she has a certain knowledge of what is to be aimed for, even if she doesn't yet have the skill to execute it. Interestingly, she seems tentative about adding oil—Katina has to tell her four or five times to add more oil to the zucchini. This is perhaps because when describing the recipe to her, her mother had told her to use "a spoonful of oil." Also note that the oil decanter has a low flow, perhaps impeding more liberal usage. Using a butter knife seemed less a safety issue and more about employing whatever happened to be to hand to accomplish the job. For example, Katina gives her daughter a low-lipped bowl to beat the eggs, so she could not beat them with much force without spilling them, even while recognizing that they are not beaten to the proper consistency. Katerina uses a spoon to turn the zucchini in the pan as is common on Kalymnos—rather than a spatula—which allows for closer control of the process but increases the chances of burning oneself.[19] Katerina also doesn't know what to do when things go wrong: while she is beating the eggs, the oil begins to burn. "What happened? Is it okay? Should I add more oil?" When she begins beating the eggs, she repeatedly refers to them as "avgolemono," a classic sauce made from beaten eggs and lemon, but not a term appropriate for an omelet. Eventually her mother tells her that lemon isn't used in this dish. On the other hand, she knows to turn (skalizo) the zucchini every two minutes to keep them from burning. Furthermore, when her mother tells her the zucchini is cooked enough, she insists that it isn't ready, that some of the pieces have taken on the right color but not enough of them. As she is saying this, she thinks of another zucchini dish that she is familiar with, made with flour and cheese, and gives me a list of ingredients, telling me, "It comes out great," even though it is something that she must have observed rather than made herself. This memory leads her to decide to try making this dish as well, which she prepares the next day for me. With both of these dishes she insists several times that since it is the first time she has cooked them, she shouldn't be judged too harshly on the results: "At the very least, it will be edible."

My overall impression here is that for Katina, teaching the skills of cooking is about teaching all the "tricks" and adjustments one must make for things to come out right. It is interesting that she didn't scold Katerina when she failed to produce the desired cuts of zucchini, but gave her positive reinforcement instead. Scolding came when Little Katerina failed in her knowledge of cooking, by using the phrase "it didn't succeed," and in displaying proper deportment in the kitchen, when she laughed while describing the dish instead of presenting it properly.

Two years later, in 2008, I filmed Little Katerina making a salad for her father. The short video "Little Katerina Making a Salad" (video example 10) shows her describing the ingredients that she is putting into the salad and then serving it to her father.[20] After roughly two years her hands displayed considerably greater confidence in peeling and cutting a cucumber, with almost none of the hesitation seen in the earlier video and easy movements of her thumb as she presses the knife through the sliced cucumber to create chunks. She is also still picking up discursive knowledge, as when I ask her whether she will put vinegar on the salad and she replies, "We add vinegar when the salad has cabbage." Her grandmother adds, "and lettuce," which she repeats, a small memory-jog that is part of her learning what ingredients go together in Kalymnian cooking. But she also displays a certain culinary knowledge in her statement "We'll stir the salad so that all the salad takes its flavor" (*na parei yevsi oli i salata*), an idiomatic expression suggestive of the way that the salad is conceptualized as tasting better because of the relationship of the ingredients when all mixed together.[21] The video also shows the playful banter between Katerina and her father, who jokes about the camera having a sense of smell so as to show off the wonderful smell of the food. When she gives him the salad he jokes with her about proper presentation of the dish, while she responds that it will be the best salad he's ever eaten.

Unfortunately, I didn't have the opportunity to film Little Katerina again until 2012. In the meantime, however, we talked about cooking, and I observed her changing interactions within the family. In 2008 she was sixteen and was making coffee more regularly. Greek coffee is, in fact, one of the first things that teenage girls learn to make. That it is considered a skill was brought home to me by the many comments I heard about how best to prepare it while preserving the all-important foam (*kaimaki*) on the top.[22] With her grandmother giving her small directions, such as "watch it boil" and "pour a little into each cup first," Little Katerina took pride in the fact that she was able to divide the foam evenly among three cups. Her mother and grandmother provided both positive and negative reinforcements depending, it seemed, on their mood and what else was going on at the time. I observed, for example, Katina telling a neighbor that Little Katerina hadn't let the water get hot enough to make proper tea. Katina noted that she didn't chastise her about it, and the neighbor insisted, "She'll learn." On the other hand, when making the Greek salad in video example 10, Little Katerina insisted to me that the salt went directly on the tomatoes so that they would release their juices. When I asked her grandmother Katerina about this, she noted that putting salt on tomatoes is for when the tomato is an appetizer. "I told her this, but she doesn't listen, she has her own opinion." Here Little Katerina had derived some knowledge from listening and observation that was seen, at least by her family, as incorrect, but that might be the subject of debate within the wider Kalymnian community of eaters, a theme I'll develop further in the following chapter.

In 2009, Little Katerina was thinking about the possibility of some postsecondary education on the neighboring island of Kos "where we have family who would look after me." But she mentioned this possibility without much enthusiasm and joked that the alternative was a rich husband. Although she had done well through high school, she told me that she didn't see much point in studying hard for college qualifying exams. She said that although she would declare her intent to study to be a grade-school teacher (daskala) or nursery-school teacher (nipia-gogos), she was not excited at the prospect of opening a tutorial school, as most girls who train in education do at least for a number of years while waiting to be appointed to a regular teaching post. And Katina saw little point in this as well, as she dismissed the prospect of Little Katerina leaving home for study or for work.

By 2011, it had been decided that Little Katerina would not pursue higher education. Instead, she had been working making jewelry to sell to tourists on Telendos, a neighboring tiny island where the family had a small summer dwelling. Katerina told me that she was able to make several thousand euros a year in this trade, an important contribution to the family as the financial crisis in Greece deepened and her father and her unwed brother went through extended periods of unemployment. She said she would occasionally spend time with a school friend in a coffee shop, but mostly she preferred to be at home, working on her jewelry or taking care of and playing with the goat they were keeping at the time or playing on the Internet. Indeed, I observed her often on Facebook, posting links to various Greek pop songs. She also took pride in having caught twice as many fish as her father in a recent nighttime spear-fishing expedition.

While we planned to make another video during my visit in 2011, as she had been cooking more often—particularly while her mother and grandmother were absent on trips to Athens for health concerns—somehow this never panned out; her mother Katina insisted on cooking for the camera instead. However, I did observe one interesting interaction when Little Katerina was helping her friend and next-door neighbor prepare a pot of lentils because the friend's mother was gone that day. I was talking to the older Katerina in her kitchen as she prepared the family meal (for clarity's sake I'll refer to them as "grandmother" and "granddaughter" in the following). After the grandmother had listed the basic ingredients, the granddaughter kept running in with questions such as what spices to add—to which the grandmother responded, "You can add some parsley if you have some." The granddaughter came in several times to ask about the washing and cooking of the lentils, how much water to add, and so on; the grandmother told her that it depended on the type of lentils you had and whether they were harder or softer, smaller or bigger; it could take an hour to cook, it could take three hours. "Such a big difference?" (*tosi megali i diafora*) wondered the granddaughter. When she had put the lentils on to cook, the grandmother reminded her about how much tomato paste to add, and the granddaughter said that she hadn't added so much. The grandmother responded that it didn't matter; it would still come out okay.

When the dish was done and the granddaughter reported that it had indeed turned out fine, the grandmother expressed a bit of annoyance—not at her granddaughter but at the friend, who was a year older and had briefly been engaged to be married. The grandmother noted, "She's practically married and she doesn't know how to do these things? You know how to make them." The granddaughter responded, "I know only how to make white beans" (*fasolia*). The grandmother reassured her in the form of a lesson: "Fava beans [*koukia*] are the same. Sometimes you need to throw out the first water from boiling to get rid of the bitterness. Chickpeas [*revithia*] are the same, but you might want to add in a bit of *manestra* [a ricelike pasta] with them."

A few things stood out to me in this exchange. First, this was not a case of hands-on teaching, as in the earlier example of the zucchini omelet; the grandmother was offering only verbal guidance from a distance. This might, then, in some ways resemble the kind of guidance provided by telephone when grandmother and mother were absent in Athens. In some ways, the grandmother's guidance functioned like a recipe, that is, as a memory jog, a reminder of specific ingredients, though within a general ethos of flexibility (see Sutton 2001, 134ff.). In other ways what was being taught, even without direct instruction, was an attentiveness to the ingredients and the environment: the granddaughter was surprised that there could be "such a big difference" in cooking times for lentils, while the grandmother was suggesting a careful evaluation of one's ingredients rather than a more automatic following of a recipe.

The other "lesson" was more abstract, but more part of the cooking discourse that is so common in Kalymnian daily life. The grandmother suggested that beans be regarded as a group, but with important variations. If you knew how to make white beans (of which there are also a significant variety in size and quality), you could also think about making other kinds of beans, keeping in mind variations such as adding pasta to chickpeas or changing water more often for fava beans. This, too, is part of learning an attentiveness to circumstances, or a "synaesthetic reason" (Paxson 2011).

One important aspect of this exchange between grandmother and granddaughter is its implications for the reproduction of gender roles. The grandmother suggests here, offhand as the comment may be, the idea of certain expectations for a marriageable woman on Kalymnos—that by the time she married she would know how to prepare lentil stew. Earlier the grandmother had told me in reference to her granddaughter that in four or five years, when Little Katerina would be in her mid-twenties, she would have learned the basic skills of cooking, cleaning, and managing family finances and bank accounts. This was still an expected part of Kalymnian female identity, reflected both in positive statements such as these, and in negative hyperbolic claims by older women that women of the younger generation are only interested in going to coffee shops and having sex with older men (see Sutton 2008). However, this socialization is also potentially quite different from contemporary gender roles in other parts of Greece. When I showed the video of Little Katerina preparing the zucchini omelet to my student Leonidas Vournelis, who grew up in Thessaloniki and in a village in Macedonia, he was surprised that she wasn't more comfortable in the kitchen already *at age thirteen!* Vournelis suggested that a twelve-year-old northern Greek girl, even one growing up in the city, would have developed many of the skills to prepare dishes. Indeed, such a girl (who didn't show her developing cooking skill by age twelve) would be excoriated by the community with the question, "Who will marry her?" (*poios tha tin pantrepsei*). This comment made me go back to interviews with his mother, Georgia Vourneli. She had begun to help her mother in the kitchen from the age when she could "understand" (about four or five). By age six she was often making things for her siblings when her parents were absent working in the fields. In a follow-up interview, Georgia claimed that still today girls in Macedonia would be expected to know how to cook by age twelve. For Kalymnian girls no such expectation was in evidence of early enculturation into cooking responsibility.

Once again this suggests that a very different dynamic of cooking and knowledge transmission may be in play in patrilocal areas of Greece when compared to Kalymnos.[23]

CONCLUSION

Let me return to the two claims often made on Kalymnos, that cooking passes seamlessly from mothers to daughters, and that the younger generation doesn't cook anymore. Both of these are idealized claims meant to comment on proper or improper social relations, but not, I think, to refer to actual, specific circumstances. The same person who might claim that "the younger generation doesn't cook anymore" will at the same time recognize many individual differences, making this blanket claim less descriptive and more a part of the general Kalymnian discourse on the felt benefits and downsides of so-called modernity (see Sutton 2008). As for cooking being passed from mother to daughter, my different examples have been meant to show that the relationships surrounding cooking and the knowledge encompassed by "cooking" are both highly variable.[24] In the different examples in this chapter we have seen cooking "passed on" in different ways, from specific verbal instruction to demonstration of bodily techniques. And I have attempted to illustrate a multiplicity of different mother-daughter relations—from cooperative to semihostile—to suggest the many different social relations that may encourage or discourage the transmission or, perhaps better, the reproduction and remaking of cooking knowledge (cf. Marchand 2010). While certain aspects of cooking are explicit and open to discussion, negotiation, and debate (as we saw with Little Katerina), certain techniques may, in Bourdieu's phrase, "go without saying because they come without saying" (1977, 167). In the former category would be all kinds of taste knowledge that circulates on Kalymnos about little "tricks" that make a particular dish tasty, as well as debates over whether to peel tomatoes or leave the skin on, to cut them or to grate them. Older women may have a greater amount of such knowledge, and there are opportunities for control of knowledge here and special tricks that make for one's community reputation, such as how to prepare bitter onions (*veryious,* see chapter 3) properly. As anthropologists who have studied secrecy have long noted, the power of secrecy lies in the impression that there are always more secrets or "tricks" to be revealed or, as Lamont Lindstrom puts it, "Conversational power depends simultaneously on a person's ability both to keep and to tell his [*sic*] secrets" (1990, 113; see also Barth 1987). But this kind of circulating knowledge can only be realized in practice, so there is a sense as well that discursive knowledge about cooking is cheap and readily moves throughout the community, among men and women, young and old, as part of daily food-related conversations. Even embodied techniques are subject to considerable verbal commentary, as the contributors to Marchand 2010 have shown at length. But at the same time, verbal commentary is very much an "education of attention" (Ingold 2000) and only makes sense in relation to the sensory training that is part of Kalymnian daily life. In the various instances of teaching Little Katerina, we see her mother and grandmother encouraging her to understand how one must negotiate the constant variations presented by the fallibility of tools and the unpredictability of ingredients and the larger cooking environment, the "mutinous unpredictability of matter."[25] In Katina's guidance of her daughter making a zucchini omelet we see how this involves what Tim Ingold terms a "guided rediscovery" (2000, 356). Nicolette Makovicky describes this process for young girls in central Slovakia learning lace-making techniques: "novices are placed in situations where they can practice, hone their skills, and gain experience by themselves. Ana [an older teacher] wanted her pupils not only to memorize specific movements, but also to understand how to respond to the visual and sensual clues generated by the thread, tools, and pillow . . . Zuzana, sitting on the lap of her great-grandmother, was taught to see the lace she made as a result of her physical activity, of which calculations, decisions, and assessments were an integral part" (2010, 82). These are the kind of judgments, or "synaesthetic reason," that make up the essence of cooking knowledge for Kalymnians.

As for the silent techniques that may be passed on without consciousness or commentary, one would certainly be the technique of cutting in the hand that I described in chapter 2. The power of this technique, as I argued earlier, is its social efficacy, but also it is not seen as a choice: Little Katerina does not consider the possibility of setting the zucchini down on a board or counter, but rather struggles to develop dexterity in this one proper way of cutting (although she does rebel to some extent by using the knife to cut the zucchini already cooking in the pan). Over the course of my research I encountered only two women who used a cutting board for cutting. One was Evdokia Passa, who said she had observed the technique as part of her training at hotel school in Rhodes. She said that they had shown how to cut onions on a board using only your fingertips, so that you wouldn't cut your fingers. While she doesn't employ that technique, she and her mother do use cutting boards (color coded for different types of food) for most cutting in their restaurant kitchen. The other was Polymnia Vasaneli, a woman in her thirties, who used it while cutting a red onion for a tomato-cucumber salad. She showed off the small, even cuts that she was able to get by first cutting it in half, then across, and then rotating the onion ninety degrees. When I questioned her about this, she said that she had been frustrated because her mother-in-law cuts them in her hands "faster than a food processor, and I can't do it." So she used to use a grater for onions until she saw someone cutting them on a board on the popular cooking show *Forgiveness with Every Bite.*

This raises squarely the issue of horizontal transmission: if "passing from mother to daughter" is not the simple, conflict-free process that the phrase implies, what kind of learning of cooking goes on not in families, but through the wider community and from other sources such as cooking shows? I've suggested throughout that a certain kind of knowledge of cooking circulates "in the air" of everyday Kalymnian discourse, without regard to age or gender. In the next chapter I look in more detail at TV cooking shows and how they frame issues of cooking, knowledge, and identity. I look specifically at how Kalymnians (along with people from Thessaloniki) watch, respond to, and cook with and against these shows. Here again we will see that what makes studying cooking anthropologically exciting is the complexity that lies beneath its seeming straightforwardness. Instead of a simple passage from mother to daughter, it can be compared to Shakespeare's view on love in *A Midsummer Night's Dream:* the course of true cooking knowledge never did run smooth!

CHAPTER 5

Horizontal Transmission

Cooking Shows, Friends,
and Other Sources of Knowledge

"Vefa or Mamalakis? Who do you watch? Who do you prefer?" These questions stimulated strong reactions among Greeks on Kalymnos and in Thessaloniki when Leonidas Vournelis and I began to pose them in 2006.[1] The hosts of Greece's two most popular cooking shows, one female, one male, each had their following. Some referred to Vefa as "full of imagination" and "golden-handed," while others insisted that Mamalakis embodied authentic Greek cooking and Vefa was a crude infomercial, or a representative of "the oppressiveness of tradition." While not everyone opposed one to the other, it was clear that many people were watching and were deeply interested in this new phenomenon, the cooking show, one of the most striking examples of cooking and recipes moving out of the localized circuits of communities and into the wider community of the nation.

The previous chapter looked at the conflicts and negotiations that constitute daily cooking within families. This chapter widens the focus to get at the ways that cooking knowledge is shared throughout a wider community. This community consists of the circle of neighbors and friends who make up the local community, as well as migrants who return to Kalymnos during the summer. Moreover, while the majority of this ethnography has been focused on cooking practices on Kalymnos, this chapter explores cooking in relation to the wider Greek society through the medium of cooking shows. Ethnographically, this chapter expands to include work done in Thessaloniki, Greece's second-largest city. We analyze the content of Greek cooking shows to get at some of the key debates over the values surrounding daily cooking in Greek society at large. We also look at how Kalymnians and Thessalonikans define their own cooking practices in relation to the wider discourses generated by these shows, what kind of knowledge they derive from the shows, and what influence the shows have on daily cooking practices. We also use this chapter to trace some of the changes in cooking shows from the mid-2000s, when the only cooking programs available on TV were produced in Greece, to the second decade of the twenty-first century, which has seen these shows complemented by foreign ones, in particular *The Naked Chef* featuring Jamie Oliver. Let's begin with a consideration of some of the ways that cooking knowledge and knowledge of other crafts circulate outside the family on Kalymnos.

A SOCIOLOGY OF GREEK COOKING KNOWLEDGE

I have suggested throughout these pages that food discourses saturate Kalymnian everyday life, as discussion of recipes and their variations are commonly shared among family, friends, and neighbors. Part of what makes Kalymnian food a "cuisine" is, in Sidney Mintz's words, that people feel a shared investment in talking about it.[2] Whether one cuts or grates tomatoes for octopus stew, whether one uses bags or jars to store one's rice, how to add flavor to a dish of green beans by mashing feta into it, the virtues of different types of containers for cooking Easter lamb, discussions of food shopping and the pros and cons of different markets—all of these make up unending fodder for Kalymnian conversations among women and men, young and old. But what about more specific claims to cooking knowledge? What kind of teaching and learning goes on beyond the family, and with what implications for food practices and identities?

It is in some ways difficult to establish a reputation as a cook on Kalymnos because one is generally cooking to feed the immediate and extended family circle. While oral discourses about recipes abound, one doesn't typically invite a friend or neighbor into one's kitchen to observe some dish or cooking skill. However, food generosity is a key social value on Kalymnos, and when cooked food is involved it does allow one to extend one's reputation so one is spoken of within the neighborhood, if not the wider community. This is not as common as you might think, however, since cooked food is more commonly offered to visitors and other foreigners rather than to neighbors, who are expected to have food available at home. Among neighbors and friends, food generosity typically involves unprocessed ingredients: fresh produce from one's gardens or fields. It is only on the occasion that a neighbor or friend passes by on the way to work, or on an excursion to the beach, that one might offer cooked food and be able to display one's talents. In some cases one does exchange cooked food with a few neighbors with whom one may have ongoing transactions of various sorts, and this is, indeed, a chance to comment on the small differences in preparation technique that make for much of the substance of Kalymnian daily conversations about food. One woman regularly shared food with a poorer neighbor who often came by asking whether she could help with tasks such as lighting candles at the graveyard (an ongoing female responsibility). When money was tighter, this poor neighbor would be offered leftover cooked food as well, and might herself bring vegetables that she had gotten from a vendor who deemed them no longer salable. This might be a time when neighbors would compare preparation techniques; one woman deferred to her neighbor's preparation of moussaka as being better because she cooked the eggplant just before assembling the dish, rather than doing it the night before and letting it sit.

Most women with whom I spoke insisted that they were happy to share knowledge of cooking as well as skills such as crocheting, sewing, and other tasks related to making a trousseau. In this regard sharing *knowledge* parallels sharing food itself, in that the important thing is for the generosity to be narrated within the community. A woman complained to me how she had taught a friend crocheting for her daughter's wedding trousseau, and had helped do much of it. The friend failed in her social task: when asked by relatives who had done the crocheting, she claimed the knowledge herself rather than defer to the woman who had taught her. The woman who had offered the help complained, "And this she did right in front of me!" However, she added, "It is not important. Do these good things and they will come back to you. I taught another friend crocheting, and she taught me some knitting stitches, even though a neighbor had told her not to teach me because then everyone would be producing the same thing. So she taught me on the sly."

This type of exchange between female neighbors and friends is not uncommon, and it may be one of the ways that skill knowledge is learned in a less-fraught context than mother-daughter relations. What is important is that the provenience of any special skill or trick be recognized and acknowledged. A woman told me how she had taught an acquaintance to make pizza—a novel dish on Kalymnos at the time—and when she ran into the woman several years later, she said, "Every time I make pizza you must sneeze because I talk of your 'trick.'" Other women mentioned that their crochet designs "are famous throughout Kalymnos." Another example comes casually at the beginning of the video "Katerina and the Can Opener," which I discussed in chapter 2. Katerina mentions that her neighbor who gave her the can opener asked her where she found *maskalies* in the middle of the summer. Katerina then explains to me that *maskalies* is a "wild local herb, very aromatic," which, when you add it to bean soup or codfish, makes it really a "traditional Kalymnian dish." Katerina tells her neighbor how she collects it and freezes it, along with other herbs, so that she can use it year-round.[3] "My neighbor Vangelio said, 'You're a real school if someone observed you.'" These are the kinds of interactions that ensure that one's reputation for skills, like one's general reputation, circulates throughout the community (see Sutton 2001, 45ff.).

Another potential source of knowledge circulation for many Kalymnians is the visits of return migrants, typically during the summer. While many return migrants are eager to eat the foods they remember from the past, they also can occasionally be a source of new knowledge of ingredients, techniques, or combinations. For example, although soy sauce has been available on Kalymnos since at least the early 1990s, it was typically something bought only by non-Greeks living on the island.[4] Soy sauce was introduced to Katerina and her family in the summer of 2005 by her grandson and his girlfriend, who were visiting from Australia and took it upon themselves to make a few dishes, including fried rice. Katerina enjoyed the fried rice and praised her grandson for his kitchen abilities. I asked Katerina whether fried rice is something that she could imagine cooking herself. She said yes, she would cook it for guests, but not for her family because of her concern about excessive sodium. Several days later, however, I saw that Katerina was using the soy sauce as a supplement to salt in a spaghetti sauce she was making. In this case the flow of knowledge (of a "new" ingredient) was from the younger to the older generation, but this was also framed by the fact that the knowledge was coming from Australia, and thus had a positive connotation of exoticism.

A few women gave examples of gaining cooking knowledge in circumstances that I would label "class-based transmission." One woman worked as a servant for two rich sisters, and she said that they shared their knowledge of how to cook with her as part of her work preparing foods for them. She noted that her mother had been a terrible cook, so she had learned very little from her, and that she was grateful for the knowledge from her employers. Another woman spoke of being a regular visitor at the home of the mayor and his wife when she was a teenager and in her early twenties: "They invited me over because I would sing and tell jokes, and I would also help the wife prepare sweets and desserts when they were hosting visiting dignitaries." She noted that many of these desserts were cakes and other sweets not typical on Kalymnos at the time, so she learned some of these preparations. She also learned other skills from the mayor's wife, such as spinning silk from silkworms. One woman got to know a rich family with whom she would normally never have socialized because the young daughters had become friends at school. She noted being impressed by the fact that the rich woman didn't "put on airs," but made her own jam, and made the birthday cake for her daughter's party rather than buy it from the store "not out of cheapness, but because she likes to do these things." Class distinctions can be somewhat submerged on Kalymnos, however (see Sutton 1998, chap. 2), so I did not hear about many other explicit discussions of the kind of cross-class knowledge transmission that other writers have seen as a key aspect of the development of traditional cuisines (e.g., Diner 2001, chap. 2).

Learning on one's own is also not absent on Kalymnos, though interestingly enough, the three cases of it that I recorded in depth involved Kalymnian women who were not residing on Kalymnos at the time. In these cases women referred explicitly to relying on cookbooks to help them. One was Vakina Roditi, who learned cooking in the context of migrating to Italy, and thus claimed to learn a combination of Greek and Italian cooking based on her memory of her mother's cooking, often combined with advice coming from Italian neighbors. Another was Polykseni Miha, who discussed a period in her life when she was helping her sister who had moved to the neighboring island of Kos as a teacher, and who had a young child to look after. In this case, Polykseni would frequently consult the classic Greek cookbook by Nikolaos Tselementes in order to help her figure out how to reproduce the dishes she had become used to from her childhood on Kalymnos. The third was Popi Galanou, whose parents were absent because they worked full-time in Athens. While she initially learned by helping her brother prepare meals (he was six years older), she remembers her excitement on receiving a cookbook at age twelve. None of the Kalymnian men I spoke with indicated that cookbooks were important in helping them learn to cook, typically in circumstances where women were absent, such as migration or being a professional sailor. Rather, they suggested that their own observational powers and creativity were key factors in their ability to master cooking, themes that appear in my discussion of male cooks in chapter 6.

Today, cooking knowledge and cooking reputation can grow from other sources as well. In 2011 the Kalymnian church had set up a "kitchen of love" to feed those on the island hardest hit by the ongoing economic crisis. Some neighborhood women from Ayios Mammas cooked food to donate to this drive, moving their domestic efforts into a more public setting where kitchen ability could be commented on. And now that birthday parties and sleepovers are more common, women have the opportunity to observe each other's food more than they might have had in the past.[5] For an older generation, as discussed in the previous chapter, cooking skill continues to mark the sign of a good woman in Kalymnian terms.

THE GREEK BETTY CROCKER VERSUS THE COOKING ZORBA

When I was doing research on Kalymnos in the 1990s, TV cooking shows did not exist, though perhaps an occasional recipe might be shown or discussed on a variety program. So by the mid-2000s I was surprised by the extent to which Kalymnians were watching, and talking about, cooking on TV, and in particular two shows: *Vefa's Kitchen* and *Forgiveness with Every Bite*. Even those who claimed a lack of interest in the shows were familiar with them and could give opinions about their content. As I began watching the shows myself, and watching Kalymnians watching the shows, it became clear to me that the programs were compelling partly because of the way they were playing with ideas about gender, nostalgia, and Greek identity. Their popularity, and the *familiarity* people felt with the personas of Vefa and Mamalakis even among those who didn't watch, suggested that they were touching on some of the key strains and tensions of contemporary Greek society. I begin with a brief description of each show before getting into some of the ways they played on cooking values in Greek society and how they were watched and discussed by Kalymnians and people from the city of Thessaloniki.

Vefa's Kitchen was a daily feature on Greek channel Antenna at 4:00 P.M. for several years in the mid to late 2000s. The show was indeed set in Vefa Alexiadou's kitchen (her studio kitchen, with an audience looking on).[6] The kitchen was outfitted with her endorsed products, and indeed, much like Martha Stewart, Vefa has an empire that includes monthly cooking magazines and stores selling a variety of kitchen gadgets. The commercials shown during her program often advertised kitchen appliances that Vefa had endorsed. Like Martha Stewart, one could say that her main focus was on presentation: decorative sweets, sandwiches shaped like animals that children would want to eat, and other such inventions were typical features of her show. Like the majority of the cooking shows in Greece, Vefa's show presented mostly variations on typical Greek food (though the sweets and desserts tended to be more "Western"). Vefa's recipes did sometimes incorporate unusual or not typically Greek ingredients into familiar Greek recipes. A salad might include such ingredients as black Mission figs, radicchio, walnuts, and a balsamic vinaigrette dressing. She tended to cook more "traditional" recipes around religious holidays, and in these programs she would also talk about religious celebrations or "the meaning of the day." She generally took for granted that all her viewers were religious and practiced Greek Orthodoxy. Thus she would say things such as, "Now that Sarakosti [Lent] is beginning, I will only show you recipes for fasting because, of course, you have asked for it, and this is the proper thing to do on these holy days."[7] On such days she would end the show with a religious blessing. She would occasionally chant a religious hymn from the day's church service on the show. She also made comments, such as "When you've come back from church at night, and you are tired, here's a quick thing you can cook. . . ."

It was clear in watching *Vefa's Kitchen* that the show tended to promote traditional gender roles and an image of the traditional Greek Orthodox Christian family. She clearly envisioned those in the kitchen as normatively female, sprinkling her dialogue with comments, such as "On your son's or husband's or child's name day, you can make," or "When you are cooking for your husband," or "Your husband will definitely like such-and-such food." In appearance on the show she came across as an urban, educated older woman, and often would bring on children, allowing her to act the role of the wise, caring grandmother.[8]

Vefa's Kitchen typically would begin with a written recipe, which she proceeded to make, sometimes with the help of an audience member or a visiting chef. Sometimes she would invite children to help her make some sweet dish, and she would occasionally have her own daughter on the show. But in all these cases, she remained in control of the kitchen. She displayed a casual conversational style: noting variations in recipes for a meat pie, she said rhetorically, "Tell me what you think would be in it, liver of course, but you can decide whatever other organ meats suit you, though naturally you will also put in ground beef." While the recipes involved precise measurements, her own descriptions were often more casual, noting for a pie (*pita*), "You know when it's done when the phyllo turns brown-orange."

Always well dressed and wearing expensive-looking jewelry, Vefa was very soft-spoken and smiling. However, compared to other similar shows on Greek TV she would generally avoid becoming confessional by telling her own stories related to food and cooking. Her language was precise and all about the food, the ingredients, and the kitchen utensils.

Vefa typically took several calls from viewers toward the end of the show, offering comments and suggestions, such as how to freeze eggs for a trip. She would also read letters from viewers, which were almost always laudatory, most of them noting that the viewer has "all your books." One letter chided her gently for referring to her viewers with the female pronoun, protesting that many of her fans were male as well.

Elias Mamalakis's show appeared over a similar period during the mid to late 2000s, daily in reruns on the privately owned channel MEGA, with a new episode at 6:00 P.M. on Sundays. The title of the show was *Boukia kai Sihorio,* which literally means "forgiveness with every single bite." This is a traditional Greek proverb that has come to be uttered when one is enjoying a well-prepared meal. Basically, one proclaims that the tastiness of the food has made one forget and forgive life's sorrows. *Sihorio* means "forgiveness," but its root meaning is "agree or be of the same disposition with someone else," suggestive of the kind of commensality that is an unquestioned part of Greek food values.

The host of the show, Elias Mamalakis, was a middle-aged man, chubby, sporting a thin, upturned mustache of the type associated with Greek intellectuals. He had a very playful and simple way of carrying himself. What was striking about the show was that only half of it was focused on the actual cooking and preparing of food. Each episode was set in a different region, most within Greece but some abroad. The shows shot inside Greece avoided any hint of professional high-class cuisine. In fact, Mamalakis rarely visited urban locations. The show was typically shot in rural areas, mountain towns, small islands, and so on. When the setting was urban, Mamalakis tended to focus on a particular neighborhood locale. He would occasionally go to restaurants within

Greece, but once again he was typically in search of a "traditional" restaurant recipe that people might remember but that was no longer available.[9]

At the beginning of each show, Mamalakis announced the episode's location. He then went on a tour of the region, focusing on the most important monuments, local architecture, local historic and tourist sites. He would talk about the geography of the area and the history of the region and its people, usually starting from ancient times and ending with more recent histories, seamlessly mixing "official" history and local lore. For the better half of the show Mamalakis functioned as a guide to the viewer and rarely as a cook. The camera shots usually focused on strikingly beautiful natural landscapes. Quite often the show would include the locals performing some folkloric song or dance.

Historical information, in the form of either major historical events or local trivia, did not stop when the cooking started. Rather, the locals would take over the history telling from Mamalakis. It was in the midst of their storytelling that the cooking process would be discussed. The cooking was rarely done in a kitchen setting; rather, it was almost always done outside, using some gas-operated small burner or a traditional stone-built oven in the back of someone's yard or, quite often, in the middle of the street in a small village. Occasionally, the show was shot in the kitchen of a family-owned Greek tavern, but once again without any trappings of professionalism.

Thus, although he was definitely the star of the show, Mamalakis rarely did the actual cooking. He would almost always wear an apron, but he was just a second pair of hands, maybe to help with washing a plate or chopping the onions at the most. This allowed him to seem less authoritarian in the sense that, unlike Vefa, he did not instruct the viewers directly. The cooking was done by the locals. They were the camera's focus, with their cooking techniques and their storytelling, as well as their appearance; the locals were almost always older women and men, occasionally dressed in traditional local clothing typically seen at folkloric festivals and the like.

When the locals were of a younger age they usually fell in two categories: either daughters and granddaughters helping their mothers and grandmothers, or males occupied with traditional professions—fisherman, goatherd, monk, the town baker, and the like. In these cases, the younger generation would be shown following faithfully in the footsteps of the older generation, even when the latter were not actually present. For instance, the town's fisherman, in his twenties, would explain his recipes by telling how they were handed down to him by the older generations; or a daughter would be cooking with her older female relative watching over her.

Whether the episode was shot within Greece or outside, the recipes were familiar. They were usually not fancy or experimental or personalized. The style of the cooking might be personal (the way an older grandmother peels a tomato or the way an older fisherman cleans the scales off a fish), but the recipes were always traditional, verging on quaint. Although Mamalakis sometimes featured a local delicacy not to be found in major Greek urban centers, primarily the recipes were local variations on common dishes like cheese or spinach pie, baked chickpeas, or Easter lamb. Another point about the recipes concerns the ingredients. There was the occasional local herb or product, but the ingredients were rarely unknown to his audience, even if not readily available all over Greece. The show, however, focused heavily on the purity of the local ingredients, whether they be a particular type of goat cheese or handpicked herbs from the nearest mountain. The person doing the cooking would be asked to share stories about his or her youth and verify what all the viewers suspected: local products are pure and healthy and they are of a superior quality, not to be found in big cities.

Mamalakis's own discourse was, in style as well as in content, an interesting blend of the "good old days" and a contemporary celebration of multicultural diversity. Being from Crete himself, he retained in his speech traces of his native dialect (archaic or village words), while his style was quite poetic. The poetic style of speech is one that is to be found in rural Greece and is hardly ever used now. It is associated with the carefree villager in touch with "nature," enjoying a simple yet happy life, and creates an imagery of playful innocence and wonder at the natural world.

The most striking examples of his poetic discourse would be exhibited when talking about the cooking ingredients or about the local mountains, rivers, lakes, and other natural features. Mamalakis would assign a will and desire to them, as if they possessed independent agency. In his language, they became actors and not inanimate things. They shared the same natural space with the people who were themselves in touch with this idyllic nature. Ingredients and local geographical features participated with the locals in the town's life. This tendency to animate nature is perhaps the most recognizable feature of traditional Greek poetry (Politis 1969), and Mamalakis's discourse was laden with it. It was perhaps his most recognizable signature, since almost all of our interviewees used the word *poetic* in describing him.

Another key feature in Mamalakis's discourse was an insistence on the primacy of the senses, not just in the actual food experience, but more generally in experiencing life. Quite often the host would stop his narration or a villager's narration to look at the camera and exhort the viewer to be quiet for a moment and listen to the food cooking, the onions sizzling, the water boiling, or the wind blowing through the leaves of an ancient olive tree. He would then proceed to talk about the colors, smells, and texture of the local ingredients and geographical features with boundless enthusiasm and awe. Thus, although some aspects of Mamalakis's persona might identify him as an intellectual, in other ways his discourses of the senses and locality identified him clearly as an "ordinary" bon vivant. Indeed, Vournelis found a number of Mamalakis's fans among working-class Thessalonikans who are typically suspicious of intellectuals. While he did not hide his culinary knowledge, his personal style served to portray him as a man who not only knew his French wines but was also able to enjoy the little things in life, such as a fresh vegetable from an old lady's garden in a mountain village. This served to undercut any air of pretentiousness about Mamalakis.

While Vefa and Mamalakis clearly displayed strikingly different styles, there was considerable overlap as well. They both focused on "traditional" Greek recipes, and often used "traditional" locales as backdrops for their shows. Both used a sensory-oriented discourse to talk about the recipes, though Mamalakis did so to a greater extent than Vefa. Indeed, it was the place itself that was in some ways the focus of his show, though food and place were shown to be inseparable. In light of these similarities, why did Vefa and Mamalakis provoke the strong antithetical reactions we observed among their viewers? In the next section we turn to general responses that we elicited from informants on Kalymnos and in Thessaloniki, before focusing on particular informants and how they incorporated these shows into their daily cooking lives.

THE COMMERCIALIZATION OF TRADITION?

In general, there were some broad indicators in people's responses to the two shows: more formally educated, middle-class informants tended to dislike Vefa and like Mamalakis, and broadly speaking, men were more likely to prefer Mamalakis, while most favorable comments about Vefa were made by women. Surprisingly, however, many who said they disliked Vefa also said they were more likely to try a recipe from her show than from Mamalakis's, that she, in fact, taught you cooking. A Kalymnian housewife in her seventies noted the way Vefa showed you how to do everything and then gave you all the ingredients and measurements, so "you'd have to be an idiot not to be able to do it."

An interesting contrast is provided by a Thessalonikan middle-class woman who, after watching Mamalakis make a Cycladic baked fish dish, commented on how good she thought it would taste. When asked whether she would try making it, she responded, "What's the point, since I don't have a backyard? Where would I cook it, on the balcony? Look at that backyard, look at that [outdoor] oven." When asked why this mattered, she said, "Everything plays a role, the sun, nature, the climate of the particular island." By and large, although it provided the featured recipes to its viewers, Mamalakis's show did not seem to encourage people to go into the kitchen, but simply to appreciate the food, as well as the wider social context in which it was produced. Indeed, the question of authenticity, or rejection of admixture, seemed key to many people's assessments. A Kalymnian young woman in college on Cyprus noted that Mamalakis's food was real Greek food, whereas Vefa would tell you to put strawberries in a salad. Another Kalymnian woman complained on a more practical level that Vefa used English or other foreign words in recipes, and you might not know what the ingredient was and make a mess of things. A young Thessalonikan woman, who admitted to not liking cooking very much, noted that she once tried to make a chocolate soufflé she saw on Vefa's show but gave up when she was unable to find some of the "curious" ingredients. An older Kalymnian woman, however, noted that while Vefa's ingredients sometimes seemed strange, "She convinces you that they would be good."

Both in Thessaloniki and on Kalymnos people responded strongly to what was seen as Vefa's commercialization: her peddling of kitchen products on her shows and in her signature stores, called Vefa's House. A Kalymnian woman in her forties, married to a manual laborer, found this one of the things that was most attractive about Vefa: she sold special tools to help decorate cakes, cookies, and other baked goods, and she illustrated their uses on her show. For her, it was these kinds of things that were most useful about Vefa, since the recipes were "all the familiar things." Her views contrasted strongly with those of a Thessalonikan woman, also in her forties, who is a housewife (and an active member of the Greek Communist Party). Noting that Vefa was more of a salesperson than a chef, she commented, "How many specialized utensils do I need? Vefa has a specialized tool for everything; that's just stupid. I don't need a special spatula to turn my fish in the pan; I can use my fork to do everything."

In her study of cooking shows on American television, Pauline Adema speculates on the pleasures of "arm chair cooking," noting that it was part of a larger cultural context in which, because of the concerns with diet and health, the pleasures of eating were *deferred* in the act of consuming television: "The home viewer defers the sensual pleasures of cooking and most important of eating what is being made" (2000, 115). It would seem that this might be the case for Mamalakis's show, in which, as we saw above, there was a reluctance to make the recipes outside of their local context. Even here, however, people might pick up techniques from the show, as with Polymnia Vasaneli, who, as noted in the previous chapter, first saw someone cutting an onion on a cutting board while watching it. Thus, both shows were part of the circulation of cooking knowledge, even if they didn't necessarily inspire people to cook the exact recipes shown, as we'll see in more detail in the next section. Moreover, many informants noted that both shows drove them, if not to make the specific recipes (though this did happen more commonly with Vefa), at least to eat. Indeed, one Thessalonikan woman complained that every time her husband watched Mamalakis, he demanded that she cook something for him. But even here, there seems to be a subtle difference. When expressing desire while watching Vefa's show, people tended to focus on the food itself, while with Mamalakis it was *his eating of the food*. Indeed, one Thessalonikan woman noted that she liked the way Mamalakis's mouth watered as the dish was prepared, the way he showed it in his mouth, the way he savored the tastes and kept the food in his mouth before swallowing. By contrast, Vefa "doesn't even eat her food, at most she'll take a bite and that's it"; she spoiled the intimacy made possible by imagining shared food consumption.

If both Vefa and Mamalakis played on nostalgia for the traditional, they did so in different ways that provoked strong reactions. Vefa's nostalgia was clearly for what is imagined as the traditional Greek family, in which the woman is responsible not only for cooking, but also for looking after the religious devotions of the family (see Hirschon 2010), set within a society in which everyone is assumed to be a practicing Greek Orthodox. This gender nostalgia fits with the Kalymnian view that women should have primary responsibility for feeding the family, even if it is more in line with the patrilineal, patriarchal traditions of

northern Greece, which, as noted, demand a much younger enculturation into cooking for girls. Setting her show within a home kitchen suggested traditional gender roles as well. However, if Vefa harked back to
an imagined 1950s version of Greece, it was an urban traditionalism,
and one that was comfortable with "modernizing" gestures—reflected
in what people identified as her consumerist ethos, in expensive and
diversified kitchen gadgetry, and in the incorporation of foreign,
particularly French, recipes into Greek cooking.

Mamalakis's tradition was, on the surface, more of the romantic
nationalist variety. This is a nationalism drawn from the folkloric tradition, so well documented in Greece, which takes common, everyday,
intimate practices and parcels them out to different ethnic or local identities. It assumes that authenticity is a condition that existed in the past,
and only its remnants can be seen in the present. Here we can incorporate many viewers' reactions to why they disliked Vefa and preferred
Mamalakis: because she often seemed to disregard or blur these boundaries, while he purified them (even while showing respect for the traditions of other groups, similarly conceived). However, it is important to
qualify the characterization of Mamalakis's show as romantic nationalist, considering that he did not treat tradition as a series of fossilized
remnants of a dead or dying past, but as very much alive and part of the
present. Thus, his show struck an optimistic note for those who might
fear that cooking is dead.

The nostalgia evoked by Vefa's show was undercut by what a number
of people on Kalymnos and in Thessaloniki identified as her commercialization of cooking. A number of people in Thessaloniki complained
that Vefa "even brought her daughter on her show." Vefa's daughter is,
in fact a celebrity chef who has her own cookbooks and other parapher-
nalia. While this seems in keeping with Vefa's theme of traditional family roles, a number of people (including Lambros, below) saw this as a
part of her inappropriate commercialization of domains of life that
should not be thought of as "for sale," including kinship and food (see
chapter 1 and Sutton 2001). Mamalakis seemed to get away with commercialization without viewer disapproval because he kept the commercial aspects of his show separate from his encounters with the food
itself, for which, as noted above, he showed a kind of quasi-religious
devotion. While Mamalakis was thus concerned with making distinctions and preserving boundaries, it should be noted that he also had a
certain playfulness, which might have helped him appeal to more intellectual Greeks. While his food remained pure and locality-specific, he

often played foreign music such as David Bowie songs during the show, a fact that one urban interviewee commented on as part of his appeal.

WATCHING AND COOKING

If the preceding tracks some of the issues raised by these two shows, in this section we address how people on Kalymnos and in Thessaloniki actually incorporated Vefa and Mamalakis into their daily lives and practices, in order to get at the larger theme of the chapter: what kind of cooking knowledge is transmitted through the medium of cooking shows? We examine two cases in detail in order to explore the complexity of ordinary Greeks' influences from and dialogues held with Vefa and Mamalakis.

Lambros is single, in his forties, and prides himself on being an excellent cook of traditional Greek cuisine. He is not a professional cook, though; he is a dock worker for the Port Authority of Thessaloniki. He is in the leadership of his union, and has traveled throughout Europe. He traces both his taste in traditional Greek food and his skill in cooking to his family origins. He is a third-generation refugee from Asia Minor, and he still identifies himself as a refugee. When asked why, he said that his "land is still over there" (*afou ta horafia mas ekei einai*). He watches as many of the cooking shows on TV as he can (even the ones he claims he does not like), but preferred Mamalakis by far.

Lambros often cooks for his friends. His house is a very sensory-intense environment, and he prides himself on paying attention to every possible detail that has to do with preparing food for guests and friends. The sounds of traditional Greek music are the first thing a guest notices on arrival at Lambros's house. Lambros also uses the same type of music to accompany his cooking well before his guests arrive. The first few times that Vournelis was invited for dinner, he was not allowed to help in any way (setting the table, bringing the wine from his wine cellar, etc.); after a few more visits, when they had developed a friendship, he would be allowed to do small things, like fetch an extra chair or maybe at most help set the table. Lambros made it clear to Vournelis that he was there only to observe and ask questions, not to help.

Although Lambros enjoys taking ownership of his creations in the kitchen—which represent both his cooking ability and the veracity of his claims to his roots—Lambros is one of the few people in our study who claimed that he did cook the recipes Mamalakis presented with any regularity. When asked for specifics, however, he noted that he rarely follows through an entire recipe, but rather "gets ideas" from watching the show of what "the old ones"—that is, an older generation of Greeks—used to do, and will sometimes incorporate these ideas into his cooking. For example, he said that he made a cheese pie, but after he took it out of the oven he covered it with butter and homemade jam—very unconventional—because he saw an old lady on Mamalakis's show doing the same thing with a homemade bread. The cooking show was not in any sense providing a recipe, but simply an inspiration for Lambros's experimentation.

Nevertheless, Lambros said he loved Mamalakis because his show was not strictly a cooking show; it was, according to him, a "documentary" of the people, the place, the customs, and the food. Lambros seemed to be attracted to the anthropological aspects of Mamalakis's show: he loved looking at the local topography, how people live, and what they eat. He said he always liked the way Mamalakis let you get to know the people and their food. This he contrasted to Vefa, who "executes recipes out of nowhere." He criticized Vefa for being "grandiose" by mixing Greek and foreign food in her show. When Vournelis mentioned that Mamalakis had shot numerous episodes featuring foreign cuisines, he answered that Mamalakis "does not try to enforce that on the [viewers]"; rather, he showed the people "what non-Greeks eat." Thus, it was Vefa's perceived boundary transgression that Lambros found objectionable.

When Vournelis asked him what was wrong with blending cooking styles and cuisines, Lambros responded that there's nothing wrong with it, but Vefa did it in a way that made him feel like he was a "poor relative to the Europeans." He said that he considered it pretentious to serve game with blueberry jam; "We don't do that here." He said that Vefa was not a real cook because the recipes were not hers. When Vournelis asked Lambros if the recipes Mamalakis was presenting in his show were his, he said, "That's a different case altogether; that is traditional Greek food." Lambros meant that traditional food falls into a category of belonging to the people rather than being the possession of an individual author or chef.

Lambros said that he liked Mamalakis because on his show "you see the people" (*vlepeis ton kosmo*). When he saw Mamalakis's episode on Asia Minor, he got goosebumps and couldn't stop crying because he saw the foods his grandmother used to make: "I could imagine my grandmother going to the bazaar and getting her spices." Lambros then recalled stories his grandmother had told him about how the Turks and the Jews and the Armenians would go to the *panygyria* and eat the food the Greeks would make, and the Greeks would go to the other ethnic groups' celebrations and eat their food.[10] Referring to the Greek army's occupation of parts of Asia Minor—a venture that ended in all Greeks being expelled from the region—he concluded that the catastrophe "was Venizelos's fault."[11]

At first it seemed that we had left our discussion of food behind and he was just talking about history. But in fact for Lambros, all these things were tied together. This was after all the reason he liked Mamalakis, and it was the same reason he did not like Vefa. When Lambros said that Vefa "executes recipes out of nowhere," he was really saying that he perceived her cooking to be out of context. For him food has history, and he was not able to see that in Vefa's show. Vournelis asked Lambros if he had ever seen Vefa cooking anything traditionally Greek and he responded that he had, usually when it was some major Greek or Christian holiday. Then her cooking would be "Greek," Lambros admitted. But he immediately added, "She will still tell people to buy her products! She never stops!"

It is interesting that Lambros echoed a number of other informants in criticizing the commodification of cooking in Vefa's show. Both shows were, of course, commercial programs and both hosts had a series of products they had endorsed. When asked why this was okay for Mamalakis but not for Vefa, Lambros and others said that Mamalakis never pitched a product *during the show*, while Vefa did so all the time. It would seem that pitching a product such as a book or a kitchen utensil, *while in the process of cooking*, was seen as particularly offensive to Vefa's critics. Indeed, notice that Lambros brought this up directly after admitting that Vefa sometimes cooked "traditional Greek dishes." It is as if he were saying that when Vefa was not transgressing boundaries between cuisines or nationalities, she was transgressing other boundaries—between public and private, the intimacy of the home and the calculation of the marketplace.

Turning to Kalymnos, I watched cooking shows for several weeks in April 2006 along with Katerina Kardoulia and her family (at which time Katerina's husband, Yiorgos, was still alive). Vefa's show was in favor with Katerina, and even more so with her daughter, Katina. Katerina said that she did not make many things from Vefa's show because her husband had his preferences and did not want any changes. She said that Vefa was "for the younger generation," her daughter and granddaughter. Katerina, Yiorgos, and Katina, however, sometimes watched the show together, along with Little Katerina. They all seemed to enjoy her show, noting how hungry it made them. In one episode we watched, the recipe was for a Greek bread called *tsoureki*. At first Katina said she would make Vefa's recipe only if she used nuts in it, but later, despite the lack of nuts, she said it looked really good. She also got excited when she saw the way Vefa cut the dough and put the pieces standing up on the baking sheet, saying that that was the "trick" (*patenta*) so that it wouldn't spill over in baking. Vefa suggested a variety of ingredients you could put inside the dough, and Katina had some other possibilities to add as well.

Two things are notable immediately. The first is that Katerina and Katina insisted on the value of such shows in that you could watch what the cook was doing: "Watch and remember. If I simply tell you, maybe you won't remember, but if you watch, it will stay with you," Katerina intoned, stressing the importance of learning through observation already discussed in earlier chapters. Second, it was clear that both mother and daughter were having a dialogue with Vefa's show; they would be excited about certain things, particularly designs or certain "tricks," but each would express her disagreement or suggest modifications for other things that Vefa did. Vefa, for example, used store-bought dough for one recipe, and Katina suggested that you could save money if you made your own dough, which she subsequently showed me how to do. It was as if Vefa were simply another voice in the familiar Kalymnian community discourse in which food choices and preparation techniques are analyzed and debated. I asked why they watched the show since they knew how to make these things already. Katina said it was for "the tricks," or maybe Vefa might suggest a different dough recipe, and that was useful. Cooking shows were no more sources of authority than friends or neighbors. Rather, the intelligent cook could glean new ideas and inspiration from these interactions.

Katerina and Katina also had an ambivalent attitude about Vefa's reliance on measurements. One day they decided to make a "fasting" dish of zucchini balls that they had learned from Vefa's show. Katerina said her daughter had written down the recipe, which she followed. She made a test ball to make sure it didn't dissolve when she put it in the cooking oil to fry; if it did, she would have to add more flour. I asked whether Vefa had said to do this, and Katerina said no. "Vefa is all about the measurements: 'Put in this many grams and it will come out right.' But I have my own ways, not worrying about timers or grams. But my cooking comes out right because it relies on experience."

Katina also commented that she liked the show because she liked to watch Vefa and "her movements around the kitchen, the way she decorates things. She has great imagination! But as far as the recipes, it's the usual, familiar stuff, cheese pies and so on." Her father, Yiorgos, was the most critical. While saying that some of her recipes might be good, he insisted that most were ridiculously expensive, full of all kinds of strange ingredients, recipes for rich people who want to be seen as rich, but don't know how to really enjoy life. Instead of taking a nice piece of meat and some potatoes, she had you putting in three kinds of cheese, cream, yogurt, strange sweet things that are meant for kids, "food for crazy people." Or she had you make a stuffed fish when you could just grill it with lemon and really appreciate the taste of it. While Katina said that Vefa had imagination (*fantasia*), Yiorgos said that she was "putting on airs" (*fantasmeni*). Not that you shouldn't spend good money on food; as he put it: "I want to eat, and want the food to *be something*. It's just a question of knowing what's good so that you don't waste money or get cheated."

At times Katerina and Yiorgos were even more pointed in their critiques of Vefa. After watching Vefa's shrimp and wine recipe with tomato balls on the side, Katerina didn't focus on the fact that the recipe was supposed to be traditional. Instead, she said that this was a new system of cooking, and Vefa played all over Greece. "The old food was beans or meat and potatoes, but a new generation of housewives will make shrimp in wine with a little rice on the side and say 'We've eaten well.'" This was said with some irony, but also with resignation, the feeling that things were changing more toward the "European" model, and that the change was both good and bad. Yiorgos felt no ambivalence, claiming that shrimp were good only for appetizers, and that tomato balls should be called shit balls (the two terms rhyme in Greek).

However, when not speaking generally but thinking about specific members of "the younger generation," Katerina had a more positive perspective. She noted that a neighbor (a close friend of her daughter's) had a daughter in her twenties who was recently married, and who had transformed her mother's style of cooking:

Her mother cooked heavy foods, bean stew and the like, but the daughter sits watching the program and writing down the recipes, "down to the gram," and she turns out wonderful things; she doesn't just make salad, but makes it artistically, so that it looks nice in the bowl, despite the fact that she's working outside the home as well. And her husband [older, already once married] is so impressed. She "shows off" in the kitchen [*apofaneronetai*]. It's good for a woman to be clean, but it's in the kitchen that she can really show her skills.

While more engaged with Vefa, the family did appreciate Mamalakis as well. One episode they watched involved Mamalakis traveling to the island of Sifnos to learn how to prepare chickpeas in locally produced clay pots. In a typical opening sequence, the camera lingered over the island, the quiet streets (never a car or motorcycle in sight), the priest, the religious imagery, the baker's oven (Katina observed that it was indoors, rather than the typical Kalymnian outdoor oven), and the ceramics shop where they showed how to make the clay pot. This got Katina thinking about a trip to another nearby island, Nisyros, where her husband had been working a few years back, and where they cooked chickpeas for one of the local religious festivals. She remembered being struck by the fact that on Nisyros they took basil from their windowsills (in Greece basil is decorative, not typically used in cooking) and threw it on the coals where the chickpeas were baking. While she didn't remember in particular the taste of those chickpeas, she did remember the color of the basil as it burned on the coals.

Katina was constantly aware of these variations on recognizable dishes associated with nearby islands, and trips to other islands were always a chance to learn twists that might be incorporated into one's cooking repertoire. For example, on a trip to Rhodes to take her mother for hospital tests, the family stayed with her son's boss, with whom they had exchanged hospitality on a number of occasions. This was a chance to observe her host making giant butter beans (*yigantes*) in the oven, a dish rarely made on Kalymnos. She also observed that on Rhodes cumin was used for grilling meats, which made it more acceptable to her when in 2012 her daughter, Little Katerina, incorporated cumin into a rice dish.

Part of this recognition of similarities and differences in recipes presented on TV cooking shows can be seen as a memory process. It was notable that both Katerina and Katina, because they assumed they knew the basics of the dishes that were being shown, would attempt to classify the dish. This was particularly noticeable if they started watching the show in the middle, after the show host had explained what was going to be made. At other times, mother and daughter would reconstruct a recipe that one of them had seen on TV, repeating ingredients back and forth to each other and puzzling over how it would turn out. This reminded me of how Kalymnians would ask me what my wife was cooking that day, and suggest appropriate ingredients or puzzle over the "odd" ideas that Americans had about cooking, such as putting carrots in lentil soup (see Sutton 2001, 25). These TV shows seemed to provide more fodder for Kalymnian comparisons and contrasts.

If a careful look at cooking practices reveals the way these shows are integrated into preexisting knowledge and techniques, how should we interpret the focus on foods from other parts of Greece, which seemed to make up an important part of the interest in Vefa's and particularly in Mamalakis's shows? Vassiliki Yiakoumaki (2006a) suggests that the new demands of European integration and consumerist agendas in contemporary Greece lead to a self-exoticization, expressed through such food tourism. Yiakoumaki is right to point out that the fetishization of "traditional" cooking practices from different parts of Greece is a new phenomenon. Indeed, elsewhere Yiakoumaki has shown how mainstreaming of Greek minorities through their food cultures tends to flatten or ignore any histories of conflict or oppression, reducing the "other" to a recognizable, palatable sameness (Yiakoumaki 2006b). Certainly we hear echoes of nationalist purifying discourse in the criticisms leveled at Vefa for mixing so-called "Greek" with so-called "foreign" food, as if these ever existed as pure, unmixed categories. However, if we listen with a careful ear, we find that our informants don't simply mimic a twenty-first-century consumerist, multiculturalist version of typical nationalist discourse. Indeed, recounting variations in customs and traditions from different parts of Greece—as Katina did, stimulated by a cooking show—is not something particularly new in itself. Rather, there have long been lively discussions of people's travels within Greece, with great attention given to recounting the details of expressive culture in different parts of Greece, their similarities to and differences from local practices (see Sutton 1998). And these discourses, while concerned with issues of continuity and change, are also often at odds with nationalist narratives. Indeed, this is very much the kind of "unreconciled historical experience," grounded in the senses, that C. Nadia Seremetakis (1994) points us to as a kind of productive embodied nostalgia that mitigates against the closures of modernity and nationalism. We saw this clearly in the case of Lambros's third-generation memories of food exchanges and good relations among different groups in Asia Minor. Far from eliminating conflict and tension, such memories keep the tensions of identity very much alive in the present. We also see it in Katerina and Katina's discussion of Turkish dishes, which they treat similarly to dishes from other parts of Greece—they are discussed for their recognizable qualities as well as for their differences.

By 2011 Vefa and Mamalakis were no longer on the air. Instead, there were a number of Greek cooking shows modeled on British and American competition shows like *Top Chef*. Katina contrasted Vefa's and Mamalakis's shows, where you always learned something, with the current show *Master Chef*: "On *Master Chef* it's a cooking school shown on TV, and it's a competition for who will come out the best. So it's all anarchy, cursing, and so on. While they say that they've gone to the school to learn cooking, they don't learn. They have no patience." For Katina, shows had moved from being opportunities for viewers to learn tricks and tips to competitions in which nothing was learned, and she watched them only out of curiosity, rather than watch "some English program full of murders and drugs."[12]

There were also for the first time a number of non-Greek shows, including several of Jamie Oliver's programs, and those of other British celebrity chefs including Gordon Ramsay and Nigella Lawson. A few Kalymnians talked about Jamie Oliver and had actually made some of his dishes, Nina Papamihail being one, as described in chapter 3. Pavlos Roditis, one of the male cooks I discuss in chapter 6, also said that he had adopted some of Oliver's salads into his repertoire. In general, I found little interest in these shows comparable to what Vefa and Mamalakis had generated. Indeed, some people were still talking about Mamalakis and the fact that he had done a show about Kalymnos in the time since my previous research. In this show he had focused on the Kalymnian version of dolmades, *filla,* known as the "Kalymnian national dish" because of people's propensity to eat it most Sundays (Sutton 2001, 105). It was interesting to watch the presentation of this dish on Mamalakis's show as prepared by Nomiki Leleki, considering how familiar a recipe it is to most Kalymnians.

A number of traditionalizing touches were performed on the show, such as the making of ground beef and pork "by hand" by using two knives to mince the cuts of meat instead of buying preground meat from the butcher. Leleki noted that cutting meat this way was "like in the old days," and Mamalakis added, "I remind you that mixing beef and pork comes from Byzantine times," encompassing local history and its oral transmission and reliance on memory in a "national" historical reference, presumably based on literate knowledge. Leleki also added fresh grape leaves at the bottom of the pan, a technique to keep the stuffed grape leaves from sticking. She also added grapevine shoots, known for their aroma, which she referred to with the local Kalymnian word *blasti.* And she added bones on top of the leaves to enhance the flavor. These are aspects of the recipe that are not commonly done in the preparation of the dish today. When Kalymnians commented on the preparation as shown by Mamalakis, they found some parts of it recognizable but others strange. Putting sliced tomatoes in the middle and on top fell under the category of "never done" for Katerina Kardoulia; indeed, she considered it ridiculous (*malakies*). Similarly for cutting meat by hand: this was simply what they did before they had the machinery to grind meat. Her daughter elaborated:

> They did it like that when I was little, and it was good, coarsely cut like a lentil or a chickpea. But slowly the children say they don't like it coarsely cut, the machines are an available luxury [*polyteleias*], and that way of doing it is gone. Sometimes we still remember it. This summer my neighbor on Telendos [a small island next to Kalymnos] didn't have any ground meat and wanted to make *filla* for her husband, so she cut it by hand. I don't have time for that, but when I get older, a grandmother, I might get bored and start remembering the old ways [*boro kai na thimitho ta palia*].

The latter claim is interesting in that it projects "the old ways" into a potential, imagined future. It also equates the act of preparing a dish a certain way with "remembering" it, rather than simply calling it to mind, once again stressing a more active version of memory.

Compared to cutting meat by hand, using bones to add flavor was something that people still did, whenever they might be lucky enough to have bones set aside for them by their butcher to add to the dish. What was most striking, however, was that Mamalakis's version of *filla* was like any invention of tradition in that it froze one particular version of what is traditional into a standard that showed both shared and idiosyncratic aspects, while leaving out others. For example, I observed Katina Miha making *filla* in 2012, and she used cabbage leaves along with grape leaves. While this is not uncommon, Katina stressed that these cabbage leaves were from Vathi, the agricultural center of the island, and that they grew from a type of seed that had been preserved through time, giving the leaves a distinct flavor that could not be reproduced using regular cabbage.

Katina was still watching cooking shows on my visits in 2011 and 2012, and she—unprompted by me—decided to make a rice cream pudding that she had seen on the Greek show *Chef in the Air*.[13] She had made it a few times previously, and her neighbor and friend Vangelio had asked her to make it, both because she wanted to have it again and because she wanted to observe. Katina noted that the recipe was from Turkey, but she and Vangelio insisted that it was very similar to traditional Kalymnian puddings because the basic ingredients were rice flour, milk, and sugar. This was a combination that mothers raised their children on "back in the days before pizza," Katina noted, and was also the basis for popular sweet-shop deserts like *galactoburico*. With a little cinnamon on top it was a popular dessert for grown-ups. But this recipe was a "modernization" of the traditional pudding, according to Katina (*se moderno rithmo*). The main difference was that the recipe called for gum mastic and rose water or orange-flower water, and after the pudding was set it was topped with a layer of jam—which, once chilled, Katina insisted, made it taste like ice cream. Here once again we see the pattern of cooking shows extending knowledge and practice around the margins of Katina's repertoire, rather than adding any radical new elements. Indeed, it was both because this recipe was familiar—reminding her of a "traditional" dish—and because it displayed "modern rhythms" that Katina decided to use it. A year later, however, she said she had gone back to the old recipe, finding this one not worth the extra fuss.

CONCLUSION

It is clear from our ethnographic observations that, for Kalymnian and Thessalonikan viewers, cooking shows offered an extension of their already established cooking practices but did not change them in any radical way. While Lambros tended to have a strong emotional reaction to the shows, particularly in terms of the memories invoked, using them to confirm his attitudes about family and national history, Katerina and Katina focused on the "tricks" that they could learn, the small adjustments that, for them, were essential to being a good cook. Thus these shows may represent a change in *scale,* but not any basic alteration in the *forms* of cooking knowledge that I have been tracking in this book. Indeed, they integrate themselves well into the kinds of discourses and practices that are typical of Kalymnian cooking.

However, perhaps a change simply in scale does make a difference. When I compared cooking practices in 2012 with those observed on earlier trips to the island in the 1990s and 2000s, it was hard to avoid the conclusion that more experimentation was occurring.[14] The number of sources of alternative recipes, from television to cookbooks and magazines, had mushroomed since the early 1990s. But perhaps more important, the different sources of authority provided by television programs, especially when associated with familiar personalities like Vefa and Mamalakis, seemed to make many Kalymnians more confident about trying different recipes gleaned from multiple sources, whether a mass-mediated one or a more local one—a neighbor, a trip to a local restaurant, a discussion of practices observed on a visit to a neighboring island.

In reviewing research on cooking in France, Jean-Claude Kaufmann sees a decisive shift between traditional and modern cooking: "The breakdown of any direct transmission from one generation to the next is [a] decisive change; that tradition has been destroyed by the growing individualization of culinary practices."[15] This may or may not be true for the French middle class.[16] On Kalymnos, as we have seen in this and the previous chapter, the transmission of cooking skill and knowledge is, and always was, anything but a smooth and direct process. But it is only through careful ethnography that we can begin to document the multiple avenues through which everyday cooking practices are reproduced, as well as slowly altered.

CHAPTER 6

Through the Kitchen Window

One of the exciting aspects of research into everyday cooking was learning how articulate Kalymnians are about their cooking practices. I suppose this shouldn't have been surprising, considering that Kalymnians tend to have well-formed opinions on most subjects, from relations with their neighbors to international politics.[1] But in reflecting on how casual cooking seemed to be for many of my friends and family in the United States, when I embarked on my Kalymnian research I was surprised to find consistency, even an aesthetic component, in people's approaches to the daily task of cooking. This consistency fitted with larger Kalymnian cultural practices in other domains—though, of course, these were not without their own contradictions as well.

In this chapter I present a number of short portraits of Kalymnian cooks. In using the term *portraits,* I take inspiration from Daniel Miller's book *The Comfort of Things,* in which he suggests that individual people can display a kind of pattern, or aesthetic, in their approach to life, similar to the notion of pattern that anthropologists once associated with cultures. These patterns are, he notes, "an overall organizational principle that may include balance, contradiction, and the repetition of certain themes in entirely different genres and settings" (Miller 2008, 293). While I would not go as far as Miller in claiming that these patterns can be more important for analysis or can even preclude larger cultural and structural influences,[2] I find his focus on the centrality of material objects to these aesthetics to be helpful in thinking about everyday cooking practices, as I have argued in one way or another throughout this book. As he puts it: "People exist for us in and through their material presence," which puts emphasis on the role of relationships, that is, not just among people, but among people and things. I would add here, perhaps, not just material presence but also sensory embodiment, to stress that objects are always apprehended in terms of an embodied and sensory enculturation, as David Howes (2003) has long argued.

Miller, for example, describes the aesthetic of Elia, a Greek-born Londoner, as revolving around the relationship among her understanding of clothes, jewelry, and gravestones, among other objects and practices (including cooking!). Objects, for Elia, are "forms that actually mediate and transfer substance and emotion between people" (2008, 37). He also notes that Elia "infuses food with ancestry" (much as we saw with Lambros in the previous chapter), and that she remembers the precise details of past meals, in particular the meal she prepared for her mother when she was dying in the hospital (2008, 40), a mnemonic ability that would be right at home on Kalymnos. My point here is that what Miller describes as Elia's aesthetic is recognizable to an anthropologist of Greece as part of a larger cultural repertoire, even if Elia creates her own particular combinations and syntheses.[3] This was my goal in chapter 3 when I explored Nina's particular relationship with her ambivalent Kalymnian identity. And I do the same here, in briefer fashion, reflecting the fact that I recorded these Kalymnians fewer times than I did Nina, although in almost every case my recordings are based on a ten- to twenty-five-year acquaintance with the participant.[4] Thus, in using the concept of "portrait" to describe Kalymnian cooks, I hope to highlight the ways that people create particular syntheses of wider, recognizable themes that resonate in different aspects of daily life. My goal, once again, is to explore the relation of everyday practices to values and shared islandwide, national, or global discourses about cooking.

POLYKSENI MIHA: EATING HEALTHY, EATING MODERN?

The notion of eating "healthy" is not a new one on Kalymnos. Since I began fieldwork on the island in the late 1980s, I was often told about the health and nutritional value of different foods: fish was full of phosphorus, good for the eyes; beans contained iron; and pomegranates offered lots of energy. There was also an extensive discourse about the contemporary risks to health represented by the growth of meat consumption, the use of pesticides and fertilizers, and the general increase in foods for which the provenience was not known. This was part of a larger discourse about the relation between "modernity" and "the good old days" that tried to skirt the dangers and recognize the benefits of each.[5] One change I noticed in the mid to late 2000s was what seemed to be a growing quantification of these health beliefs, objectified in measures such as cholesterol numbers (cf. Yates-Doerr 2011). As I suggested in chapter 1, the notion of "healthy" food needs to be seen as a total social fact, part of a larger landscape of beliefs about what makes food good. But how do these ideas about health, which can be elicited by interviewers, play out in everyday practices in the kitchen? I began to get a sense of this when I filmed Polykseni Miha making moussaka. Polykseni is a nursery school teacher, who lives with her husband (from Kos) and her teenage son on a hill overlooking the neighborhood of Ayios Mammas. I had known Polykseni since she befriended me on one of my first research visits to Kalymnos in the late 1980s. At that time she was living with her parents in the center of Ayios Mammas, just off the main square; we were introduced by her neighbor, someone I had known since my first visit to the island in 1980. Polykseni took an interest in my research and, as a teacher, was patient with what was at the time my beginner's Greek. Polykseni's wedding in 1992 was the first Kalymnian wedding I attended. Even though they lived about a half-mile distant, Polykseni's mother, Eleni, in her mid-eighties, often prepared daily meals for them during the week, when Polykseni was working. Polykseni herself might cook something more elaborate on the weekend and share it with her mother.

When she agreed to have me film her in 2008, she decided to make dishes that were not out of the ordinary, but still not everyday food, which was why she chose moussaka (and, on another occasion, mushroom pies). Over coffee we talked about current changes on the island, and Polykseni raised concerns about the invasion of "fast food." As many others told me, Polykseni insisted that the desire for meat every day was the biggest change in eating habits, with all the negative health consequences that accompanied this shift. As a teacher and a parent of a teenager, she was particularly concerned with children's eating habits, especially the snacks that children now consumed (which contrasted with the typical snack of "the old years": a slice of bread with olive oil and tomato). Indeed, she had told the parents of her class that she didn't want to see potato chips, ready-made croissants, and other ready-made snacks in her classroom—or at least not on a regular basis, noting that if you completely deprive children of something they desire, this can lead to a worse reaction. She said that fast food hadn't really inundated Kalymnos since there was no McDonald's or Goody's (a Greek hamburger chain) like they have on Kos, but that when Kalymnian students went to Athens, they went crazy for fast food, and since their bodies weren't used to it, it affected them more.[6] She insisted that I write all this down. The discourse on fast food paralleled discussions of the influx of drugs on the island, something unprecedented that young Kalymnians simply weren't prepared for, and that parents had not provided the proper guidance in teaching their children to avoid.

When we begin filming, Polykseni once again shows her awareness of the context of my research, directing comments about my long acquaintance with Kalymnos to the colleagues at my university who, she assumes, would be viewing the video. She also introduces her kitchen, noting that the house was completed in 1983, and that she had put in a special Greek-made marble for the counters, which had held up extremely well over the previous twenty-five-plus years. She also "introduces" the dish she was going to make, noting, "We think of moussaka as a Greek dish," though others suggest that it was perhaps brought from Turkey after the population exchange following the Asia Minor catastrophe. She states that she will first present the ingredients, and then show "in practice how we make it." In some ways this introduction paralleled Little Katerina's presentation at the beginning of her zucchini omelet video, as discussed in a previous chapter. But in this case there was no note of mimicking Vefa, or cooking shows in general; rather, Polykseni's introduction to her dish seems structured more like a school lesson.

Halfway through the list of ingredients, Polykseni pauses to note the issue of the potential "heaviness" of this dish: she uses Vitam, a butter substitute, because "in olden times [palia] people prepared things in an extremely fatty way [para poli pahia], because they ate meat only once a week." In modern times, Polykseni notes, cholesterol has reached new heights. This has led people like us today to raise our children in a more healthy manner, by banning butter and replacing it with olive oil and with corn oil for frying, and by buying meat with little fat on it (indeed, later she shows me how lean was the ground beef she had bought, admitting that there was still some fat, but that was unavoidable). Always aware of contrasts, Polykseni says that there are still families today who use lots of fat, especially in dishes like Kalymnian filla (stuffed grape leaves); they use pig fat, put bones at the bottom of the pot, "They insist on making it this way!"

This discourse on fat provides a backdrop for Polykseni's cooking, and she refers back to it throughout the presentation. But, to my surprise, her discussion becomes more nuanced when she is actually illustrating the process of cooking. As I found with Nina, Polykseni justifies each of her decisions—whether health-related or otherwise—in relation to a larger community that might practice different variations. She uses potatoes only as a bottom layer, while other families put several layers of potatoes in the dish. Noting other possible variations (e.g., adding zucchini), she insists on her own preference for eggplant as the central ingredient. When it comes to health, however, Polykseni's initial insistence on concern for fat is modified when she describes her own practice as being less extreme than that of some women she has heard of, who don't fry the vegetables before putting them in the casserole: "Even the idea of this I don't like to think about. But since I don't make it often, when I make it I want to feel it!" While Polykseni can't imagine not frying the vegetables, she is equally insistent on using several layers of paper towels to absorb as much oil as possible, noting, "The more oil that remains in the eggplant, the heavier the dish gets, and we don't want that." Other small moments of health concern are expressed in cutting up onions for the dish: "lots of onions, because they make the food both healthier and tastier." As she cooks, Polykseni moves between talking about food and analyzing society, saying that while it is more difficult for women nowadays to balance the demands of jobs and home, people are also suffering what she calls "occupation syndrome" (*katohiko syndromo*), in which the older generation, who had lived through the privations that came with occupation during World War II, don't want their children and grandchildren to suffer the same, so they work harder than they need to.[7]

An interesting moment comes when Polykseni is adding salt to her tomato sauce. She turns to me confidentially and admits that her husband doesn't want her to use salt, and she knows it's not good for you, "but I like it, I want it. It makes the food tasty, without it the dish would be useless [*ahristo*]! So, I know it's not good, but. . . ." When I ask her about other spices, she says that she doesn't use cinnamon, because her husband thinks he's allergic—"He has the idea, whether it's true, I don't know. But I will add nutmeg; I don't think it will bother him."

When it comes to making the béchamel sauce, a careful balancing act of fats and choices come into play, once again with awareness of a larger community of people who might do things differently. Polykseni uses half full-fat and half low-fat milk, noting that sometimes she uses all low-fat milk, but this time she is making it special (presumably because of my presence). She takes a 500 g (about 1 pound) container of margarine from the refrigerator, noting that it is "made from oil, not animal fat," and says, "Of course, we don't use the whole thing." She uses about three-quarters of the package though others use only half to make it lighter, she says, but she finds three-quarters to be the right amount. Later she reflects that using actual butter is tastier, but, of course, makes it too heavy "for those of us who have cholesterol."

All this leads Polykseni once again to reflect on how moussaka used to be made in the old times (*palia*), when it was done differently: they would pile the pan with two full layers of ingredients, potatoes-eggplant-meat sauce-béchamel-potatoes-eggplant-meat sauce-béchamel. This was "much tastier," she said, moving her hands in circles to emphasize her point. "But slowly the nutritional habits [*diatrofikes sinithies*] have changed, and we said, yes, we should eat, but not quite so richly."

For Polykseni the road to health was through maintaining a balance: a balance of "good" and "bad" foods, as well as a balance of "modern" and past practices. Everything should be done in some moderation, she believes, whether that means using three eggs in her béchamel, rather than the two or five that others use, or using fresh tomatoes in her sauce rather than canned tomatoes. She says she does this because the canned tomatoes are full of preservatives; however, the fresh tomatoes are not ideal because "they are far from the ones we used to know, but we must try as much as possible." This leads to memories of the tomatoes that her father used to grow in his garden without fertilizer, noting, "Things have changed for the worse, always they change for the worse." While this is part of a common Kalymnian view that vegetables (and most foods) were tastier in the past (see Sutton 2001, chap. 2), it also contains a critique of some of the contemporary prescriptions for health that elsewhere she subscribes to. She remarks, "We say 'This is healthy,' but it is only in theory that is healthy. In essence [*stin ousia*] . . . who knows?" She expresses similar sentiments in relation to the question of whether to bake bread at home to ensure its healthfulness: you may see what ingredients are in the bread, but you don't know about the flour and its provenience. She says the one time she baked bread that she could trust completely was when she was living on Kos and had found a mill where they ground fresh flour. In the news at the time was a scandal in Greece in which cooking oil had been cut with motor oil, feeding into Polykseni's perception (and that of many Kalymnians) that the further you were from the processes of production, the less trust you could have in the health and safety of a product.

In focusing on health, we see how healthy cooking is infused with many larger ideas about tradition and modernity, continuity and change, and the reasonableness of choosing a middle course between extremes, once again with a strong awareness of the range of acceptable Kalymnian practices. Interestingly, this middle path for Polykseni is negotiated during the cooking process itself, as prescriptions to use less salt are balanced against her desire to make the food "tasty," and her husband's concerns over spice allergies are given some sway—no cinnamon—but ignored when it comes to nutmeg. Indeed, at one point she enlisted me to tell her whether she had added enough salt to the tomato sauce, deferring to my claim that it tasted fine. Polykseni's embrace of contemporary health knowledge and discourse is always tempered, then, by a commitment to balance, and to a wider belief in traditional authenticity and the potential in the present to be deceived by appearances.

ANGELIKI RODITI: I COOK FOR THE CUSTOMERS

We last met Angeliki in chapter 4, when I talked about her in relation to her daughter, Vakina, and Angeliki's unusual claim that she learns from her daughter, rather than vice-versa. Angeliki was an interesting interlocutor. While she clearly took pride in her cooking, it was often hard to get her to talk about the details of the taste of food in the way that other Kalymnians did. I filmed Angeliki on more than a half-dozen occasions between 2005 and 2012, but I also spent many afternoons in her kitchen, and stayed in her home for more than a month during 2011 and 2012. In following Angeliki's kitchen practices, I found an overwhelming emphasis on the social nature of cooking, one that was a familiar dimension of Kalymnian culture, but that seemed to receive its strongest articulation in Angeliki's cooking.

Angeliki was shaped by the loss of her father when she was a child and her mother when she was a young woman, which put her in the position of cooking and caring for several of her brothers before they were married. Angeliki also lived together with her mother's sister, a teacher who never married. This aunt was known on Kalymnos as "the teacher" for her devotion to religious instruction on the island, as well as for her lively sense of humor. She became a second mother to Angeliki, living with her and her family for many years, even after Angeliki's marriage. Angeliki told me that she learned much of her cooking from

FIGURE 13. Angeliki Roditi in her kitchen (2014). Photo by Dimitris Roditis.

her aunt who, she proudly told me, was known as the "first feminist on Kalymnos." Her aunt had broken the gender line in coffee shops at the time by insisting on sitting down and being served. And she didn't choose just any coffee shop for her act of protest; she chose the one in the center of the harbor that served as the island's cultural center.

Because of a longstanding family dispute, Angeliki and her husband, Yiannis, were never able to extend their yard beyond a small space (roughly ten by twenty feet) used for planting flowers, hanging clothes, and placing a table and chairs when they wanted to eat outside. Thus, Angeliki's situation was unusual in that there was no second kitchen or outdoor processing area in her kitchenspace, and she used her kitchen sink for cleaning fish, unlike many other Kalymnians.

Angeliki's cooking was very much oriented toward hospitality and generosity: she referred to her son and husband as her "customers," and also joked that she was the "most inexpensive restaurant on Kalymnos." The humor in this joke came from the fact that for Angeliki, cooking food is as far from an economic transaction as she can imagine. But it also referred to her adjustments to the tastes of her family members. She took pride in her ability to cook typical dishes in ways that satisfied them, such as putting a whole onion in her lentil stew so it would be easy to remove later because her son didn't like the texture of cooked onions. She also mentioned preparing stuffed grape leaves without the leaves—in other words, as meatballs (*youvarlakia*)—as per their preferences. She said, laughing, that she made these adjustments in order to "satisfy the appetites of all of the clientele." Her wording had a formal ring to it, which was part of the humor: *yia tin ikanopioisi tis orexis olonon ton pelaton*. For the lentil stew she had rinsed a bowl of lentils in water. She said that the new machines clean the lentils, while in the old days you had to clean them yourself: "But I still rinse them, just to be sure" (indeed, she found a little bit of dirt in the water). As she transferred the lentils to the cooking pot in handfuls, she explained that she was counting a handful per person, but she always estimated the amount first for the invited guests; this way she never had to throw away food, which is a sin.

Any discussion of cooking with Angeliki focused on the issue of generosity, and she regularly fed certain people (including myself) who could not feed themselves. While some Kalymnian women took pride in feeding many different passing strangers, Angeliki's house was on a side street off the harbor of Kalymnos town. So it was usually personal relationships that she cultivated, and she would feed a few extra people regularly rather than many people occasionally.

Angeliki has had to adjust to cooking for herself over the course of the past several years. Her husband, Yiannis, secretary to the mayor for many years and a recognized local artist, died in 2006.[8] Her son, Dimitris, was married in 2007, so by the time of my research he only very occasionally ate at his mother's house. Her goddaughter, who used to come by frequently for a meal, was now a student studying in Cyprus. For a while she cooked for a needy—unemployed and disabled—neighborhood man who would stop by several times a week, until she found out that he had become a drug addict. She looks forward to visits from her daughter and son-in-law—who live in Italy, and who often bring friends with them to visit Kalymnos—as a time to display her cooking skills. But in the main, her "customers" have become scarce in recent years.

Angeliki's daily cooking was suffused with memories of past acts and gestures. Even small gestures, such as the peeling of an onion that made her tear up, reminded her that her son told her not to buy the red onions because they are stronger. Preparing *filla* without meat (with a zucchini stuffing), she was reminded of how much her daughter in Italy and her friends enjoy this dish, and how she brought grape leaves with her when she visited Italy so she could make it there. Food memories are mixed with other memories of generosity. Looking out the kitchen window at her yard, she noted that there used to be a lake where their yard is, that's why the chapel is called Panayia I Limniotissa (The Virgin Mary of the Lake), and she knows this because a plant that is hard like a straw and normally grows in lakes sometimes comes up there. This led her to think about her aunt, the teacher, climbing the big fig tree and picking figs to distribute to everyone in the neighborhood, even though the milk from the figs bothered her skin, thus emphasizing the self-sacrifice that generosity demands. Angeliki found an old censer under the fig tree, but she gave it away to someone who asked her for it: "I never was scheming [*den eiha pote afti i poniria*] to try to benefit from something like that, and my daughter's like that too, always giving; she could have a nice house in Italy, but she doesn't because of her generosity" (once again implying the importance of self-sacrifice).

There was an antimaterialist thread to Angeliki's views, and she was often critical of other islanders whom she saw as interested only in making money and building houses, rather than contributing to the island either through religious good works or through artistic achievement. It is not the building of houses in itself that Angeliki dislikes; indeed, she praises all the little houses that have been built by Italians, Swedes, and other visitors to the island "because they love Kalymnos." It is the self-regard and egotism of some Kalymnians that draws her critique. In this context, food is simply one of many potential channels of generosity that make for proper social relations in Angeliki's view. But there is always the potential for a lack of reciprocation, or ingratitude, in such relations, as illustrated in the case of the young man who turned out to be a drug addict and who, after Angeliki's long investment of care and feeding and even enlistment of other family members to help him, ended up demanding large sums of money from her to pay off his drug debts. Such "ingratitude" does not alter Angeliki's generous practices, though it contributes to her view that "the world has changed," and that there are few good people left on Kalymnos. She tells of her husband, when close to death, warning her to take care not to be taken advantage of in this changed social environment on Kalymnos.

One interesting touchstone in Angeliki's memories is that of her mother cooking for German officers during World War II. Angeliki was a small child at the time, and they were living in Athens, facing the worst of the famine that ravaged the city during the war.[9] Before the war had begun, she recalls, her father had opened up a restaurant along the Piraeus harbor. The restaurant was a failure, Angeliki said, laughing ruefully, because many Kalymnians came to it and her father insisted on feeding them for free. I realized that this was not a critique of her father's business skills, but rather intended to situate her family's generosity as including both of her parents. Overgenerosity was not a flaw in Angeliki's eyes: when she spoke of the former mayor of Kalymnos, Yiorgos Oikonomou, she said that he was the best mayor that Kalymnos had had, as shown by the fact that he was so generous that he never even owned a house (i.e., he had never saved enough to buy his own house, according to Angeliki).

During the war, her father was killed when he was struck by a German officer while trying to get a little wine that was spilling from a boat in the harbor at Piraeus. Her mother had to care for her and her four brothers, and indeed her younger sister died during this period. The others survived thanks to the fact that some German officers staying near them took on her mother as a cook, and she was able to bring home extra food that she had prepared. Thus, cooking even extended in this case to the enemy, though certainly in desperate circumstances. The Germans fed them as well. She remembered the officers giving her mother lots of food for the family—boiled eggs came to mind for her— because they thought so highly of her cooking. She also told of the generosity of a number of prostitutes living in the neighborhood. They had been paying her mother to do laundry for them, and they offered to pay for the funerals of her husband and her young daughter, showing that generosity and humanity knows no social class or occupation.

While I have written about Kalymnian food generosity in my previous work (Sutton 2001, chap. 2), thinking about Angeliki's practices leads me to some further conclusions. Implicit in many of Angeliki's statements is a dichotomy between surface and depth—hence her criticisms of the shallow materialism of Kalymnians who accumulate money instead of turning that money into value by using it to give back to the wider community. The distinction between surface and depth is reflected in Angeliki's preference to talk less about the flavor of food or even the details of food preparation—though she would provide recipes for me when I asked—and to focus rather on the social good that comes from cooking and sharing food. I noted similarly that Angeliki did not seem interested in cooking shows when they came on TV, and would flip the channel looking for something "educational," such as nature, art, or history programming. And it was also reflected in her stories about the foreigners whom she had come to know through her daughter and son, and how they were never pretentious, showing off their knowledge or wearing fancy clothes. She talked about serving meals to doctors and professors from around the world who would dress in shorts and T-shirts.

These comments reminded me of some of Katerina Kardoulia's reflections on hospitality. Katerina recalled a man from Sweden, "a huge man with big teeth," who had seen her milking a sheep and asked her about it. When she offered him some sheep's milk, they had begun talking, and she had invited him to have lunch. She was cooking fava beans that day, and he had never tried them before, didn't know what they were even though he had traveled all around the world and despite her attempts to offer the word in several different languages. Eventually he joined her and her husband, offering a bottle of retsina that he had bought. After that encounter he sent them regular postcards from Sweden at Christmas and Easter for a number of years. Her conclusion about such encounters had a religious twist. She noted that in our origins "humanity is one" (*I Anthropotita einai mia*), and that only much later were we divided into different races and different languages. Hospitality, Katerina implied, recognizes our shared humanity as an ideal value. This sentiment would certainly be recognized by Angeliki, though her discussions of hospitality focused on respecting the value of particular people despite their humble appearance, in effect echoing the ancient Greek maxim that you should always be generous to strangers because you never know which one might turn out to be a god in disguise.

Cooking and sharing food is then, for Angeliki, part of creating a value that circulates through acts of generosity in the community and allows for the possibility of others to contribute to the kinds of values that transcend money and crass materialism. Sometimes, however, I believe Angeliki wondered if she could have made some other kind of cultural contribution. While we were watching a show about a Kalymnian woman who had become a singer, she reminisced, "Imagine if my uncle from the United States had taken me to New York when I was a girl to become a singer as he had promised [*laughing*]. Forbidden! I had to remain here on Kalymnos and do the laundry of my brothers."

NOMIKI TSAGGARI: LIVING TRADITIONS

While "tradition" is a popular touchstone in talk about Kalymnian cooking, and indeed we saw its influence in Polykseni Miha's practice, no one I filmed illustrated the importance of this category more clearly than Nomiki. Tradition was present not just in her discussions of cooking, but in multiple aspects of her daily life. Nomiki, in her mid-forties when I made a video of her in 2006, lived with her husband, Mihalis; Nomiki's mother; and one teenage daughter, Maria. Their older daughter, Popi, having started college on Cyprus the previous year, was at home for the Easter holidays while I was there. Mihalis works as a civil servant in the mayor's office, while Nomiki's father had been a carpenter (he died in a tragic dynamite accident), and her mother does part-time sewing, producing "traditional costumes" for sale to Kalymnians in the United States and Australia to use for holiday celebrations. While neither of Nomiki's parents had gone to high school, Nomiki had studied music and had the option of continuing study after high school, but had dropped out when she decided to marry. Several years earlier, Mihalis and Nomiki had gone in on a partnership with a friend and opened a pizza restaurant on the harbor, catering mostly to tourists and young Kalymnians. By 2011 they had closed the pizza restaurant but opened a restaurant and café with Nomiki's sister, Polymnia Vasaneli, near one of the tourist hubs of Massouri.

They had invited me over to video the preparation of and then partake in Sunday lunch, an elaborate meal of stewed fish and pastitsio, the popular noodle and meat casserole with béchamel sauce. It was the first time I had seen their new house, as on previous trips they had lived in Nomiki's parents' house. Most strikingly, the house was designed in some respects to re-create the traditional Kalymnian home. The typical parlor for greeting guests opened onto a *krevvato* or *krattho,* a large bed with storage area underneath that is a key feature of "traditional" Kalymnian homes. Renée Hirschon describes a similar feature still found on Karpathos, where it is called a *soufas:* "The great architectural feature of the Karpathiot house is the elaborately carved sleeping platform, which can be said to constitute the house itself. It is the center of attention, both for the owners of the house, and visitors" (2008, 570–71). Families sleep on the *soufas* platform, which is also used for displays of family wealth, its treasures, and for special festivities such as weddings. This was the first of its kind that I had seen in a recently built house on Kalymnos, as most Kalymnians have adopted "Western-style" beds. However, a number of people mentioned that this feature was making a comeback in the past five or six years in newly built houses. Interestingly, in the case of Nomiki and Mihalis it no longer had one of its original functions as a sleeping area for the entire family: the daughters slept on it, but the parents slept in their own room. When asked about it, Nomiki noted that they saw it as really for the grandchildren, so that they would have a sense of being close, instead of being isolated in separate rooms.[10] On Kalymnos, the "traditional" is not simply discursive, or relegated to special occasions, but incorporated into mundane, bodily practices such as sleeping arrangements. However, while the *krevvato* remained the central visual feature, it no longer took up the entire house as it once would have. In Nomiki and Mihalis's house, this area also opened directly on the right into the kitchen, with a corridor leading to an indoor bathroom.

Other "traditionalizing" features included the second-floor fireplace built into the corner of a wall, and the outdoor oven in the front courtyard. Mihalis was using this oven to bake the pastitsio for lunch, the first time they had used it for something other than lamb. He showed me the special kindling he had gathered from particular mountain shrubs to infuse the food with a unique smell while it was cooking. After asking me to notice how nicely it caught fire, he noted, "Thus, back then the old ones made [their fires]. They didn't have lights, electricity, nothing. Therefore, in order to survive they needed to cook their bread, their food, their sweets in outdoor ovens." Similarly, when I asked Nomiki about the meat sauce for the pastitsio, which she had prepared the night before and left on the stove, she said, "It doesn't hurt to leave it overnight. That's what the old ones did, since they didn't have refrigerators, they cooked things in a pot for a long time." At this point she turned to her mother and asked, "Was it with oil?" When her mother affirmed this, she said, "Yes, they cooked it this way to preserve the meat." What was interesting was that neither husband nor wife was present for the other's comment, and yet they used almost the exact same phrasing, "thus did the old ones . . ." (*etsi kanane oi palioi*). This discursive reference to the past as justification for present practice rolled off the tongues of Nomiki and Mihalis throughout the afternoon: Nomiki, for example, showed me a vegetable appetizer that Mihalis had preserved in salt, noting, "Back then people would make this for appetizers. And Mihalis made it [now]. It's called *toursi,* and is made with carrot, two kinds of pepper, cauliflower . . . and they used to make it. It's preserved with a little oil on top, and it keeps for years." Here the continuing of tradition is metaphorically embodied in the object itself, which "keeps for years." But it is also marked by the use of the past imperfect tense to refer to something in the present: Nomiki was holding the object in her hand while talking about it as part of the past. Contrast this to U.S.

popular usage, in which to "enter the past tense" is "to literally cease to exist."[11]

An interesting moment came when Nomiki and her older daughter were listing for me the ingredients the daughter had put in the ground beef for the pastitsio. Not hearing it mentioned, I asked Nomiki whether there was nutmeg in it, which I had previously noted in other people's preparations. She responded, "Some have gotten used to using that, but a long time ago those things didn't exist, they came later to Kalymnos, those ingredients. Like curry, all that stuff. Those didn't exist." At this point her mother interjected, "They did have nutmeg."

Nomiki: Eh, it didn't exist, nutmeg. In the food?

Mother: It did. Nutmeg, cinnamon, pepper. Whoever liked it put it in.

Nomiki: Ah, I didn't know, perhaps, perhaps . . .

In each of these two examples, the past is a direct reference and justification for present practices (of commission and omission). In the case of the nutmeg, it's interesting that her mother corrected Nomiki, noting that there was also choice in the past, challenging the typical suggestion about tradition that it is uniform and accepted by all, and only in the present do some deviate from the norm. Later, while preparing béchamel sauce for the pastitsio, Nomiki reiterated that she didn't like to use nutmeg, though this time she said it was because it overpowers the other spices and you don't get to "hear" them as well. I noticed that Nomiki was preparing her béchamel differently from the way Polykseni Miha did, as she did not brown the flour in butter first, instead adding it directly to the warming milk. I asked her about this and she insisted that both ways were acceptable; indeed, sometimes she did it the other way, but it made no difference to the flavor. Similarly, Nomiki referred to the number of eggs one adds, saying that some people add more so that the béchamel has a more yellow coloring, but this didn't matter to her because she was interested in the flavor. On the other hand, she referred to the possibility of making béchamel from a ready-made powder that you buy at the store, noting simply, "It's nicer to do it yourself."

So for Nomiki the keys to cooking seemed to be a concern for tradition and for variations that affect flavor. I might have thought that the references to tradition were made for my benefit if not for the fact that they fitted completely with the decor of the home: objects such as the TV and microwave were not displayed prominently; instead, the house was decorated with all kinds of objects representing the past. These included a number of kitchen items—pans, casserole dishes, sifters, bread boards, bowls for allowing bread to rise in (which she claimed still to use), all of which were displayed on walls, in corners, or on top of cupboards in the kitchen, or in various spots in the front yard. She even claimed that she hoped to buy an old-fashioned Kalymnian refrigerator, which she asked her mother the proper name for (*fanari*)—a box suspended in the air from a string—which she would display for decorative purposes. I had heard about *fanaria* in other Kalymnian accounts of the past, but Nomiki was the first person who suggested using one in such a way.

Also displayed in the front yard were several farm implements that Nomiki had found abandoned in fields on Kalymnos. She referred to these, as well as to some of the kitchen implements, using their local, Kalymnian names (identifying them even more with the past). Finally, all the furniture that she bought, both for her use and for her daughters' dowries, were antiques, though not all from Greece. In relation to these last Nomiki said, "I don't like getting these modern things. Everything here is made of wood. I want to know the history of the furniture," noting that the set she had bought for her elder daughter was made in the 1930s, owned by a doctor in Switzerland, and that the chairs had pigskin coverings. While keeping old things is not uncommon—indeed, some homes on Kalymnos display ancient Greek amphorae brought up by sponge divers—new houses more typically tend to be sparsely decorated, such as the home of Polykseni, who had on her walls a few icons, locally done paintings of Kalymnos harbor, and a few handcrafted plates. For Nomiki these claims on tradition extended to everyday practices as well. She has encouraged her younger daughter to learn the *sandouri*, a Byzantine instrument (somewhat like a xylophone), and with Nomiki playing accordion, they perform in traditional music groups on and off the island. Her daughters had also participated in the local dance school, dressing in costumes that represented the different Dodecanese islands.

In talking about cooking, Nomiki dismissed cooking shows like *Vefa's Kitchen,* which she saw as failing to uphold traditional Greek cooking. Her daughter piped in that Vefa's salads were particularly awful. Nomiki agreed that Vefa "mixed things up," admitting that she needed to do this on her show for variety. She contrasted this to the proper traditionalness of Mamalakis's show, *Forgiveness with Every Bite.* Although she said she hadn't cooked any recipes from his show, she intended to make a kind of cheese pie from Epirus, which had a sauce (*krema*) mixed in with the cheese. She wasn't sure about it, though, because it called for a lot of mint, and she wasn't a big fan of mint. Nomiki proudly showed off a cookbook of traditional Cretan recipes that she had bought on a trip to Crete; she said she liked it because the recipes were linked to the seasons and to holy days, and described the associated traditions, that "it was more about traditional life than about food."[12] Indeed, she said, recipes were not that important, you could add what you wanted to any particular dish, as long as you showed concern and care for the food, tasting things as you went along, doing things not with indifference but with passion (*na to frontiseis, na proseheis to fagito; meraki*).

Nomiki was one of the few women of the younger generation who knew how to make the labor-intensive Greek funeral food *kolliva* (Sutton 2003). An older neighbor had showed her how to prepare it, as her mother had not learned either, many Kalymnian women feeling that this tradition is too "sad," and preferring to buy prepared *kolliva* from the store. Nomiki had felt guilty about buying prepared *kolliva* for her father's memorial, and had heard a priest say that not preparing it yourself was like inviting your ancestors to eat and taking them to a restaurant. Of course, there was a certain irony here, considering that Mihalis and Nomiki own a restaurant. Their restaurant, which they referred to as a good investment for difficult times, was seen as a place mostly patronized by young people, who had learned to eat things like hamburgers, souvlaki, and other snack foods, foods that Nomiki and Mihalis saw as inappropriate on a regular basis for their own children.

A number of authors have suggested that the revaluation of "tradition" has been an undertaking of the middle classes, a project of symbolic capital and class distinction.[13] Here, however, it is important to note that many of Nomiki's practices, such as learning to make *kolliva*, or to build a house with a *krevvato* and with the living space built for her daughter on the second floor of their house (rather than a separate house), are not necessarily given status by the community. Indeed, when I repeated Nomiki's comment about the priest who said that you should not buy *kolliva* prepared by others, people were highly dismissive, one man calling that "bullshit" and classifying *kolliva* not as a valued tradition, but as a stupid superstition.[14] Even in the realm of food and expressive culture, then, there are traditions and there are Traditions. There are many other aspects of Kalymnian life in which it would make no sense to embrace "tradition." Despite the traditionalizing features of their house, Nomiki and Mihalis did not reject indoor plumbing, for example, despite the fact that for many older Kalymnians, bathroom practices were the site of a kind of nostalgia for community intimacy (Sutton 1998, 37–38). Nor did they reject opening a pizza restaurant, despite its association with fast food, tourism, and the antisocial aspects of "modern" eating. It makes more sense, then, to see the views and practices of Nomiki and her family as ontological attitudes about time, about the problem of facing the present appropriately, rather than as calculated displays of authenticity as symbolic capital or dressing up for tourists. This is also implied in the amount of tradition that is "embodied" in memories of taste, as well as in sleeping and other spatial practices. I address issues of time and temporality more specifically in relation to the timing of cooking in the next section.

POPI GALANOU: IF THERE'S TIME . . . .

In 2008 when I made a video of Popi making octopus stew, she was in her late thirties, married with two small children born to a sailor who was absent for several months out of the year. I had known Popi's family since my fieldwork in the early 1990s. Popi's father—a cousin of Yiannis Roditis, Angeliki's deceased husband—had run one of Kalymnos's fish farms at the time. Her mother was active on the cultural scene on Kalymnos, organizing performances, and had run a "traditional" coffee shop and venue for local artists from 1999 to 2003. Her brother Pavlos was the director of the Kalymnian Transportation Department. Sadly, her mother had died fairly young, in the mid-2000s. The family had a certain cosmopolitanism about them, reflected in the fact that the children had grown up in Athens. Before marrying her current husband, Popi had been briefly married to a German man whom she had met while he was visiting the island, and had lived for a short time in Germany until their marriage dissolved.

Time and timing are, of course, always part of the calculations of cooks. Nomiki Tsaggari complained about how in contemporary times it seems as if you were always checking your watch. But time can have different experiential dimensions in different contexts and settings. As Jean-Claude Kaufmann notes in his writing on cooking in France, the French woman "is always juggling two contradictory injunctions: something quick, something good. . . . To that extent, she is a perfect illustration of contemporary family life, with all its contradictions and its difficult juggling acts" (2010, 85).[15] But with two small children, a husband often gone at sea, and no female relatives to share labor with, Popi felt the temporal dimensions of cooking particularly acutely as they structured her cooking discourse and practice.[16]

In the video, the issue of time is immediately raised by Popi because she is using a pressure cooker to soften the octopus. She notes that using the pressure cooker isn't as good as cooking the octopus slowly, but it saves time. She says she uses it often, for certain types of beans like chickpeas or other beans, which take a long time (*argoun para poli*). For the octopus, to make up for the speed of the pressure cooker, she adds soda water (which she has to hand, and which she says works as a substitute for baking soda), in order to help "the poor thing" to soften more while cooking. While the pressure cooker is regarded by Popi as a second choice—if she has time she won't use it on things such as white beans—she notes that for most meals she does use it.

Shortly after discussing the benefits and problems of the pressure cooker, Popi begins to prepare some tomatoes to add. In this case she notes that she normally tries to buy the nicest, freshest tomatoes, and, indeed, that's what she has done this time. "But when you don't have time it's difficult, because the right thing to do is to be able to remove the skin and any hard parts inside so that it cooks easier." She says this as she is peeling the tomatoes by hand, so I ask her whether she ever grates them. She says that she plans to grate them, or rather to blend them using a small blender, "which is the most modern version of grating, and which helps a lot." But she returns again to the issue of not always having time, and says that of course it is possible simply to blend them with the skin on, but that is a bad solution. Note that the issue of tomato skin is something not everyone agrees on; as Nina mentioned in chapter 3, many Kalymnians prefer the skin left on, but once again it is seen as one of the decisions that *matter* in Kalymnian cooking. Later Popi notes that the best way to prepare the tomatoes is to grate them, but she has gotten used to the blender. Here, as throughout, she mixes a sense of "best" practices with the ever-present constraints of time.

Because Popi is concerned with feeding her young children properly, I ask her what "healthy food" means to her. While she begins with the issue of "heaviness" or fat discussed by Polykseni, issues of time quickly enter in as well. She raises the issue of not overboiling vegetables to keep them from losing their vitamins, but at the same time, she says, one needs to boil the vegetables to kill microbes and other things they might contain: "There are ways to avoid this overboiling. But I think that because modern life doesn't give you the time—I mean, I've learned some of these ways, and I do them when I have time. When you soak greens for a long time in vinegar, all of those little bugs (*zouzounakia*) leave by themselves. But you have to do it two or three times, it takes two hours. Especially if someone is working, they won't be able to do this, thus they would prefer to boil the vegetables a bit longer to be sure."

Even within the constraints of "modern life," however, Popi insists that she would never consider buying preprepared food at the super-market. At most they might go out for an occasional pizza or souvlaki when her husband is in town. She is insistent that not only she, but hardly any Kalymnians, would buy such food from the supermarket. Only perhaps a single man might buy it, but, she suggests, he too would probably have someone to cook for him. She is convinced that such food is perhaps used in Athens, but on Kalymnos even if a woman works full-time she will find the time to cook; "That's why there are few of these ready-made meals in Kalymnian supermarkets." Popi claims that at most you will find ready-made pasta sauces, but even with these it's easier and quicker to make them yourself—since the ingredients (for carbonara, for example) are things that every kitchen has—rather than take the time to go and buy it at the supermarket. However, she does find acceptable frozen pearl onions, which she tried recently and found were a convenient way to make the Greek-style stew known as *stifado*.

Popi's sense of time creeps into her cooking in that she stops at sev-eral points to review what she has done so far and what she still needs to do. She says that this happens often; because cooking is automatic, she sometimes forgets steps. That's why she puts out all the ingredients in advance, so that she is reminded to use them. At one point while she is reviewing, she remembers not that she has left out bay leaves, but that she hasn't taken them out of the cupboard so they would be there when she needs them. As Kaufmann notes for French cooks: "cooks con-stantly rely on objects that act as signs telling them what they have to do next" (2010, 181).[17] Timing also played a role: while she is frying the onions, Popi is cutting up the boiled octopus to add it in, but she takes a bit too long so the onions begin to burn. Here she notes, "I shouldn't have left it so long, but it happens, the damage has been done." Even for small gestures, timing plays a part. When I ask why she uses a spatula rather than a fork to stir with, as other Kalymnians tend to do, she says that a spatula gets it done faster, though in this case perhaps it was the smallness of the onions that made her choose a spatula, because she adds that for some things she does use a fork.

While a number of the women I interviewed talked about time as an issue, Popi's consistent references to time seemed striking. In part, no doubt, this reflected the fact that, as noted, she was caring for two small children without help from relatives and with her husband absent for much of the year. Indeed, while we were cooking, Popi's aunt was watching her two-year-old daughter, and both children came into the kitchen several times as Popi was preparing the meal. Popi mentioned that she often cooked with her daughter clinging to her leg.

However, another element of Popi's time consciousness became clear when she talked about her mother and her experience growing up. When I asked Popi how she had learned to cook, she immediately insisted that it was through her mother. But when I asked her whether it was through helping her mother prepare the daily meal, she complicated the picture. When Popi was a child they had lived in Athens, and her parents were both working full-time—her mother as a real estate agent—and Popi had been home with her brother, who is six years older. Thus, she explained, while her mother sometimes found time to cook the night before, on many days it was she and her elder brother who prepared dinner. But, she told me, her mother had "a gift for cooking," and loved to do it; she cooked or prepared food for guests in a way that concerned not only the taste of the food, but also the appearance and all of the sensory aspects. I sensed from Popi's description that her mother had struggled with finding the time for cooking, and that this was part of her culinary legacy that Popi had adopted.[18]

Interestingly, when she contrasted her mother's cooking with her own, Popi immediately thought of her own shortcuts—using the pressure cooker and adding soda to the octopus to help soften it—things she said her mother would never have done. She contrasted her pressure cooker with her mother's pot with a tight-fitting lid, which she said was healthier because it kept the substance of the food from escaping through the steam. The pressure cooker represented for Popi her own, "modern" attempt to deal with issues of time, though one that she regarded with ambivalence as lacking authenticity, because she had brought it from Germany from her time living away from home and family. Even her grammar reflected the omnipresence of time concerns. When she described being at home with her brother learning to cook while her parents were at work, she stated, "We helped a lot because there wasn't time from our parents" (*voithousame k'emeis epidi den ipirhe hronos apo tous goneis mas*). This sentence is grammatically incorrect in Greek because the verb *iparhei* (to be, to exist) doesn't take an object, but its usage reflects the fact that Popi has made "time" the subject of the sentence rather than her parents (i.e., she could have said "because our parents didn't have time").

I was also struck by the way time entered into her discussion of other issues, in particular the death of her mother and her uncle, which she referred to by saying, "So many important people left us in such a short space of time, I can't take it in that they no longer exist." Shortly after making this remark, however, she noted that her daughter, who following the Kalymnian tradition was named after her mother, had been born just twenty-five days after her mother's death, and how important that had been in helping her come to terms with the loss of her mother: "For me, Katerina [her daughter] *was* my mother. For all of us."[19] In these two examples we see larger time trajectories at work, in one case acting cruelly to take away the important people in her life, and in the other providing the "medicine" that allows Popi to deal with her losses.

Kaufmann writes of the constant struggle of French cooks against time: "Women of working age who have to cope with the demands of work but who still have family responsibilities often have to do everything in a rush and are always short of time." At the same time he sees this experience as part of modernity in which "we" are constantly "project[ing] ourselves into the future" and imagining "so many possible scenarios" that there is never felt to be enough time for mundane cooking chores.[20] I do not think that this adequately captures the experience of time pressure for Popi and other Kalymnian women. Cooking may be a burden, but it is not a chore in the sense that Popi does not see it as secondary to other pursuits. Time is a problem not because cooking is seen as something to be dispensed with quickly so as to pursue other activities—"eating, relaxing, working" (Kaufmann 2010, 184)—but because doing cooking in a proper way, one that respects tradition, the senses, and health concerns, takes time. Popi doesn't always have that much time, thus necessitating various types of shortcuts, from pressure cookers and spatulas to soda. When I asked Popi about whether she cooked from cooking shows or recipes, she complained that the TV recipes were inconvenient or expensive, always calling for some ingredient that might not be available on Kalymnos, might be prohibitively expensive, and might be used only one time. On the other hand, Popi told me, when she has time she likes to try new and unusual things, like trying a recipe from a magazine for pierogi that she and the children both enjoyed. "It was something special, not the usual stuff" (*kati idietero, ohi to sinithismeno*). Moreover, Popi saw things moving not toward the death of cooking, as others insisted, but rather toward people spending more time on growing and cooking their food: "The world is moving back toward nature" (*olos o kosmos yernai pros tin fisi*) as people become increasingly concerned with the problems caused by industrial food. "Even if you don't have time, you're going to try to make things more naturally." She mentioned that she had begun to bake bread "because they told me that the things that are used in making bread are really bad, and it's very easy for me to make bread once a week and freeze it so that we have it for the whole week." She said she hadn't done it this week because she hadn't had time, but she had done it a couple of weeks earlier, and planned to do it more regularly. Time may take battling with, but Popi seemed up to the task.

MALE COOKS

When Popi was contrasting her brother's cooking with hers, once again her phrasing suggested the importance of time. Rather than claim that her brother's cooking is inventive while hers is traditional, she said that her brother's cooking is more "spontaneous," while hers follows a "typical procedure," which in Greek implies following a certain order in which you can predict how things will go, once again stressing the temporal, processual dimensions of cooking. While I was not able to capture video of many male cooks during my research, what I did learn about male cooking conformed to the idea that it did not deal with the everyday, or the temporal constraints that Popi was so aware of. Rather, when men cook, it is by definition a special occasion.

I've suggested throughout that Kalymnian men take seriously the value and importance of cooking, even if it has been by and large an exclusively female domain. When I ask women about men cooking, they typically assimilate this practice into discourses about the "old years" versus today. For example, when I asked Evdokia Passa about male cooking, she responded:

> In my mother's generation the man would not have cooked, even if he knew how to cook. In my generation I see that Dimitris [her husband] and others of his age will cook to give their wives a break, or else because it makes them happy [yia na efharistisoun]. And so I think that slowly this [i.e., the old way] will change. But for sure, even if the man starts cooking, he won't be cooking every day, the basic cooking will still be done by the woman. But at least we're taking steps, we're progressing.

Another woman made a similar comment, noting that at a "competition for taste" for island cookery that occurs yearly on the island of Patmos where groups of islanders prepare and present traditional dishes, while the other islands had male cooks, the Kalymnian team was all female:

"Forget it! Kalymnos is a little backward, the men here are only interested in going to the coffee shop, hunting, gambling [zogos], and prostitutes!"

When I spoke with men, however, I got a more complicated picture. Even among the generation of men in their mid-forties to mid-sixties (the age range of most of the men I spoke with), there was a variety of distinct attitudes about and practices of cooking. Certainly there were some men who did not cook at all, as Evdokia suggested, or who might only "cook" when it involved grilling fish or using an outdoor oven, the Kalymnian equivalent of male barbecue expertise. These men were not totally divorced from food, however, as many of them, like Nikolas Mihas (Katina's husband), played an active role in food provisioning through activities including hunting (birds, rabbits), casual fishing, collecting snails, and gathering sea salt and other occasional finds. Thus if they did not cook, they still might "prepare" food by cleaning sea urchins or pounding an octopus on the rocks for a friend or guest.

I interviewed Pavlos Roditis, a Kalymnian in his late forties. Pavlos is the brother of Popi Galanou, whose description earlier of the two of them cooking on their own as young children while their parents were gone at work first prompted me to talk to him about cooking. For Pavlos, however, childhood was not the period that he referenced in explaining how he learned cooking. As he noted offhandedly, he "came into contact with cooking" as a child, but learned only to make "simple things, out of necessity." Nor did he cite his mother's cooking as a touchstone, as did his sister. Instead, Pavlos saw the period when he was going to college in Italy as his most formative period. During this time, he explained, he lived in an apartment far from the student union, so he had to take on daily cooking for himself. As he put it, "I started to learn some of the local dishes, especially pasta and different sauces, from watching others, and asking advice from some of my neighbors and friends. I didn't use a cookbook, I learned orally." Interestingly, the idea of not using a cookbook appeared in other brief discussions with men. It seems to follow a pattern of claiming to be able to absorb knowledge by watching and listening, which, while not exclusively male, did seem to follow typical male patterns of craft learning in Greece (see Herzfeld 2003). Italy was formative for Pavlos as well in shaping his style of cooking, which I discuss further below.

Pavlos was married with two young daughters, and his wife worked importing solar panels to Kalymnos. While at the time I interviewed him Pavlos cooked typically only on Sundays, he insisted that this was a matter of circumstance. Several years earlier, when he worked in his own business and his wife ran a clothing store, he cooked at least three or four times a week. Now that he had set hours working as the head of the Kalymnian Department of Transport and his wife had flexible hours, things had shifted so that he was primarily a Sunday cook.

I asked Pavlos how he used to decide what to cook when he was cooking more regularly. He responded that it was decided in discussion the night before with his wife (a discussion that increasingly included his daughters), but also by following a typical Kalymnian balance among fish, meat, and vegetables (they didn't eat beans because he was allergic to them). When I posed the question of what kind of cooking he did—what he had learned in Italy or the typical Kalymnian dishes—he responded by insisting on the key importance of freshness in his cooking:

> *Pavlos:* More Italian style. Because it's lighter and more healthy. But over time I've begun to mix Italian and Greek cooking. Because Greek food can be healthy if you fix it with all fresh ingredients, in other words, you buy your ingredients every day and don't let them sit in the refrigerator for a week or two, and if you eat the food you have cooked that day, and don't cook it one day and eat it the next day.

> *David:* In Greek cooking typically you use tomatoes, garlic, onions, and parsley as the base of the dish. What do you use in Italian cooking?

> *Pavlos:* The same things. It's simply that you may use less water in Italian cooking, or use certain ingredients like balsamic vinegar, more garlic, and you always use fresh tomatoes, not all the tomato paste that is used in Greek cooking.

> *David:* Your sister tells me that your cooking is more spontaneous—

> *Pavlos* [laughing]: Yes, even now I improvise.

> *David:* For example?

> *Pavlos:* I just made a grilled meat dish with carrots, nutmeg, and a preparation of local herbs. Then I add a lot of wine while it's grilling. The nutmeg gives a depth to all the other flavors, as long as you add just enough so that you "understand" it; if you add more it becomes heavy. Nutmeg was used in ancient Greece, so it's not strange, but most people now use it only in making sweets.

Pavlos's comments on nutmeg had echoes for me in the discussion between Nomiki Tsaggari and her mother about the "traditionality" of nutmeg, except that Pavlos was referring all the way back to the traditions of ancient Greece. Because Pavlos was cooking only on Sunday at this time, he was typically cooking meat dishes, grilled or otherwise. However, when he cooked more regularly, he often cooked vegetarian meals. He said the most important aspect of cooking, whether it be meat, fish, or vegetables, was that all the ingredients had to be fresh. This was a slight variation on the theme of "healthy" food that I elaborated earlier with Polykseni. Indeed, Pavlos also insisted that his cooking was "fresh and healthy" and that he used only oil, no butter or margarine, and he didn't sauté the food so that it became heavy. But his discourse was less aimed at Kalymnian community norms, and more toward his personally acquired knowledge of Italian food.[21] Pavlos embraced a certain cosmopolitan localism in his view of cooking. In the pursuit of health and flavor, one should cook with the freshest, most local ingredients possible. He contrasted Kalymnos with other Aegean islands he had spent time on such as Leros and Mytilini, where, he claimed, they had a richer cuisine based on their own specific local vegetables, herbs, and other ingredients. It's this kind of cosmopolitan localism that we saw in the last chapter represented by Mamalakis's cooking show and some of the audience reactions to it.

At the end of the interview I posed the question of male cooking directly: whether it was looked down upon on Kalymnos. Pavlos echoed the temporal view of male cooking that I had heard from women, saying, "Perhaps it was like that in the past, but now [male cooking] is seen as something natural." Perhaps this view does capture the fact that women are increasingly working outside the home so that, as was the case with Pavlos, the husband might step in to take over the primary cooking duties if the wife was unable to.[22]

However, there were other aspects of Kalymnian life in the past that might foster male cooking knowledge. Manolis Papamihail, Nina's husband (see chapter 3), embodied a number of these different factors over the course of his life. His mother died when he was three, and he lived with his father's sisters and several cousins. One aunt was blind. He would help her cook while the other aunts worked during the day as agricultural laborers. Like Pavlos and Popi in an urban context, Manolis took on learning to cook at an early age. While he did not describe this period of his life in detail, he said that he learned by watching his elders. His aunt was a good cook—he remembered her sautéed eggplant with fondness—and so he picked up whatever he could from watching and helping her. As he became an adult, Manolis found work as a seaman, another context in which men might cook, certainly learning to make things like grilled octopus, fish soup, and other foods from the sea.[23] Later in life Manolis became a seasonal migrant, traveling to the United States on a regular basis to do painting and other odd jobs in

Brooklyn, New York. Living on his own for several months of the year, he cooked regularly, "mostly vegetables, but some fish and meat too." Thus, throughout his life Manolis has been in situations that required him to develop his cooking skills if he wanted to eat well.

Unlike Pavlos, Manolis saw himself as cooking in a traditional Kalymnian style, and he told me that his cooking hadn't changed in any significant way since he first learned as a boy. His nostalgia about the past revealed some mixed feelings. On the one hand he recalled the poverty of Kalymnos, when people didn't put carrots in fish soup because carrots were a luxury. He also recalled that you had to wait for summer to eat tomatoes. But while tomatoes were now available year round, they were very different from the summer tomatoes of his youth: "Back then you cut open a tomato and you could smell it! And inside it was full of little balls [*volarakia,* a Kalymnian term] of sugar. Now when you cut open a tomato, it is like a vegetable."[24] Manolis also had interesting memories of the endless supply of food available on some of the ships he worked on, and recalled one day grilling seventeen pounds of shrimp and another day seventeen lamb chops for his own consumption.

Manolis still cooks on occasion when Nina is not able to, or when he has a particular desire to make something. He is also in charge of grilling fish and meat, as well as cooking dishes in the outdoor oven, and he sometimes prepares whatever food is being cooked in the outdoor oven (stuffed vegetables, for example). If Nina is tied up during the morning with appointments of some kind, Manolis will prepare the afternoon meal. When Nina went for ten days to Athens for medical tests, Manolis did do some cooking, yet neighbors and relatives also brought him food on the assumption that a man on his own would need to be fed. He complained to me, though, that he had received meat from everyone, so he got tired of eating meat every day. He made himself a simple pasta dish with oil and ate that for two days.

One aspect of Manolis's discussion of cooking that stood out was his focus on the importance of process for making a dish turn out right. When he makes fish soup he cooks the vegetables in the broth first. Then he strains the broth and uses it to cook the rice. In this way, he can make sure that everything is cooked to the right degree of doneness, while still allowing the flavors to meld properly. He doesn't add much oil to the soup because while it is simmering the oil will "jump" out of the pot. Instead, he adds oil to the fish once they have been removed from the soup for serving. He also describes adding the fish to the soup in a way that keeps them from breaking into pieces. And Manolis told me about

FIGURE 14. Manolis Papamihail demonstrating the secret to making the best Greek coffee: bring it just to a boil, pour the foam into a cup, and then give the remainder a good boil (2013). Photo by Nina Papamihail.

a "trick" for making Greek coffee that he had learned when he was a seaman: boil the coffee in the standard way, but after pouring the much-desired foam into the coffee cup, return the pot to the flame and let it reach a rolling boil again.[25] He claimed it is in this second boil that all of the scent of the coffee is released (*bgazei to aroma*): "That little extra boil at the end brings out the scent. And it makes a difference, I have noticed it. I find it better than the other system. The more you grow, the more you learn." Nina mentioned to me another example of Manolis's concern with process: he was always telling her to wilt onions in a pan *before* adding the olive oil. She wasn't sure why he did this, but when I followed up with him, he said that this method gives the onions more flavor (*mirodia*, literally, "smell"). He explained that the onions cook better in the oil if they have softened in the dry pan instead of putting them into the oil "live" (*zontana*), that is, raw.

It is interesting to examine Manolis's interest in process in relation to his claim that his cooking hasn't changed since he was a boy. This reflects an overall allegiance to traditional Kalymnian dishes, even if one can always be on the lookout for new "tricks" to improve them. Thus Manolis's approach is very much like what I discussed in previous chapters as key to Kalymnian women's view of cooking. The difference might be that Kalymnian women's "tricks" extend to the social aspects of cooking in relation to the different tastes of the family and in relation to cooking while taking care of other daily responsibilities. I might suggest, though this would await further ethnography, that men's tricks are more narrowly focused on the process of cooking itself. This would fit with the fact that many men like to discuss cooking and recipes even when they don't cook, as in discussions reported earlier about how to remove the proper amount of salt from an octopus in preparing octopus stew.

One other difference stood out in my research on Kalymnian male cooks: the tendency to think of cooking as a hobby rather than as a daily necessity. Mihalis Tsaggaris (Nomiki's husband) used the word *hobby* in describing his own apprenticeship in cooking. He learned from his grandfather when he was a young boy because he liked spending time with him, and cooking was a "game" for him. As he got older, Mihalis started experimenting by cooking with wine and other things, and so "what began as a game stayed with me and became a hobby." Mihalis used this characterization despite the fact that he cooks quite regularly, as he and his wife own a restaurant and they share cooking for home and work on a daily basis. Pavlos Roditis didn't use the word *hobby,* but he suggested a similar idea in claiming that men on Kalymnos tend to be better cooks: "For women, cooking is a routine, so they get tired of it, and they lose the feeling that they are doing something special. Whereas for men, since they don't cook constantly, they are more interested in what they are doing." The notion that while men may increasingly cook, cooking—with all its burdens and its rewards—is still a woman's primary responsibility seems to be very much alive on Kalymnos.

CONCLUSION

In this chapter I have used cooking portraits to present some of the different meanings and values that Kalymnians attach to cooking, and some of the different ways in which they go about it. While I have focused on a different style, or theme, in each of these portraits, I have also suggested that there are considerable overlaps, in concerns about health, tradition, time, and so on. Indeed, these values are quite general, and it might be possible to generate a fairly similar list of themes in looking at discourses about cooking in France, the United States, or elsewhere.[26]

But what is interesting is how these values are put into practice in very different cooking landscapes. Thus the significance of the value of "health" for cooking practice will look very different for a middle-class American than it does for a Kalymnian steeped in notions of the traditional Mediterranean diet. The same goes for time pressures, which will be experienced differently in a normative nuclear-family household, as contrasted to the Kalymnian matrilocal household. And if there may be said to be a correlation between healthy food and one political ideology on the one hand, and "traditional" food and an opposing ideology on the other, in the United States,[27] it would be hard to find such correlations on Kalymnos. Quantitative studies that measure the frequency in appearance of different values in cooking discourses cannot capture the nuances of the *interrelation* of these values, both with one another and with the distinctiveness of cooking practices, that I have documented in this book.

Conclusion

So, What Is Cooking?

Knowing is always bound up in one way or another with the
world: a person does not leave their environment to know,
even when she is dealing with the most abstract of proposi-
tions. Nor does she *stop* in order to know: she continues.

—(Harris 2007, 1; emphasis in original)

Recent authors have drawn on reflections on cooking, and reflections
while cooking, as a way of capturing life histories, gender relations and
gender performances, social change, and political struggle. And in these
pages I have suggested some of the ways that cooking helps us understand otherwise submerged gender conflicts and hierarchies within matrilocal families, for example. I have described how watching cooking
shows, or simply making moussaka with a little less butter, can index
ongoing debates about the existential value of living life "traditionally"
or in a "modern" fashion, or finding ways to combine the two. And I
have suggested here, and elaborated elsewhere (Vournelis and Sutton
2012), some of the ways that the contemporary political and economic
crisis can be read through cooking and through food practices more
generally.

But to conclude that cooking provides only a good "window" onto
other topics of importance would be to miss my central point: cooking
is valued by Kalymnian men and women *in and of itself,* because taste
matters. For Kalymnians, and presumably not only Kalymnians, cooking is an everyday, significant practice that generates so much discourse
precisely because it matters. And it is in an attempt to distill some of this
significance that I have focused my analysis on understanding the ways
that cooking takes place as an interaction among humans, tools, and a
larger social and material environment, as well as the ways that embodied skills and knowledges are reproduced and transformed in the course

of this repetitive, everyday practice. Cooking, like knowing, is "bound up with the world, " as Mark Harris puts it. What Harris says for "knowing" in the epigraph to this chapter applies to cooking as well: one doesn't cook by stopping what one is doing; rather, one continues. In this concluding chapter I take another look at some of the questions I've raised along the way, and in particular "What is cooking?" (in both senses of the phrase).

OBJECTS WITH AGENCY?

Before getting to "what is cooking," let me briefly return to the question raised in the introduction about the so-called "agency of objects" related to food and cooking. In discussing cooking tools, I have shown the ways that Kalymnians experience the *distributed agency* of rolling pins, can openers, and outdoor ovens, among other things. Distributed agency, the recognition of the crucial role of these tools in producing certain kinds of actions and results, is clearly displayed in many examples in which Kalymnians described their relationship with tools. It is there in Katerina's explanation, given in the medial-passive voice, in which neither subject nor object is fully responsible for an action. It is there in the claim by Georgia Vourneli and her mother that "the thin rolling pin and the dough wrapped around it is good for making thin phyllo." And this is indeed the point: that distributed agency is not a foreign concept to Kalymnians, it flows from an experience in which tools are embedded in a particular materio-social environment, not—or at least not for the most part—objectified and commodified. It is also an environment that, Kalymnians recognize, can actively aid or thwart our intentions, and that we must adjust to, as Katerina did by modifying the can after she had created risky spikes that "could cut your hand." And there is something in the Kalymnian way of cutting vegetables that recognizes such reciprocity and distributed agency as well—or, as longtime colleague Laurie Hart put it to me, "There is something dialogic about holding that onion in your hand, maybe feeling its resistance with a dull knife as opposed to putting it on a board and using your sabatier."

At a conference I attended on material objects and the senses when I was just beginning to think about this project, I was struck by the question raised by one of the participants: "What does food want?"[1] Personification is, of course, a much discussed and debated trope in anthropology, and we find it as much in movies about non-Western "others"—such as *Like Water for Chocolate,* in which the protagonist could quite literally cook her emotions into her dishes—as we do in U.S. advertisements with dancing cereal and Keebler elves. The question "What does food want?" puts me in mind of the advertisements for Starkist from the 1970s featuring the talking tuna named Charlie, who was always trying to show that he had "good taste," only to be informed, "Starkist doesn't want tuna with good taste, Starkist wants tuna that tastes good." The idea of a fish that wanted to be eaten always puzzled me as a child. In the more cynical but perhaps realistic present times we are offered no Charlies; instead, a campaign for fast-food chicken sandwich purveyor Chick-Fil-A features cows holding up signs that say "Eat Mor Chikin." (Apparently communicating cows are as bad at spelling as the company founders.) Indeed, cows do occasionally "protest" the horrendous conditions of contemporary slaughterhouses by attempting a "break-out."[2] But what of ingredients lacking a brain and central nervous system? No doubt they too encourage or discourage their own consumption—by humans among others—through the variety of flavors, colors, and other sensory impressions they offer. When these are wedded to human agencies and intentionalities we have powerful possibilities for either the "enchantment" of well-executed "culinary traps" (Adapon 2008, 38ff.) or "surprise acts of betrayal" (Janeja 2010, 164). All of this makes cooking not simply a burden or a creative act, but deeply "hazardous collaborative work" (Janeja 2010, 164). This is true, as I've shown, not just regarding special dishes or the kind of "dense objects" (Weiner 1994) that act as inalienable possessions of families and groups—such as the Kalymnian outdoor ovens—but also regarding the more mundane dishes and ordinary tools, anonymous knives, rolling pins, can openers, and the like, that we find participating in the daily struggles of Kalymnians as they work both to reproduce and sometimes to alter familiar flavors.

The point, for me, of these reflections is not to reach an ultimate solution to the question of the ontological status of nonhuman animals and other edibles (much less the so-called inanimate objects that go into making kitchen tools of various kinds). Rather, it is to suggest that for Kalymnians, and no doubt for many others, it makes no sense to think of these as part of a fundamentally different type of story from the anthropological one we have been telling, and thus these *things* should be a central part of our analyses. In other words, as Bruno Latour nicely puts it, "Toddlers are much more reasonable than humanists: although they recognize the many differences between billiard balls and people, this does not preclude them to follow how their actions are woven into

FIGURE 15. Katerina Miha making coffee for her mother and father. While not a fan of Greek coffee herself, Katerina often makes it for her parents, who describe her as an "expert" in the art (2014). Photo by author.

the *same* stories" (2007, 76 n. 88; emphasis in original). If we treat food, taste, and cooking tools, then, not as some rhetorical flourish to liven up ethnographic writing, but as equally central to understanding the ways that people are living, reproducing, and transforming their everyday lives, we will, I think, see a whole new analytical terrain open before us.

KATERINA IN THE KITCHEN

Katerina (no longer referred to as Little Katerina by the family) was clearly more confident than ever in her cooking abilities by 2012. Her brother Vasilis had declared her pastitsio superior to their mother's.[3] And Katina talked of her daughter's abilities to make "new" dishes like sautéed vegetables and ham or sausage with rice and curry, and was clearly impressed. In the short video "Little Katerina Describing a New Dish" (see video example 11) you can see her talking about how she puts together the ingredients.

She recognizes the possibility of using prepared frozen vegetables from the supermarket, but insists that she doesn't do this, she cuts everything by hand. She also recognizes other possible procedures, such as cooking the rice and vegetables separately and then combining them afterward. As we saw with Nina and Polykseni, each cooking decision is taken against a background of other possible practices. Also notice that when describing stirring and other procedures, she makes the hand gestures that she imagines doing when actually preparing the dish, once again making the recipe transmission process a multisensory experience. I was curious about the origins of this dish, which didn't sound like anything I had seen on Kalymnos before. I thought, when her mother had first mentioned it, that it was perhaps something she had learned on television. In fact, she told me that she had learned it from her brother's wife. And where had her brother's wife learned it? From her mother. And where had her mother learned it? She thought it was from one of her sons who works as a chef in a hotel restaurant on Kos. Horizontal knowledge increasingly makes inroads into the more "traditional" base of Kalymnian recipes.

Since I had by this time put up some of my videos on YouTube, I showed a few to Katerina.[4] As soon as she started watching the video of herself making a salad from four and a half years earlier, she said, "I remember this. I said that the salt should go directly on the tomatoes, but my dad said it didn't matter. But I was right, I heard someone saying the same thing on TV recently. Even though I was little, I figured it out!" The fact that she remembered this—before it came up on the video— was certainly impressive in itself.[5] She was clearly pleased that she had come up with this technique (she claimed, in retrospect, to have thought of it by herself) and had later been vindicated by the authority of a television chef. More important, perhaps, this incident suggests that Katerina has learned that it is such small techniques or "tricks" that are seen to make up a significant part of the domain of cooking knowledge on Kalymnos.[6]

I asked Katerina what would happen if she had a job when she got married—would her husband cook? She said, "No! If I can't cook in the morning, I'll cook when I get home or the night before." She also responded in the negative to my question about whether cooking was men's work. After thinking about it for a bit, however, she added, "If he wants to and knows how, well, I don't have a problem with that."

Katerina planned to cook one of her new dishes for the camera. But because I was on Kalymnos only for a short time it was difficult to fit a regular meal into the family schedule (Katerina cooked only when her mother was unavailable to do so). So instead, Katina decided that Katerina could make the sweet that she had been planning to make. The sweet in question was a variation on the dish *kadaifi*, a concoction made with shredded phyllo dough (store-bought) soaked in sugar syrup and topped with several layers of custardlike cream, frosting, and a final layer of nuts.[7] Even though a number of the key ingredients were pre-processed, including the phyllo dough and the custard and frosting (which were made from mixes), this was still a complicated recipe requiring timing and a number of discrete procedures, as Katerina soon found out. As Katerina began the dish, she asked for instruction from Katina since she had never made it (nor many sweets of any kind) before. Soon Katina took over a number of the procedures, leaving small parts for Katerina to do. Once again, it seemed hard for a mother to give up control in the kitchen, even if in this case it was justified by the daughter's lack of skill and knowledge. The dynamics at play here were mostly in a joking frame. At one point Katina used the phrase, "Who will marry you if you can't make sweets?" though it was said with a clear humorous inflection. At other moments Katina mitigated any criticism of Katerina by saying that it is through mistakes that you learn, and that in any bakery the helper is always watching and learning from the baker.

Indeed, much of Katina's instruction focused on how to solve problems, such as how to thicken the custard once Katerina had added the milk all at once instead of slowly while stirring, or how to scrape off the top of the phyllo dough, which had gotten slightly burned in the oven. Katerina herself commented at several points, "Cooking is my specialty, not baking," and she promised to cook for my camera before I left Kalymnos (unfortunately, we weren't able to arrange this). Katina also was teaching Katerina about the imprecision of measurement, as Katerina's questions about how much of one ingredient or another to add were always met with the phrase "eyeball it" (*me to mati*). Katina's more serious criticisms of Katerina came invariably in terms of *attention*: that Katerina was not focused enough on the process at various moments and was instead occupied with music or other frivolities. This once again is a reminder of the key idea that learning skill is an *education of attention*, as I will emphasize in the next section.

One other interesting lesson that came out of this cooking session was the idea that it was better to cook things at home than to buy them ready-made. Katerina raised this issue after asking her mother how much they had spent on the ingredients for the *kadaifi*. They made a rough calculation of 7 euros, leading Katerina to compare it to the 2 euros she had paid for a small sweet at the local bakery. Katina added that the bakery sweets were often stale or made from unhealthy, cheap ingredients. But Katerina interrupted, saying that wasn't the point, that if a whole family wanted to get sweets it would cost you 10 euros and some. This showed the ongoing importance of cooking in the home, as opposed to eating out, and its relation to proper household management, which is tied to Kalymnian female gender identity.[8] Indeed, Katina picked up and expanded her daughter's comment as she was washing the dishes they had used for making the *kadaifi*. She said that this was one easy way they could save during difficult times.[9] Buying sweets from bakeries or fast food was something they would do only for some urgent need so as not to be deprived (*yia na mi sterithoume*). She expanded on this to suggest that the "younger generation" had been ruined by too much time in coffee shops and that fast food had replaced the ability to make what was needed in the home. She claimed that divorces happened because of this—girls who hadn't learned house-keeping and "were only for going out—coffee shops and sex. We're not like Athens with equality, men and women both cooking. It's expected for the woman to know how."

This last comment is a good jumping-off point for summarizing some of the main points I have been making about cooking and gender in previous chapters. Kalymnians care deeply about cooking; of all the values expressed in relation to cooking, the most important is the overriding sense that cooking *matters*, and should be taken seriously. It is perhaps precisely because cooking matters that rumors of its demise tend to be greatly exaggerated: fear of the loss of cooking knowledge seems to go to the heart of Kalymnian concerns about living in the contemporary world while maintaining a respect for tradition. Because cooking is a shared value on Kalymnos, not a demeaning chore as it is seen to be in some cultural contexts,[10] it interlinks power—in the sense of influence and prestige—and aesthetic pleasure for those who control it. On Kalymnos nobody—male or female—would dismiss a discussion of cooking, the flavors of food, the sources of ingredients, or the myriad "tricks" that make up the shared or secretly held knowledge of the skilled cook as unimportant or trivial. But cooking may also be a burden in its everyday demands on time and concern. And it is a burden that falls disproportionately on women as part of hegemonic views of gender identity enforced by both women and men in Kalymnian society.[11]

Katina's contrast of Kalymnos and Athens is a recognition of this hegemony: women and men, on Kalymnos, are not seen as "equal," by which she means the same, as she imagines them to be in Athens.[12] Thus, if girls do not learn how to cook, they are in some sense at fault in a way that boys are not. Katina's statement represents the conservative end of an ongoing discourse on gender on Kalymnos and elsewhere in Greece. It is a discourse that, perhaps influenced by the mass media, seems to ignore some of the complexities of the Kalymnian gender system in imagining a "past" male dominance giving way to increasing "equality." It ignores Kalymnian kinship structures in focusing on the nuclear family rather than the matrilocal couple, which is still common on Kalymnos. It poses the issue of cooking for a new couple purely in terms of whether it is done by the wife or the husband, ignoring the equally likely possibility—as we have seen throughout this book—that cooking will be undertaken by the wife's mother or even the husband's mother, regardless of whether the wife is employed outside the home.[13] Furthermore, there is irony in claims about the heedlessness of the "younger generation," considering that, as I have shown, the desire of mothers to teach their daughters (or sons, for that matter) is often fraught with ambivalence and power struggles.

Finally, I have argued throughout this book that cooking is a practice that combines both explicit, conversationally based learning and implicit, embodied skills and training of the senses. While Katerina might not embrace all of the conservatism implied in her mother's discourse, she has certainly learned many of the *unspoken* lessons of Kalymnian society, as reflected in her taste for home-cooked food, her desire to make food for her brother and father, and her embodied assumptions about the proper deployment of tools and techniques such as cutting in the hand.

One interesting moment in the making of the *kadaifi* came when Katerina had left the kitchen and Katina was looking for something to use to crush the nuts for sprinkling on top. Not finding a food processor to hand, she wrapped the nuts in a cloth towel, put them on the counter, and started whacking them with an old pot, saying, "I'll do it like old times" (*san ta palia*). When Katerina came back in and saw her mother doing this she started laughing hysterically and went to tell her grandmother what her mother was doing. I interpret this moment as the inverse of the can-opener incident described in chapter 2. Just as Katerina's grandmother had used an old technique to define herself as "traditional," the laughter here stemmed from the disjunction between most of the tools they had used in preparing the *kadaifi* (the handheld electric blender, which Katerina clearly deployed more comfortably than her mother) and this low-tech, "old-fashioned" way of getting things done. Keeping in mind that Katina had always been a supporter of replacing old tools, such as aluminum pots, with new ones, the image of her smashing the nuts with an old pot was particularly incongruous to her daughter. Certain things change, but the idea of women drawing a crucial part of their identity from their kitchen practices has been passed down from grandmother to mother to granddaughter. And Little Katerina has internalized the view that places prime importance on developing cooking skills as part of what is expected of a Kalymnian young woman.[14]

SOME LAST THOUGHTS ON COOKING SKILLS AND FOOD AS AN "OBJECT WITH AGENCY"

What, then, makes Kalymnians competent cooks? If my ethnographic approach is valid it is because cooking skills and knowledge are not abstractable and quantifiable but rather embedded in a particular social and technical environment (the kitchen). Cooking skills are exercised, reproduced, and changed in a context in which Kalymnians observe their own and others' practices, share and hide secrets, praise and criticize procedures and results, and carefully taste, compare, and remember what Kalymnian food *should* taste like. Thus, as Tim Ingold has argued, a skilled cook, like a skilled practitioner of any sort, "is continually and fluently responsive to perturbations of the perceived environment. . . . This is possible because the practitioner's bodily movement is, at one and the same time, a *movement of attention;* because he watches, listens, and feels even as he works. It is this responsiveness that underpins the qualities of care, judgment, and dexterity that are the hallmarks of skilled workmanship" (2001, 135). We have seen the multisensory engagement that is prevalent in Kalymnian kitchens as béchamel is stirred, phyllo dough is rolled, and octopus is seasoned. Kalymnian women, and some men, are skilled cooks to the extent that they have undergone an *education of attention* that allows them to apply dexterously embedded techniques like cutting in the hand, recognizing that no two potatoes or onions are ever exactly the same. And when some Kalymnian women complain about the younger generation not knowing how to cook, they are expressing concerns specifically about how the younger generation's attention may have not been educated, but rather distracted by the availability of fast food and the time devoted to Facebook and other activities that lack any clear connection to traditional Kalymnian gender-coded abilities. Discussions of the fate of cooking always take place in the context of some of the key values that

I have detailed in this book: following tradition; cooking lighter, healthy food; knowing the origins and provenience of one's ingredients; exercising proper exchange and sharing relationships.

Interestingly, Ingold argues that his approach to knowledge stands in opposition to those who see knowledge in the form of recipes for action that are essentially separate from action. He criticizes the approach of cognitive anthropologist Dan Sperber, who uses the idea of a recipe for Mornay sauce that is transmitted from one brain to another as an instance of the circulation of cultural knowledge, seen as a set of shared representations. Such a view consigns the practice of cooking itself to "the mechanical execution of a predetermined plan" (2001, 135). I'll return to this phrase in a moment. Between representation and execution, Ingold suggests, lies a yawning gap that can only be filled with the careful, contextual understanding that ethnography provides, and that I have tried to suggest in word and video as Kalymnians navigate their kitchen environment, with full sensory engagement and with an ever-developing set of "tricks" and other embodied (conscious or unconscious) skills.

One other key ingredient in the definition of Kalymnian cooking that I have suggested at different points in this book is the notion that cooking is *risky business*. Thus, when Katerina (the grandmother) points to the risk of cutting your hand on a can opened with an "old-fashioned" can opener, she is suggesting one tip of what I believe to be a larger concern with a person's willingness to engage life in a certain manner. The significance of risk as an existential aspect of Greek culture has been explored mostly for men in Michael Herzfeld's work on sheep theft (1985), Thomas Malaby's on gambling (2003), and my own on Kalymnian dynamite throwing (1998). The notion that cooking might share some of the same aspects of risk on a more mundane level may seem strange. But in the same way that Kalymnian women slice bread holding it against their chest or that Katerina embraced her dangerous can opener, it is argued that many Greek men attempt to engage, rather than minimize, risk as part of making life meaningful—that in dealing with the "pervasive indeterminacies of experience ... risk ... rather than tamed and quantified, is engaged and performed" (Malaby 2003, 21). In other words, there is a "poetics of risk taking" (23) that is very much tied up with Greek notions of personhood, as in Katerina's meditations on how the "traditional can opener" made her a "traditional person." And risk need not involve physical danger and the potential risk to life and limb, as in Kalymnian dynamite throwing, to be seen as meaningful. Risk is part of the significant business of Kalymnian cooking whenever someone adds a new ingredient or tries a new technique in order to face the constant challenges posed by the cooking environment, with the risk of failure—a bad meal and attendant comments by family and neighbors—ever-present.[15] Indeed, cooking in this sense is like other performances such as magicians' rituals, in which risk is required "as a precondition for satisfactory performance" (Jones 2011).

In the time that I have been doing research on Kalymnos, a major change has been that risk is not simply attendant on tools, ingredients, or other social challenges (how to feed ten people who show up unexpectedly, for example), but on one's openness to change and alteration. Katina, for example, told me how she first saw Greek eggplant salad (*melitzanosalata*, what in the United States is called baba ghanoush) at a restaurant where she went for a wedding celebration. She thought at the time that it looked like vomit. But after seeing it more often, and observing a friend preparing it when she was staying on Rhodes, she started to make it for her family, noting, "We took the risk." Risk here is seen as a willingness to expand food horizons, to continue learning new ways of preparing the familiar or variations on traditional recipes. But it is also simply an extension of the notion that the skilled cook is always adjusting to circumstances: the availability of ingredients, the desires of different people, the small variations in cooking processes and even changing times, which now include the growth of new sources of knowledge such as the TV cooking shows discussed in chapter 5.

It is the ability to face these different kinds of materio-social variations with dexterity that defines a good Kalymnian cook. In 2012, Katina was telling me about a small alteration she had made to her moussaka that she had been very pleased with. Instead of leaving the béchamel sauce as a layer on top of the rest of the ingredients, she stirred it in so that it pervaded all the layers. She said she had discovered this trick on one occasion when she had made too much béchamel and was afraid it was going to spill out of the pan, so she stirred it to allow some to sink down in the pan. In describing this to me and to her neighbor, she illustrated the stirring motion by grabbing what was nearest to hand, a paintbrush and a roll of tape, and mimicking how she would do it with a real moussaka, reminding me once again of the crucial importance of the visual and kinesthetic elements of learning. The advantage, she said, of this technique was that it allowed the flavor of the béchamel to pervade the entire dish, instead of having the béchamel sit like a "brick" on top of the rest. When I asked if she thought other Kalymnians would adopt her trick, she said, perhaps, "but some people have their own ways of cooking that they stick to out of self-regard (*eghoismo*), they are not interested in taking a risk to improve their cooking."

Regardless of whether these Kalymnians exist, Katina's comment points to the expectation that cooking skill and knowledge *will not stand still*. As Harris puts it in the epigraph to this chapter, "Nor does she *stop* in order to know: she continues." Kalymnian cooking is encapsulated in David Pye's notion of the "workmanship of risk," a type of approach to craft that once again stresses the idea that "the quality of the result is not predetermined. but depends on the judgment, dexterity and care that the maker exercises as he works" (1968, 4). Pye usefully contrasts this to what he calls the "workmanship of certainty," in which the end result is largely predetermined before the process of making begins. It is this contrast, I believe, that goes to the heart of Kalymnian concerns about the replacement of cooking with preprocessed and fast food, a type of preparation that promises exactly the same, standardized product each time. Despite its lack of deep inroads on Kalymnos thus far, the threat of fast food is the threat of replacing the risk that makes skill and embodied knowledge valuable with the certainty of industrial products that are simply the execution of a preset plan.

Certain aspects of high-tech "modernist" cooking that I discussed in the introduction tend in this direction as well, and are equally antithetical to the notion of skill developed here. *Sous-vide* cooking is an example in which "you have none of the normal sensory cues that a meal is cooking: the smell of garlic sizzling in oil, the *blip-blip* of risotto in a pot. . . . You set the water bath to the required temperature, vacuum seal the food in the bag, submerge the bags, set the timer, and wait for the bleep. No stirring, no basting, no prodding or tasting. No human input at all" (Wilson 2012, 253–54).[16]

This is similar to the approach identified with the magazine *Cooks Illustrated,* which focuses on rigorous testing in lablike conditions and controlling variables to produce recipes such as "the best soft-boiled egg." Here the point seems to be absolute control of variables so that perfection is guaranteed, as long as you follow the recipe to the letter.[17] A profile of *Cooks Illustrated* founder Chris Kimball in the *New York Times Magazine* (Halberstadt 2012) was titled with his quotation: "Cooking isn't creative, and it isn't easy." Kimball's promise to his readers seems to be that he and his staff will do all the trial-and-error work in "America's test kitchen," and will provide you with the error-free result. As it is described in his profile, "What the magazine essentially offers its readers is a bargain: if they agree to follow the recipes as written, their cooking will succeed and they will be recognized by family and friends as competent or even expert in the kitchen" (Halberstadt 2012, 68). There is something gendered male about the attempt to define abstract and context-free cooking knowledge that such approaches represent, even if they have circulated as part of U.S. female cooking culture in the form of the food industry's claims to create "foolproof" mixes for all kinds of culinary staples, recipes that taste the same every time.[18]

The most theatrical version of this approach is labeled molecular gastronomy, the ultimate in futuristic cooking. Is molecular gastronomy simply a sideshow, designed to appeal to devotees of food television programming or the wealthy patrons of restaurants like elBulli and The Fat Duck, featuring wonders like mustard ice cream? I suggest that the answer is no, that this movement is part of a larger tendency toward abstraction in many areas of contemporary life, from education to Wall Street trading. There is an ongoing struggle between context-situated knowledge and the creation of recipes or algorithms of practice that allow for the reduction of the "risk" that is part of human engagement with the world—or, as James Carrier puts it, "a general desire to replace individual skill, experience, and knowledge of context in decision-making with procedures that are seen as impersonal and objective, the 'best practice' of modern management-speak" (2012).[19] This is also what culture critic Evgeny Morozov dubs "technological solutionism, or "recasting all complex social situations either as neatly defined problems with definite, computable solutions or as transparent and self-evident processes that can be easily optimized" (2013, 5). We see these trends in education, for example, in the growth of massive open online courses (MOOCs), which tend once again to project knowledge as product rather than process, and abstract learning even further from the face-to-face contexts in which they have occurred through most of history. I would note that one of the classes that Harvard University plans to offer online is titled "Science and Cooking" (Heller 2013, 13). As one practitioner describes the model for MOOCs (at least so far): "'to the extent that learning requires some degree of interactivity, that interactivity is channelled into formats that require automated or right-and-wrong answers'" (quoted in Heller 2013, 91). Morozov also discusses a food-related example that he sees as prototypical of technological solutionism: designs for "smart" kitchens that will observe cooks' movements and inform them "whenever they have deviated from their chosen recipe" (2013, 11). In the name of efficiency, the very joys of cooking represented by a sense of mastery are sacrificed for the presumed improvement in taste.[20] On Kalymnos, "right and wrong" is always embedded in a sensory and social context.

But this raises another point: what applies to processes of cooking also applies to "taste" itself. At a time when taste is seemingly becoming ever more rarefied, with the molecular gastronomy or "note-by-note" movement at the forefront of literally separating taste from food and molecularizing it into an object for infinite play and manipulation,[21] I have argued throughout this book for an approach to taste that understands it as an experience deeply shaped by culture, history, and memory. As a sensory experience, taste cannot be separated from the panoply of other senses. I would reject the view that taste can be manipulated in the laboratory to produce anything more than the kind of addictive fast food that is the financial silent partner of molecular gastronomy.[22] Studying taste on Kalymnos, I am struck by the extent to which it is deeply shaped by not only culture, history, and memory but also locality and a long, tacit practice of enculturation. Instead of seeing taste as an abstract chemical process, I have suggested that it is a central part of Kalymnian social life, as mothers and daughters negotiate whether nutmeg is part of the Kalymnian tastescape, and Kalymnian cooks make decisions about cutting or grating tomatoes, always with the implied input (and watchful judgment) of the larger community. I am thus sympathetic to the view presented by *épicier* Lev Sercarz, as described in Halberstadt (2013), noting that "when he designed blends for clients, he learned as much as he could about their backgrounds and how they lived. 'Sometimes I feel like an investigator,' he said. The things we eat as children haunt us as adults 'whether we like it or not,' he added. 'Some people embrace where they come from, some rebel, but in the end it really doesn't matter.'" This "haunting" suggests that our senses are deeply tied not only to tacit knowledge but to memories, that memory itself might be seen as a sense.[23] But it also reaffirms a key point in my research: that if we want to understand the significance of everyday cooking, we must see it in relation to everyday eating, and the significance placed on the flavor of food. This significance was ever-present for me in my research on Kalymnos.

While binary contrasts are notoriously slippery in contemporary anthropology, it is hard not to see these objectifying trends as representing the opposite of Kalymnian cooking, which, to quote Nomiki Tsaggari, "requires hands" (and all the senses). Most Kalymnians would be on the side of many of the *New York Times* readers who wrote in to disagree with *Cooks Illustrated* founder Kimball about what constitutes the essence of cooking. As one reader put it: "I am certain though that any meeting about getting into print the problems of boiling an egg to perfection so misses the point of making that egg. By its very nature cooking is an imperfect pursuit. That we cannot make a dinner for our families and friends without standing under clouds of doomed imperfection says as much about what we actually think we are doing when we cook."[24] Kalymnians, perhaps, would be more at home with Alice Waters's plea to let local ingredients shine than they would be with any of these high-tech transformations of nature.[25] Indeed, when I asked Evdokia Passa, whose restaurant was discussed in chapter 1, whether she saw cooking as essentially art or science, she responded, "Neither: cooking is *soul*" (*to mayeirema einai psihi*).[26]

While I was writing this, I noticed a Facebook post from Evdokia's husband, Dimitris Roditis, about the exorbitant price of the common sweet-shop cookies *kourambiedes* (a concoction of butter, flour, and powdered sugar similar to Mexican wedding cookies), something that in the past people would often bring as a gift when visiting, or for someone's name day. What started out as a comment on the economy, however, soon became a discussion of the essence of *kourambiedes* in the comment stream that followed. As Dimitris wrote, in response to a friend's post about his favorite version of the cookie: "*Kourambiedes* are ONLY my friend Katerina's version! Anything else is simply the execution of a recipe." Here the execution of a recipe is seen as essentially antithetical to cooking, lacking all personal touch, emotion, "love," or embodied skill. When I asked Dimitris about Katerina's *kourambiedes,* he wrote back, "*Kourambiedes* are usually drowned in baking soda and rose water and then topped with fine sugar, so much of it, it looks like Scarface's wet dream! Katerina makes them small, irregular in size, with butter as the major taste that's blinking at the cloves and tip-dancing almonds!" I'm still ruminating over this last metaphor, which once again seems to capture the *agency of food* to influence humans and their social relations.[27]

THE LAST WORD

I decided to ask Dimitris about an article I had read about Japanese robots, known as mombots, that have been designed to make dishes including sushi, ramen, and omelets (see Daly 2010). I knew that most of my Kalymnian cooks would dismiss such an idea out of hand, just as they are skeptical of the kind of prissy nouvelle cuisine they see on TV, which doesn't satisfy the tongue or the stomach. I was curious, however, about Dimitris's reaction because he considers himself a technophile. He had basically single-handedly introduced computers to Kalymnos in the early 1990s, and is a fan of science fiction and cyberpunk in particular. He often complains about the unwillingness of the older generation of Kalymnians to comprehend the significance of the computer revolution, as well as the irrationality of the political system and those who hew too strictly to "tradition." On the other hand, Dimitris is involved in the running of his wife Evdokia's restaurant Harry's Paradise, taking pride in telling me about the careful sourcing of their ingredients such as buying from the small-scale cheese makers on Kalymnos and neighboring islands, seeking out beans grown by an organic cooperative in northern Greece, and using vegetables raised on goat-dung fertilizer by their neighbor. Would mombots represent the wave of the future for Dimitris? I showed him a video of the mombots in action.[28] Somewhat to my surprise, Dimitris was horrified by the prospect of eating the product of a mombot. He told me that he found the idea of robot cooks deeply disturbing, at first commenting that a dish is simply *not supposed to be the same* each time. After reflecting, he added, "Cooking is too much part of our humanity. A robot can't produce that." I couldn't have said it better myself.

Epilogue

Cooking (and Eating)
in Times of Financial Crisis

By 2012 Greece was already five years into a crisis that seems to be without end. While in other parts of Greece this crisis had led to attempts to challenge and rethink the food system,[1] Kalymnians told me that there had been no radical changes in their diets. Many insisted that Kalymnos was still livable, not like Athens or other urban centers. Kalymnos had been fortunate to have opened up a new tourist market just prior to the beginning of the crisis, centered on rock climbing. An international rock-climbing festival was now drawing hundreds or even several thousand additional tourists to Kalymnos. Yet many Kalymnians were still struggling and jobless. Roughly twenty-five hundred Kalymnians were reported to have migrated to Australia by October 2012, and others were seeking ways to follow.[2] This was on a base population of roughly twelve thousand. And this figure did not include illegal migration, Kalymnians coming to the United States and overstaying their tourist visas in pursuit of work. Kalymnos had a very different feel in 2012 from what it did in 2005 when I began the current research project. Many of the clothing stores that lined the main street had closed, along with many other stores (including the local branch of the housewares store Vefa's House).

In 2012 I tried to trace how the crisis had affected some of the families I had worked with. Katina Miha's husband, Nikolas, in his mid-fifties, had not had steady work for the past two years, after years of working in construction for the municipality. While their elder son had a job working for a courier service, he had married several years earlier; living in the typical Kalymnian matrilocal pattern, he no longer contributed to the family's finances. Their younger son had been working in construction like his father and, also like his father, was finding only occasional work. They had not been able to arrange for a visa for him to migrate to Australia.[3] They were also living on Katina's mother's pension. To try to make up for their loss of income, both Katina and her daughter, Little Katerina, had been making jewelry to sell to tourists,[4] while Katerina also was going to evening school to learn accounting. Katerina admitted to me that she would have preferred to train as a beautician, but since she had already invested a year in studying accounting, it seemed frivolous to switch now.

What kinds of effects was the crisis having on family food and cooking practices? Some people had told me that they were eating more beans and less meat, a diet associated with the "old years" on Kalymnos (see Sutton 1997), so I asked Katina if perhaps they were doing the same. She insisted that this was not a strategy that would work for her family. Some families, she said, would make a pot of beans on Wednesday, and then eat the leftovers on Friday, the two official "fasting" days of the week. But because her husband and children had always expected freshly made food, it might even cost less to cook a small piece of meat and some potatoes than a big pot of beans, which might be eaten once and the leftovers thrown to the hunting dogs that Nikolas kept. Katina said that by and large their cooking and eating hadn't changed as a result of the crisis; rather, most of the alterations came at the level of more careful shopping. Knowing how to shop for the best deals made a big difference. Others disagreed, telling me for example that people were no longer buying fish because it had simply become too expensive to feed a whole family on the amount of fish you would need to buy. However, fish still entered the diets of many families through fishing, or connections with fishermen, part of the "free" food that supplements the Kalymnian diet (see Sutton 2001, chap. 1).

During my stay I also noticed some interesting modifications of past practices involving "free" food. For example, one night in early October the first heavy rain of the season fell. Often after the first rain Nikolas and the children might go out the next day to hunt snails for a meal, considered a local delicacy, made by Katerina (the grandmother). If they got more than they needed, they would give them away to friends or relatives. This time, however, they collected as many snails as they could and returned by midday with a haul of about forty-five pounds. They agreed with a friend who is an itinerant vegetable seller to have him take twenty pounds to sell and split the profits. They figured that they could sell the rest themselves to neighbors. This ended up going very well, and they quickly sold out of snails. So they went out collecting again the following day, and came back with about half as many, which they also sold. Katina and Nikolas consulted with the elder Katerina about how to preserve the snails properly so they wouldn't die while they were arranging to sell them. All in all they netted nearly two days' typical construction wages for their snail excursion—not much, but it represents the kind of supplemental activity that used to be done for fun and gifting, but is now seen as a source of some ready cash. Katina also had to consult with her mother, who was severely ill in bed and thus was not cooking the snails, a dish that had always been in her purview. Katina went over the cooking procedure for snails several times with Katerina: how long; what temperature the water should be so the snails don't squeeze themselves down in their shells, making them difficult to extract; and so on. These were "tricks" and cooking knowledge that Katerina had retained not because she was necessarily hiding them from her daughter, but simply because she was the person in the family who had always undertaken the cooking of this once-or-twice-a-year traditional dish. Now they were exchanged with her daughter, as Katerina was in no condition to prepare food.[5]

If the selling of snails was a commodification of something that had in the past been a gift, one example of the many "free foods" that were a central part of Kalymnian sociability (see Sutton 2001, chap. 3), other crisis-driven food practices pushed in the opposite direction. For example, Rinyo,[6] a neighbor, often stopped by in the morning or afternoon to visit with Katina and share news. For several years Rinyo had been lighting the candle at the grave of Katerina's husband, Mastro Yiorgos, since Katerina couldn't go to the cemetery on a regular basis. While some families paid her for this service, she had a different, more personal relationship with Katina and Katerina. Katina had been giving her some of the leftover food that the family did not wish to make a second meal of. Rinyo, in turn, would go down to the harbor to shop from the vegetable stand of "the woman from Kos," who was known to have some of the best prices on the island. The Koan woman would often give Rinyo extra vegetables or fruit that was overripe and could not still be sold. She would pass on some of this to Katina: a half-dozen green bell peppers that had begun to get soft spots on them, or some slightly wilted eggplants. These might spur Katina to make an omelet with green peppers for the evening meal. These sorts of exchanges were very much in line with typical Kalymnian provisioning, as I described in chapter 1. The shift here is that during the crisis an increasing number of families might be supplementing their shopping with these kinds of no longer salable foods, which then became part of the typical gift exchange networks.

Growing one's own food was also touted as one potential solution to the economic crisis, as news reports had become common of people in Athens moving back to their ancestral villages to work the land. A few days after the snail excursion, Katina's son Vasilis was digging in their backyard, planting a few rows of broccoli, cauliflower, cabbage, and romaine lettuce. While the yard already had an olive and a pomegranate tree growing, the latter especially had been an irregular producer since the family was often gone to the neighboring island of Telendos during the summer months. This was the first time they had used their yard space for planting vegetables; it had been up till then a place for Nikolas's hunting dogs to run around. Nikolas joked that they would survive the crisis and the political corruption in the country with their little vegetable garden. But Vasilis insisted that he knew a number of people who had gone so far as to tear up the cement in their backyard to have soil for planting. When his mother worried that the cost for watering the garden would erase any savings, Vasilis reassured her that he had worked it out with the neighbors to use their cistern water for watering until the autumn rains came. A month later they were harvesting their first heads of romaine lettuce, and Vasilis was planting onions and talking about expanding the garden to the small plot of land that he owned on the neighboring island. It would be interesting to pursue these practices in terms of what Nafsika Papacharalampous refers to as "the link between hardship and the exoneration of the local" in Greek cooking practices.[7]

Clearly, Katina and her family were for the time being managing to survive amid reduced circumstances, as were most of the other families I knew. However, people did tell me about the plight of some families and individuals on Kalymnos, who didn't have enough for food and were being served by the church's "meal of love" program, in which one could get a daily meal either on-site or delivered to one's door by the Greek Orthodox Church and numerous community volunteers. A recent, crisis-inspired twist on the "meal of love" was a free meal for several dozen non-Kalymnian schoolteachers living on Kalymnos. These teachers have seen their paychecks slashed by the Greek government to the point that Kalymnian church leaders felt that food charity would be a help to many of them.

Some of this charity work is supported by donations from Kalymnians working in Australia. Others donate various food items in memory of a dead relative, a common memorial practice in Greece.[8] And some of the grocery stores and supermarkets are making canned food and other groceries available for free to needy Kalymnian families. I was told that the families who rely on these sources of food are concentrated in the neighborhoods of fishermen, such as Ayios Stephanos and Ayios Nikolas, traditionally some of the poorer neighborhoods on the island, and perhaps further affected by a recent decrease in fish stocks in the Aegean.

Some Kalymnians, however, complained about the lack of a more focused solution to poverty and job creation. Aside from the general complaints against politicians local and national, which were at an all-time high by 2012,[9] some still complained that Kalymnians are not willing to exploit the opportunities that exist on the island. Yiannis Gavalas, who has long been one of the leading beekeepers on the island, said that there was available land on the mountaintops for cultivating crops like figs and prickly pears. Figs and prickly pears are traditionally crops that people grow in small quantities for their own consumption or for exchanges among family and neighbors. But Yiannis said that when he had gone to Italy to promote his honey, he had seen figs and prickly pears for sale in local markets for 1 euro apiece. This was an amazing price to him, because Kalymnians will often consume fifteen or twenty of these fruits at a sitting when they ripen in the summer. He said that the figs for sale in Italy had been imported from Israel, and although they were very large, they were tasteless because they had been watered, which makes them big but ruins their flavor. He suggested that since Kalymnos has an ideal climate for producing these fruits, Kalymnians could take advantage of this market. But nobody has done so, he believed, because after the hardships of the past, no Kalymnians want their children to have to "dig in the ground" for a living.[10] I heard Yiannis's complaint echoed in different ways by others in 2012. Pavlos Roditis, for example, believed that the crisis had not yet hit bottom. His analysis was that Greece had gone from producing "real things" to producing "air." And thus the crisis was an opportunity to see the mistakes that had been made and to return to producing things again. Whether such opportunities do exist on Kalymnos, and whether people will be pushed to find more creative ways to survive in the coming years, remained unclear to many.

NINA'S TRIP

I called Nina in early March 2012 and heard the excitement in her voice. "We're coming to America," she practically shouted. One of Nina's cousins, who still lived in Seneca Falls, was celebrating her eightieth birthday and had offered to pay for Nina and Manolis's tickets to come stay with her. Along the way they would stop for a couple of days to visit with Manolis's friends and family in Brooklyn, as well as in London to stay with a British friend of Nina's and her Kalymnian husband. This would be Nina's first trip outside of Greece since she had moved with her parents to Kalymnos in 1971. As the trip was coinciding with the end of my semester, I arranged to go to New York during the time they would be in Brooklyn and show Nina around my hometown. When I met Nina and Manolis for coffee in Bay Ridge, Brooklyn, Nina was already enthusiastic and full of observations about the airports, the cleanliness of the streets of Bay Ridge (contrasted to the streets of Kalymnos), and the fact that cars got out of the way of ambulances (once again, unlike Greece). It was two days into her visit and she said she felt reconnected to the United States in many small ways, such as saying hello to police officers that she passed on the street. One important moment for Nina was seeing a Catholic church in Bay Ridge that had a memorial in front of it to the 9/11 events. The memorial had a piece of the World Trade Center in it and a plaque with the names of victims who had come from that congregation. She told me that she had cried when she saw this, and planned to go back to take a picture of it.

While their time in New York City was short and largely taken up with visiting Manolis's family, we did arrange to spend an afternoon together, accompanied by Julia Koullias and her children. Julia was a non-Greek American who had married a Kalymnian, Mihalis Koullias, and they lived part of the year in New York and part on Kalymnos.[11] We spent a few hours at the Museum of Modern Art (Nina loved it, especially the Diego Rivera special exhibition) and then went down to Chelsea Market and took a walk on the High Line. While at Chelsea Market, we stopped in at one of my favorite shops, where they sell flavored salt, balsamic vinegar, and olive oil, since she had asked me in the past to bring her special salts and peppercorns. Nina was less taken with the salt there, but loved the balsamic vinegar, and so I got her a bottle of blueberry-flavored vinegar to take back with her to Kalymnos. We headed up to the High Line to enjoy a quick stroll before Nina had to be back in Brooklyn to meet Manolis for dinner with his family. In the midst of our walk Nina overheard two teenagers talking, one saying to the other, "Where you live is who you are." Nina was upset by this phrase, and repeated it several times to me and Julia. Nina said, "That's just not right! People don't always have a choice where they live."

Clearly Nina felt that this phrase didn't apply to her, that Kalymnos didn't define the extent of her identity. I was curious how she would react to going back to Seneca Falls. I received a letter from her a few weeks later with reflections on her trip. She thought Seneca Falls was "clean," like Brooklyn and unlike "Kalymnos, the garbage dump." This brought to her mind a childhood memory of hearing about Ladybird Johnson's campaign to "keep America beautiful" by empowering police to arrest people who threw litter from their cars onto highways.[12] And it made an impression on Nina that you had to cut your grass or the town would come and do it and charge you for it. But she was also sad to see how run-down the town had become because of its high unemployment rate, like much of northern New York State: "Lots of houses need repair outside, lots for sale, some fallen down, empty for a long time." She also noted that the Greeks of Brooklyn "cook and eat well. The Americans [friends in Seneca Falls] do not." She made a coconut cream pie while she was staying at her aunt's. She said it didn't turn out as well because she didn't have cornstarch, and she struggled to figure out how to use the electric stove. "And of course, it's not my mother's famous pie," she said. But it turned out okay. She bought more coconut to take back with her to Kalymnos so she could make it properly when she returned.

In the letter Nina sent when the trip was over, she noted that she and Manolis had a lot of work to do to get the garden in shape after their three-week absence. I got the sense that she felt it was good to be "home" and back to her familiar routines. There were many good things about Bay Ridge and Seneca Falls, but America was no paradise. When I spoke with Nina a few weeks later, she was clear about one thing. Although she still preserved her shared allegiance to America and her sense of difference from other Kalymnians, she had no illusions that staying in the United States would have led to a better life course. She told me that her aunt had asked her point-blank whether she was glad her parents had brought her to Kalymnos forty-one years earlier. "Oh, yeah!" she responded, matter-of-factly.

Notes

1. See Sutton 2001, chap. 3. The phrase "hear the smell" is familiar in other areas of Greece, such as Crete (Eleana Yalouri, personal communication with author).

2. Cruikshank 2005, 256; see also Perley 2013 on the struggle between decontextualized approaches to knowledge that seek to "preserve" Navajo language versus those that try to keep it alive and relevant in new and changing contexts.

3. Roosth 2013: 8. Hervé This describes his approach as "note by note" cuisine and suggests that it must overcome the tendency of humans toward neophobia (the fear of the new), so that "traditional" cooking is preserved "even when the 'virtues' of traditional foodstuffs are not demonstrated" (This 2013, 3).

4. Cited in Roosth 2013, 8. Roosth discusses some of the gendered aspects of molecular gastronomy in this article, which seems to me to parallel much of so-called "modernized" knowledge, in which traditional female practices are abstracted and standardized by men.

5. See Hernandez and Sutton 2003; Sutton and Hernandez 2007.

6. Greenfield 2004; Maynard, Greenfield, and Childs 1999.

7. Tim Ingold argues for a focus on "materials" as opposed to the "materiality" favored by Daniel Miller. Ingold argues, for example, that materials "do not present themselves as tokens of some common essence—materiality—that endows every worldly object with its inherent 'thingliness'; rather, they partake in the very processes of the world's ongoing generation and regeneration, of which things such as manuscripts or house fronts are impermanent by-products" (2007, 9).

8. The notion of affordance in relation to tool use has been developed by Tim Ingold, and is discussed below.

9. Marx cited in Graeber 2001, 268. Also see Shove et al. (2007, 35), who discuss specifically the way that kitchen equipment should not be seen "as entirely passive tools with which individuals realize aspects of their identity. Instead, the point is that new demands, injunctions and forms of practice arise as social and technical systems co-evolve."

10. See Hoskins 1998; Weiner 1992.

11. Carsten 1995; Weismantel 1995.

12. See Seremetakis 1994; Sutton 2011.

13. That appellation is disputed by some, however (see Pink 2010).

14. Downey 2005; Hahn 2007; Geurts 2003; Howes 2008; Feld 2003; Parr 2010.

15. The notion of *terroir,* "the taste of place," also can be seen as capturing a notion of gustemology, that is, taste as a crucial way through which we know places (Trubek 2008).

16. See also Keller 2001; Keller and Dixon Keller 1999.

17. Wrangham's book is a synthesis of his work and that of other biological anthropologists. For a fuller review of *Catching Fire,* see Sutton 2013.

18. There are many reviews of the literature on food in anthropology, but a good starting place is Mintz and Du Bois 2002.

19. See Yanagisako and Delaney (1995, 16), who note that "superficial assessments of similarities in the roles and sentiments of women in different societies can lead to the naïve conclusion—rampant in U.S. white feminist scholarship in the 1970s—that all women can readily comprehend each other's suffering, sorrows, and joys." This scholarly lacuna has by and large remained unfilled until recently. In her study on female Mexican cooks, Christie notes, "It is truly amazing that scholars—feminists among them—can continue to exclude women's contributions to 'the archives of knowledge.' Many respected books presenting recipes and other cultural aspects of *la cucina Mexicana* rarely mention the gendered nature of food preparation spaces or the women who accumulate and transmit cultural and technical knowledge from generation to generation" (2008, 264). See also Short's discussion (2006, 53ff.).

20. See, e.g., Adapon 2008; Allison 1991; Counihan 2010; DeVault 1997; Murcott 1983; Williams 1984.

21. Avakian 1997; Abarca 2006; and see also two special issues from 2006 of *Gender, Place and Culture* devoted to kitchens (vol. 13, nos. 2 and 6).

22. See Inness 2001; McFeely 2001; Shapiro 1986, 2004, 2007; Hayden 1982.

23. See Kaufmann 2010 for an ethnographic elaboration of these issues.

24. See, e.g., Harper and Faccioli 2010.

25. Kirsh 1995; de Léon 2003a, 2003b.

26. See also Clarke 2001 on Tupperware and domesticity. A number of scholars, including Miller 1988, Parr 1999, and Freeman 2004, provide ethnographic explorations of the design of kitchen technologies and kitchen spaces. Scholars of housework have noted that the vaunted "labor-saving technologies" have often simply rearranged family divisions of labor (children no longer being sent to the store to pick up things for Mom) and displaced female labor into different low-valued activities (driving the kids to soccer): Cowan 1983; Strasser 1982.

27. See Hernandez and Sutton 2003 and Sutton 2006 for elaborations of these points.

28. See also Meah and Jackson 2013.

29. Counihan 2004, 2010; Finn 2004; Hauck-Lawson 1998; Abarca 2006.

30. Grasseni 2004, 12; see also Herzfeld 2003; Pink 2005; Relieu et al. 2007.

31. See Sutton 1998, chap. 6; 2001, chap. 3.

1. EMPLACING COOKING

1. It differed on Kalymnos because of the addition of dried bread rings, moistened with water, called *kouloures*.

2. Estimating population on an island of seasonal and longer-term migration is notoriously difficult. If I asked how many lived on Kalymnos, people would respond, "In what month?" Government figures on population have been unreliable and, since the financial crisis, nonexistent.

3. Thanks to Russ Bernard for this observation. See Galaní-Moutáfi 1993 for a comparative discussion of this phenomenon.

4. Extensive studies have not been done, but see Vernier 1987 for a comparison of inheritance practices on different Dodecanese islands.

5. For more details of this practice and its ramifications, see Sutton 1998, chap. 5.

6. See Sutton 2001, 105ff. for a fuller description of meal and snack patterns.

7. UNESCO Convention for the Safeguarding of Intangible Cultural Heritage, application for "The Mediterranean Diet," nomination file no. 00394. For a vivid anthropological account of daily life in an outdoor food market in Turin, Italy, see Black 2012.

8. The fruit merchant's family had bought property from the buyer's family, a small piece of land for a prefab summer home, which meant that they were neighbors both in their regular homes and in their summer getaways.

9. See Sutton 2001, 23ff. On gender and grocery shopping, see also Miller 1998.

10. On the ambiguous ideas about meat, masculinity, and tradition, see Sutton 1997.

11. See Sutton 1998, chap. 7. As noted, Angeliki's stress on generosity does not mean that she doesn't perceive slights and acts of ingratitude. For more, see my discussion in chapter 6.

12. I am reminded here of E.P. Thompson's description of the "moral economy" of English society, in which profit-making on bread or grain, the staple food, was long seen as inherently antisocial. Thompson writes, for example, that in much of England at least through the eighteenth century, "There is a deeply-felt conviction that prices *ought*, in times of dearth, to be regulated, and that the profiteer put himself outside of society" (1971, 112; emphasis in original).

13. In the context of arguing that people "know" nutritional advice but don't follow it, Kaufmann writes, "Ideas come from outside and are stored in a separate mental stratum that may be either active or dormant and which is divorced from our actual practices. They have no immediate effect on the underlying mechanisms that govern our practices which reshape the things that make individuals what they are day by day" (2010, 23).

14. Found at www.unesco.org/culture/ich/index.php?lg=en&pg=00335#6.41 "Consent of Coron Community, Greece," accessed August 15, 2001, but the page has been subsequently taken down. Visit www.unesco.org/culture/ich/index.php?lg=en&pg=00011&RL=00884 for the current status of this application.

15. See Yiakoumaki 2006a, 2006b; Ball 2003.

16. See Sutton 2001, 59ff., for a discussion.

17. See www.aegeancuisine.net/portal.

18. I filmed Evdokia and Aleka on several occasions between 2008 and 2012. I incorporate only one of these videos into this study, however, because of my focus on home cooking here. I will consider the relationship between restaurant cooking on Kalymnos and "Mediterranean cuisine" in a future publication.

19. See Sutton 2001, chaps. 3 and 4, for discussion and examples.

2. TOOLS AND THEIR USERS

1. Hernandez and Sutton 2003; Sutton and Hernandez 2007.

2. *Kaloriziko,* more literally translated as "may you [and it, i.e., the appliance] have a fortunate destiny."

3. See Cockburn and Ormrod 1993; Parr 1999; Silva 2000.

4. All the videos are available at www.ucpress.edu/go/greekkitchen, and at www.youtube.com/channel/UCZhvwUWSdxHSHM0Frx3J17Q/videos.

5. For the dynamite throwing, see Sutton 1998, chap. 3.

6. *"Einai loksa, den me volevoun."* Both of these phrases in Greek suggest a relational and contextual character to human-tool interaction that will be discussed further in the section below on can openers.

7. Cf. Meah and Jackson's suggestive description of gendered conflict over the design of kitchen counters, cupboards, and stoves in their U.K.-based study (2013, 591).

8. See Shapiro 1986; Hayden 1982.

9. Maynard, Greenfield, and Childs 1999; see also Janeja 2010, 54, on the class-based practice of squatting while cooking in Bengal.

10. Mann et al. 2011, 233. This quote is from Priya Satalkar. She also notes in a personal correspondence that when she learned cooking in India, chopping was done in a kneeling position and with a special chopping tool, a board with a blade attached to it by a hinge. As she further notes, "at home [in India] we always cooked together, either with my mom, brother or father," whereas cutting vegetables in her current home in the Netherlands is a time "when I can block almost all stimuli from outside and turn inwards" (2012, personal communication with author).

11. *Kopeckhi* are sweets made in honor of the king of Denmark (Kopeckhi = Copenhagen).

12. Ingold's reflections on Lefebvre's notion of "rhythmicity" seem relevant here. As Ingold notes, rhythmicity "implies not just repetition but *differences within repetition.* Or to put it another way, fluent performance is rhythmic only because imperfections in the system call for continual correction. . . . Inexperi-

enced practitioners, by contrast, could not maintain a rhythm" (2011, 60, emphasis in original).

13. Her mother came from the village of Monastiraki in the district of Dorida (Fokida Prefecture).

14. The importance of balance, stance, and use of hands is explored in detail by Patel in her thesis on the work of bakers (2008). She notes, for example, "The haptic or the tactile-kinesthetic touching with the hands and indeed with the body is central to cooking. It is through active touch . . . what I refer to as 'analytic touch' with the hands that a baker knows the quality of the dough and how to work with it" (137).

15. Georgia Vourneli, from Thessaloniki, gave a different recipe for *sfoliata*, but agreed that the point of this technique is to make the phyllo lighter and crunchier (*tragana*).

16. Yogurt is not a typical ingredient in phyllo dough, but it was part of a number of acceptable variations typically associated with the dish *boureki* (as I noted above, Polykseni claimed to have multiple phyllo dough recipes that she used).

17. Interestingly, I learned from Nina Papamihail that when her family moved back from the United States to Kalymnos in the early 1970s, before making pies had become popular on the island, Nina's father, a chef by profession (see chapter 3), had found a carpenter to cut and sand a broomstick handle for him so he could have a proper rolling pin.

18. This description is drawn from Hernandez and Sutton 2003, in which we also describe the entire process of making a leek pie.

19. Cf. Patel's description of several bakers making cannolini shells using thin sticks (2008, 123). As she notes of one, "He appears to be exerting a gentle pressure, letting the dough do the work. His fingers and the stick move in tandem appearing to be an integrated working unit."

20. I found a YouTube video of this process, using a thinner rolling pin, at the following link: www.youtube.com/watch?v=vvNzAi9w6TU&feature=youtube_gdata_player.

21. For a description of the *sofra*, and its significance as an inalienable possession, see Sutton and Hernandez 2007.

22. I was staying with Katerina and her family at the time that I shot the video discussed in this section, and so had complete daily access to their kitchen activities.

23. Cited in Sutton 2001, 129. For further discussion, see 129ff.

24. In Greek, the exchange went as follows:

Katerina: Της Κατίνας το άνοιγμα θα δείς τώρα. αφού έχουμε το εργαλείο πιάσε τώρα να μην ρημάξουν τα χέρια: Α πα πα νεύρο. Για να μην καθυστερήσω τώρα . . . εγω το ανοίγω . . . σωστά. μάλιστα, τι να κάνουμε, τα είπαμε, είναι δικιά μας ο,τι και να την κάνουμε, δεν γίνεται αλλιώς. να φας τα χέρια σου είναι το πράμα; Μπορεί να κόψεις τα χέρια σου. ένα λεπτό με τη ανοιχτήρι,

David: δεν παίρνεις από το καινούργιο?

Katerina: έχω, μου έδωσε η Βαγγελιά έχω, αλλά δεν το μπορώ, δεν το επιδεξεύομαι, δεν το βολεύω πως το λένε . . . εγώ είμαι παραδοσιακιά . . . παραδοσιακιά. Τι να κάνουμε.

25. The interesting phrasing "eat your hands" will be considered in the conclusion.

26. Jean-Pierre Warnier provides a similar anecdote about Marcel Mauss puzzling over how a Kabyle man can run downhill in slippers. Warnier suggests that it is because slippers "are incorporated into his motor habits by apprenticeship. . . . He is a man-with-slippers" (Warnier 2001, 7). In this case, Katerina is a woman-with-can-opener. Thanks to Eleana Yalouri for pointing me to this.

27. Bourdieu 1990, 73. See also Warnier's argument for "a kind of synthesis between subject and object in motion, to such an extent that the subject *identifies* with his embodied objects" (2009, 467). Technological action, according to Warnier, should be seen as efficacious action directed toward both objects and subjects.

28. See, e.g., Downey 2010 for a discussion and critique of Bourdieu's formulation of the habitus.

29. Many of the older pots are made of aluminum, and Kalymnians are aware that these may pose health hazards, but many kitchens on Kalymnos still contain these pots, and I often saw them still in use.

30. Indeed, outdoor ovens became a desired feature not just on Kalymnos during this period, but throughout Greece. One might compare this with the renewed popularity of fireplaces on Rethymnos, Crete, as described by Herzfeld (1991, 230–32). But while Herzfeld sees contemporary fireplaces as having a largely symbolic motivation (represented by their placement in the more public living room rather than in the kitchen), outdoor ovens clearly are much more than primarily decorative.

31. Freeman 2004; Shove et al. 2007.

32. While the Saturday before Easter is still a fasting day, many Kalymnians don't observe the fast on this day. Men in particular are known to eat meat and consume alcohol during the afternoon. On Easter dynamite throwing, see Sutton 1998, chap. 3.

33. Cf. Fajans's comment on Kayapo ovens, in which "the house and oven are a unit and are called *ki kre* ('the space of the oven') and represent the social living space of the family" (2012, 54).

34. See the discussion in Portisch 2010, 68ff.

35. Contrast this orientation to a typical specification of kitchen tools from the classic textbook *Household Equipment:* "Every utensil should be judged on construction, efficiency, and care required. It must be well made and of a material fitted to the purpose for which it is to be used. It should be durable, simple in design, and suitable in size and shape. The material and design should contribute to ease of cleaning. It should be designed to accomplish the task for which it was made efficiently, without undue expenditure of effort" (Peet 1975, 51).

36. On sponge diving and risk, see Bernard 1976. On dynamite throwing, see Sutton 1998, chap. 3.

3. NINA AND IRINI

1. Nina pronounces her name with a hard *ī* rather than an *ē* sound. Her last name is given in the typical "formal" transliterated version, rather than the

more informal Papamichali. She told me that as her husband had spent considerable time as a seasonal migrant in the United States, on legal documents there he used the spelling "Papamaechel," as that is what "an illiterate friend" told him to use.

2. This is also part of Nina's frugality. She often talks about how she keeps everything, every plastic bottle as well as all the beautiful hundred-year-old china. On one visit to her summer house in 2009, she showed me and my wife some of the stuff she has scavenged from family and neighbors who were throwing them away—pretty pottery, a mallet that she thought her aunt might have used for tenderizing meat, old furniture. She recounted how Manolis used to bring her back shoes and clothes from the States but doesn't anymore because he could never pick out the right thing. But he fills his duffel bag with stuff he collects from the apartments that he refinishes after the people move out (from an ongoing job in West Point, New York)—plastic wall hangings that say "home, sweet home," even nails used to hang pictures and spare door hinges. Nina refers to these things with a smile as "the crap that Manolis brings back for me," but she keeps them all. She has a storeroom for furniture, keeps old stuff in her dresser, and hangs up everything she can on the walls: "country" plaques, a wooden spoon with an elephant on the handle. She often asks if I think it's good that she keeps these things; do my wife and I do the same? At one point, she wondered to me whether she keeps all this stuff because she doesn't have children. But she's also extremely pleased when she finds uses for things she has saved: an old plastic milk bottle that she uses to give me a gift of olive oil to take back to the States.

3. Manolis has two grown daughters from a previous marriage who live in the United States.

4. Baked foods like pastitsio and moussaka were the province of the rich in this time period.

5. When they moved to the States in the late 1940s, Nina's father had left money with his father-in-law to renovate the house and to switch the living room and the kitchen (the living room was originally a larger space than the kitchen). When they moved back to Kalymnos in 1971, they moved the traditional kitchen storage closet (*doulapi*) into the outdoor kitchen and had cabinets installed on an American plan. They also brought their large refrigerator with them from the United States, making their fully outfitted kitchen a rarity for early 1970s Kalymnos. As time went on they used the living room less and less for formal occasions, instead serving guests around the large table in the kitchen).

6. This was one of the few aspects of Nina's father's professional cooking that became part of their home-cooking repertoire. As Nina noted, her mother was always interested in cooking, so she was pleased to master the art of making pies and pie crusts.

7. For example, Nina's uncle weighed the pros and cons of keeping the water from boiling the octopus, which would be full of sea salt, or throwing it out and adding table salt to the dish.

8. I consider the relationship of cooking, control, and death at greater length in Sutton 2001, 154–55.

9. A spoon sweet is a Greek sweet made from various fruits or nuts preserved in sugar water; it is typically served with coffee. Note that meat with quince is not uncommon in parts of northern Greece but was not typically known in Kalymnian cooking.

10. See Salamone and Stanton 1986 for a rich discussion of the meaning of *nikokyra*.

11. The process involves slicing cherry tomatoes from the garden and the *vergakia* (Roma-type tomatoes from Vathi), putting them on a tray with a paper towel underneath and a *touli* (a kind of nylon cloth with holes in it) on top, and putting them in the sun. You bring them in at night so they don't get wet. The whole process takes about a week. Then you put them in a jar with oil and spices.

12. Manolis also cooked spaghetti with shrimp on January 31 when they had his niece over for supper. Nina noted that Manolis is better at dealing with shrimp than she, since she has always found them to be fussy to peel and clean. Manolis seems to follow a pattern of cooking the occasional evening meal, as during the day he would be more likely to be occupied working in the garden. For more on Manolis's cooking, see chapter 6.

4. MOTHERS, DAUGHTERS, AND OTHERS

1. This story was reported on the Association for the Study of Food and Society (ASFS) members-only listserv, July 18, 2008.

2. Crick 1982; Barth 1987; Tuzin 1997.

3. It is notable that much of this anthropological work focuses on male knowledge, in largely ritual contexts. Seremetakis 1991 provides an interesting exception in her ethnography of female control of mourning practices. She provides explicit consideration of questions of transmission through practices such as antiphony, yet, as with Lindstrom, learning is of explicit discursive material; and while embodiment is certainly part of Seremetakis's concerns, questions of skill transmission are only examined schematically, as in her discussion of visits to "grandmother's house" (Seremetakis 1994).

4. While interested in questions of "reproduction" of knowledge, such studies rarely address actual processes of learning, assuming that the intensity and heightened awareness provided by ritual ensures transmission. Some exceptions are Whitehouse 1992 and Rowlands 1994, which offer explicit discussions of processes of memory in relation to ritual knowledge and transmission. Barth does consider questions of the appropriateness of particular ritual imagery to carry knowledge. Much of this is seen in terms of questions of consistency, that is, in relation to a larger tradition of knowledge that each ritual element belongs to (Barth 1987, 34ff.).

5. Although indeed there has been a rise of cooking schools in Greece in recent times, these cooking schools tend to focus either on non-Greek recipes or on "traditional with a twist" recipes, not on learning classic dishes like moussaka. They would also insist on typical Western practices such as cutting using a board and a chef's knife (I owe these insights to Nafsika Papacharalampous).

6. Early functionalist ethnographies such as Audrey Richards's classic *Land, Labour and Diet in Northern Rhodesia* (1939) discuss the female transmission

of cooking knowledge in the context of broader enculturation and learning of gender roles. Richards, for example, notes the stress placed on observation and the construction of "play frames" for young Bemba girls. Interestingly, she observes that most direct teaching is done not by mothers but by siblings, and in some cases grandmothers. She does not discuss competition between mothers and daughters over cooking, but does suggest that such competition exists between cowives, noting that cooking is a key source of power: "The Bemba woman's prestige largely rests on her power to provide porridge and relish for her male relatives and to serve it nicely" (129; see also Gelfand 1971). Written as it is in functionalist generalizations, however, it is hard to assess the process of learning with any specificity.

7. Argenti 2002; Dilley 1999; Herzfeld 2003.

8. Some ethnographies of apprenticeship that look specifically at sensory-based learning are less about making things and more focused on bodily transformation through various disciplines. See, e.g., Hahn 2007 on Japanese dance and Downey 2005 on the martial art *capoeira*.

9. Indeed, they suggest that "kneeling" is a recognized stage in a child's development akin to crawling or walking in Western societies.

10. A red sauce includes onions, garlic, and tomatoes.

11. Cf. Sutton 2001, chap. 3, for a discussion.

12. Steinberg 1998; see discussion in Sutton 2006.

13. I realize this naming pattern may be a bit confusing for non-Greek readers. Little Katerina is named after her grandmother, but often referred to with a diminutive attached to her name. The name Katina is *not* a derivative of Katerina, but a shortened version of the Kalymnian name Kalotina. For an extended discussion of Kalymnian naming patterns, see Sutton 1998, chap. 8.

14. Cf. Sutton 2001, 29–30.

15. She used the word *sinenoisi*, which suggests an understanding that has come after discussion rather than arising spontaneously (*katanoisi*).

16. Along these lines, Little Katerina asked her mother at the beginning of this video why the dish is called "zucchini mincemeat," since there is no "meat" in the dish. Katina explained that *mince* didn't refer to meat, but rather to the fact that the zucchini is cut up small, i.e., "minced."

17. Cf. Leynse's study (2008) on the agency of children in learning cooking.

18. Indeed, she tried cutting some of the pieces using a sharper knife against the pan while they were still frying, in effect improvising a response to the task as it demanded one. This is a nice reminder again that no recipe can be completely specified in advance, and everyday improvisation is always part of adjusting to the circumstances presented by cooking. Cf. Hallam and Ingold's discussion of the significance of improvisation: "Because no system of codes, rules and norms can anticipate every possible circumstance . . . the gap between these non-specific guidelines and the specific conditions of a world that is never the same from one moment to the next not only opens up a space for improvisation, but also demands it." (2007, 2ff.).

19. Once again, note the "risk" involved in cooking that I discussed in chapter 2, which Kalymnians learn from the beginning to manage rather than to minimize through technology and "proper" procedure.

20. As this video was shot near Eastertime, you can hear dynamite exploding in the background, part of Kalymnian Easter celebrations.

21. *Parei yevsi,* rather than *yinei nostimo*—which would literally mean "become tastier"—is a phrase suggestive of the salad becoming what it is, and something that we, through our senses, can understand.

22. I was reminded of the skill that goes into coffee-making by Angeliki Roditi when I stayed at her house for several weeks. When she would go on early-morning errands, she insisted that it was okay for me to prepare my own freshly squeezed orange juice [using her electric juicer], but that I should wait till she returned to have my coffee because "you don't know how to make it."

23. Kalymnos shares an Aegean island cultural pattern that tends toward matrilocal residence and a stress on matrilineal or dual inheritance, though with distinct variations among islands as well. This is in contrast to the patrilocal and patrilineal stress of many areas of mainland Greece. For discussion of these differences, see Dimitriou-Kotsoni 1993; Sutton 1998, chap. 5; Vernier 1987.

24. See also Meah and Watson's suggestive study (2011), which questions linear transmission and notes the "diversity of sources through which culinary competence is constituted."

25. I take this lovely phrase from Paul Auster (2008, 38). But see related ideas in Keane 1997; see also Bennett 2010 on the agency of food and Bogost's discussion of the ways food escapes human intentionality as portrayed on TV shows such as *Ace of Cakes* (2012, 116ff.).

5. HORIZONTAL TRANSMISSION

Leo Vournelis did research in Thessaloniki during approximately the same period as I was examining these issues on Kalymnos. For a discussion of methodological issues, see Sutton and Vournelis 2009.

1. This ongoing, collaborative project with my student Leo Vournelis was originally published as Sutton and Vournelis 2009. Vefa is Vefa Alexiadou of the television show *Vefa's Kitchen;* Mamalakis is Elias Mamalakis of *Forgiveness with Every Bite.*

2. Mintz 1996. See Sutton 2001, chap. 4, for a more detailed discussion on this point.

3. Compare with Martine Perrot, who notes the role of freezers in preserving "traditional" foods in France: "In effect, far from having eliminated traditional forms of conservation, the freezer proposes an additional one. It participates in domestic production and makes possible, in both rural and urban areas, a rediscovery of the rhythm of the seasons by encouraging the conservation of fruits, vegetables and poultry" (1993, 367).

4. I discuss the first appearance of soy sauce on Kalymnos with Julia Koullia, an American woman married to a Kalymnian, in the video "Nina Making Octopus Stew" (video example 7).

5. In the past, birthdays were not celebrated, but rather "name days" (Hirschon 2010).

6. Very occasionally, Vefa traveled to different parts of Greece to highlight local and regional recipes.

7. All of these quotations are translations from my fieldnotes, recorded while watching the show in April 2006.

8. Thanks to Vassiliki Yiakoumaki for these observations.

9. The show did occasionally work with professional chefs, but typically this was when Mamalakis was showing the cuisine of non-Greek countries.

10. For an excellent account of intercommunal relations in Asia Minor, see Doumanis 2012.

11. Eleftherios Venizelos was prime minister of Greece for several terms in the early twentieth century.

12. She admitted that you could learn a little from *Master Chef* since at least they provided recipes. She contrasted this with the show *Something's Cooking* (*Kati Psinetai*), a competition in which five contestants gather at one another's houses and rate one another on their cooking, which was "all irony and criticism and nothing to learn about cooking," according to Katina.

13. This is different from rice pudding, which is also popular on Kalymnos, but which involves using cooked rice rather than rice flour.

14. Admittedly, cooking was not the focus of my research during the late 1990s, so my notes are less systematic.

15. Kaufmann 2010, 201. Kaufmann does qualify this stark contrast; see pp. 203–4.

16. For a critical discussion, see my review of Kaufmann (Sutton 2013).

6. THROUGH THE KITCHEN WINDOW

1. I discuss this topic in Sutton 1998, chap. 6. See also Brown and Theodossopoulos 2000 for a more general discussion of Greek views of international politics.

2. Indeed, I would have problems with Miller's claims about people making up their own moral or aesthetic orders "rather than just inheriting [them] as tradition or custom" (2008, 293). His dismissal of class and gender as analytic categories is problematic as well.

3. Other aspects of Elia's portrait that are familiar themes in the anthropology of Greece include issues of debt and betrayal (Miller 2008, 38) and the central place of cemeteries and ongoing relationships with the dead (40ff.).

4. The number of recording sessions ranged from one to roughly a dozen in different cases.

5. See Sutton 1998, 2008.

6. She said particularly their livers, though I'm not sure what the genesis of this claim was.

7. On the way that notions of World War II suffering and famine infuse understandings of the present day, see also Knight 2012.

8. See some of Yiannis's pictures in Sutton 1998, 49; Sutton 2001, 44, 160.

9. For an account of the famine in Athens, see Hionidou 2006.

10. James and Kalisperis's study of the nearby island of Chios (1999) suggests that this layout is unusual. They note that the Chiots "prefer to have a

formal area, separated from the family living area by walls and doors, in which to entertain guests and strangers." They also note that bedrooms on Chios are "very private," seen by most nonfamily members only on the ceremonial occasion of "dressing the bed."

11. Roland Haas, referring to his book *Enter the Past Tense: My Life as a CIA Assassin* (2007) on BookTV (C-Span), September 1, 2007.

12. On Greek regional cookbooks, see Ball 2003 and Yiakoumaki 2006a. On Kalymnians' view of the relation of food, seasons, and holy days, see Sutton 2001, chap. 2.

13. See Argyrou 1996; Gefou-Madianou 1999; and Stewart 1989.

14. This could be compared with debates about the "traditionality" of dynamite throwing; see Sutton 1998, chap. 3.

15. Kaufmann (2010) generalizes across class, ethnicity, and locale to an ideal-typical French middle-class urban experience.

16. de Léon (2003a) also examines the temporal dimensions of cooking, but from a strictly cognitive perspective focused on timing and task organization.

17. See also de Léon 2003a, 2003b; Kirsh 1995.

18. Indeed, while they lived in Athens, her mother was in a similar position to Popi's of not having female relatives nearby for sharing domestic labor.

19. Popi's statement reflects the relation between naming children and the rebirth of the person for whom the child is named, which I have explored elsewhere (see Sutton 1998, chap. 8).

20. Kaufmann 2010, 184. Note that Kaufmann does contrast weekday cooking, which is seen as a chore, with weekend cooking, when French cooks give their imagination free rein. I found no such distinction on Kalymnos.

21. Pavlos also told me that he watched an Italian cooking show that used to air, and got ideas for different spaghetti sauces from it. And he liked Jamie Oliver for some of the salads that he presented.

22. Note too that in the case of Pavlos there was also no grandmother on hand to take responsibility for the primary cooking. Pavlos's mother-in-law lived in Australia, and his own mother had died several years earlier.

23. Wilk and Hintlian suggest that some seafarers' cooking is cut off from female traditions and is "a cuisine of ingredients rather than preparation" (2005, 162). This is clearly not the case for Kalymnian sailors, who take their cooking seriously and draw on the food and preparation techniques with which they are familiar. For a detailed discussion of Kalymnian sailors' preparation of fish soup, see Riak 2012.

24. The reference to "like a vegetable" indicates the lack of sweetness of contemporary tomatoes.

25. Sometimes he would repeat the first step several times: bring just to the boiling point, pour off the foam, bring to a boil again, pour off the foam. Then he would allow it to reach a rolling boil.

26. On France, see Kaufmann 2010; on the United States see Trubek 2008. For an interesting comparison of food values in France and Sweden, see Bildt-gård 2010.

27. See, e.g., Wasserman 2011.

CONCLUSION

1. This question was posed by Aldona Jonaitis. See Jonaitis 2006 and Edwards, Gosden, and Philips 2006.

2. See the description at the beginning of Pachirat 2011.

3. She told me that she had used the store-bought béchamel the first couple of times, but once she hadn't wanted to go to the supermarket and decided to make it herself, and since then she had been doing it on her own.

4. Her Internet connection was spotty, so we watched only a few, shorter videos.

5. Except that the details are somewhat off: according to my notes, at least, it was her grandmother who told her that you put salt directly on the tomatoes when they are appetizers, while for salads the salt could go anywhere.

6. When I spoke to Little Katerina by phone in the summer of 2013, she bragged that she had made *filla* that day that were "just like my grandmother's." She told me that she follows all the advice her grandmother gave her, and that her dishes are often "better than my mom's." This was nine months after the death of her grandmother, perhaps one part of the reason that she might at that moment emphasize the explicit oral transmission of knowledge.

7. Other variations that Katina described to me include simply the shredded phyllo dough covered in honey and nuts, which she said was from Turkey and called *ek-mek,* and another variation that was a sweet cheese pie made with the Greek cheese *myzithra.*

8. For a discussion of restaurants and eating out on Kalymnos, see Sutton 2001, chap. 4.

9. Katina told me that she, along with many others, no longer bought sweets from the bakery when visiting a friend's or relative's house. Instead, she would bring homemade sweets, or perhaps some juice, or fish caught by her husband. To the extent that this is true, it represents a real shift from earlier, better economic times, when gifts of bakery-bought sweets were standard practice. However, Katina's comments about not eating out at restaurants or getting fast food during difficult economic times were simply a reassertion of what most older Kalymnians have always known—that home cooking is always the better option than public eating.

10. See, e.g., Christie 2008 on the way men deride women's cooking abilities.

11. Compare this to Williams's discussion of Tejano cooking (1984), in which the demand that wives cook for husbands is enforced by the entire kin group, at the same time that women's cooking is recognized as a key source of female prestige and influence.

12. Two important studies of changing urban Greek gender relations are Halkias 2004 and Kirtsoglou 2004. It is interesting that despite tremendous changes in Greek society, some of the same issues are raised by these studies as were highlighted in Cowan's 1991 analysis of Greek gender discourses of twenty-plus years ago.

13. This is true even for women who are excellent cooks. For example, Evdokia Passa, who runs a restaurant during the summer months, told me in 2008 that during the winter she takes a vacation from cooking, and she and her husband eat on alternate days her mother's cooking and her mother-in-law's.

14. Of course, as noted in chapter 4, on Kalymnos these expectations are very different from in other parts of Greece, where a girl might be expected to learn cooking in her preteen years.

15. See also McCabe and Malefyt's discussion of indeterminacy and "tweaking" in cooking in the United States (2013). *Risk* itself is a dangerously polyvalent word, as Mary Douglas, among others, has argued (Douglas 1992; see also Boholm 2003). I intend to address the relationship of risk and cooking more fully in a future publication, tentatively titled *A Theory of Cooking, or, How "Natives" Cook, While Thinking, for Example.*

16. Modernist cooks seem to fetishize science and technology and ridicule the human, "female" elements of cooking. See Wilson 2012, 257–58.

17. Thanks to Amy Trubek for these insights.

18. See Shapiro 2004; McFeely 2001.

19. See Ouroussoff 2010; Scott 1998; Carrier and Miller 1998.

20. I should note that Morozov explicitly exempts molecular gastronomy from his critique of technological solutionism because he says that all the additional technology introduced makes cooking more challenging rather than simpler. This is an important point to consider; however, as Sophia Roosth's ethnography (2013) suggests, this technology is, in fact, being employed toward the goal of perfectibility, and of transferring the skills associated with tradition into the laboratory setting on the model of reproducibility.

21. Instead of using fruits, vegetables, and meats, note-by-note cuisine uses "compounds," and there are exponentially more possible compounds than there are ingredients: "If we assume that the number of compounds present in the ingredients is about 1,000, and that the number of compounds that will be used in note by note cuisine is of the order of 100, then the number of possibilities is about 10 to the 3000. And, in this calculation we have not considered that the concentration of each compound can be adapted, which means that a whole new continent of flavor can be discovered" (This 2013, 5).

22. See Roosth's discussion of the funding for molecular gastronomy laboratories by large food companies. As she notes, "By following either the money or the chemicals, one traces a path from frozen French fries to foie gras foam" (2013, 10).

23. This is a point that I develop more fully in Sutton 2011.

24. Bud from Portland. www.nytimes.com/2012/10/14/magazine/cooks-illustrateds-christopher-kimball.html.

25. For a discussion of trends among leading restaurateurs such as Ferran Adrià and René Redzepi, see Davis 2012. Davis argues that these chefs are using their differently styled high-tech creations to access the links among taste, memory, and the senses in a way that is similar to what Seremetakis 1994 describes for rural Greek culture. In the absence of an ethnography of the restaurant customers, I would say that I reserve some skepticism.

26. I translate the Greek word *psyche* as "soul" here because both words are deeply multivocal.

27. See Janeja's discussion of food and agency (2010). This could also be seen as part of the "analogic thinking" that I have described as the essence of Kalymnian historical consciousness (Sutton 1998). The connection of such food meta-

phors to historical consciousness, however, awaits further thought and ethnographic elaboration.

28. Available at www.youtube.com/watch?v=EPRumYmy9PQ&noredirect=1.

EPILOGUE

1. One example is the "potato movement," which has been challenging the role of middlemen and supermarkets in setting prices and attempting to provide direct exchange between producers and consumers (see Rakopolous n.d.; Vournelis and Sutton 2012).

2. To migrate to Australia one needs to have an employer willing to guarantee a job upon arrival.

3. By August 2013 he had left for Australia on a temporary visa.

4. Katina's parents had long worked as craftspeople, tanning leather and making leather products mostly for sale to tourists.

5. Katerina passed on in November 2012. In the fall of 2013 they once again collected snails. But this time Katina prepared them using a method she had learned from a neighbor from the island of Astypalia, which involved potatoes rather than rice. Katina said it came out very tasty.

6. A pseudonym.

7. Papacharalampous 2012 discusses this in reference to the rerelease of a World War II cookbook—Themos Potamianos's *Cooking to Suit the Times*—in 2012. This cookbook, which received enthusiastic reviews in the press in 2012, advocates creativity and flexibility in using local substitutes for ingredients that were unavailable during wartime and, by extension, during other times of hardship. See also Knight 2012.

8. See Sutton 2001, chap. 2; Panourgia 1995.

9. Indeed, Katina's mother, Katerina, who had been a strong supporter of the socialist PASOK in the 1980s and 1990s, told me that she hadn't voted in the past two elections and was disgusted with all of the political parties. For an analysis of the political aspects of the crisis in Greece, see Vournelis 2013.

10. *Na skavei*, a phrase suggestive of hard living.

11. Mihalis owns a furniture factory with branches in Queens and Manhattan.

12. An ongoing debate on Kalymnos concerns whether the garbage on Kalymnian streets is the fault of the poor social services provided by the mayoralty, or the fact that Kalymnians refuse to follow rules about putting out garbage on a particular day because, as Nina puts it, "Greeks do not want to have anyone tell them what to do." For further discussion of these issues, see Sutton 1998, chap. 2.

References

Abarca, Meredith. 2004. "Authentic or Not, It's Original." *Food and Foodways* 12: 1–25.

———. 2006. *Voices in the Kitchen: Views of Food and the World from Working-Class Mexican and Mexican American Women.* College Station: Texas A&M University Press.

Adapon, Joy. 2008. *Culinary Art and Anthropology.* New York: Berg.

Adema, Pauline. 2000. "Vicarious Consumption: Food, Television and the Ambiguity of Modernity." *Journal of American Culture* 23, no. 3: 113–23.

Allison, Anne. 1991. "Japanese Mothers and Obentos: The Lunch Box as Ideological State Apparatus." *Anthropological Quarterly* 64: 195–208.

Argenti, Nicholas. 2002. "People of the Chisel: Apprenticeship, Youth, and Elites in Oku (Cameroon)." *American Ethnologist* 29, no. 3: 407–533.

Argyrou, Vassos. 1996. *Tradition and Modernity in the Mediterranean: The Wedding as Symbolic Struggle.* Cambridge: Cambridge University Press.

Auster, Paul. 2008. *Man in the Dark.* New York: Faber & Faber.

Avakian, Arlene. 1997. *Through the Kitchen Window: Women Writers Explore the Intimate Meanings of Food and Cooking.* Boston, MA: Beacon Press.

Bakken, Christopher. 2013. *Honey, Olives, Octopus: Adventures at the Greek Table.* Berkeley: University of California Press.

Ball, Eric. 2003. "Greek Food after Mousaka: Cookbooks, 'Local' Culture, and the Cretan Diet." *Journal of Modern Greek Studies* 21, no. 1: 1–36.

———. 2005. "Toward a Greek Ecocriticism: Place Awareness and Cultural Identity in Pandelis Prevelakis's Οι δρόμοι της δημιουργίας." *Journal of Modern Greek Studies* 23, no. 1: 1–37.

Barth, Fredrik. 1975. *Ritual and Knowledge among the Bahktaman of New Guinea.* New Haven, CT: Yale University Press.

———. *Cosmologies in the Making: A Generative Approach to Cultural Variation in Inner New Guinea*. Cambridge: Cambridge University Press.

Bennett, Jane. 2010. *Vibrant Matter: A Political Ecology of Things*. Durham, NC : Duke University Press.

Bernard, H. Russell. 1976. "The Fisherman and His Wife." In *Oceans: Our Continuing Frontier*, edited by Henry William Menard and Jane L. Scheiber, pp. 304–9. Del Mar, CA: Publisher's Inc.

Bildtgård, Torbjörn. 2010. "What It Means to 'Eat Well' in France and Sweden." *Food and Foodways* 18, no. 4: 209–32.

Black, Rachel. 2012. *Porta Palazzo: The Anthropology of an Italian Market*. Philadelphia: University of Pennsylvania Press.

Bogost, Ian. 2012. *Alien Phenomenology, or What It's Like to Be a Thing*. Minneapolis: University of Minnesota Press.

Boholm, Åsa. 2003. "The Cultural Nature of Risk: Can There Be an Anthropology of Uncertainty?" *Ethnos* 68, no. 2: 159–78.

Boivin, Nicole. 2010. *Material Cultures, Material Minds: The Impact of Things on Human Thought, Society, and Evolution*. Cambridge: Cambridge University Press.

Borthwick, Fiona. 2000. "Olfaction and Taste: Invasive Odours and Disappearing Objects." *Australian Journal of Anthropology* 11: 127–40.

Bourdieu, Pierre. 1977. *Outline of a Theory of Practice*. Translated by Richard Nice. Cambridge: Cambridge University Press.

———. 1984. *Distinction: A Social Critique of the Judgment of Taste*. Translated by Richard Nice. Cambridge, MA: Harvard University Press.

———. 1990. *The Logic of Practice*. Translated by Richard Nice. Stanford, CA: Stanford University Press.

Brown, Keith, and Dimitrios Theodossopoulos. 2000. "The Performance of Anxiety: Greek Narratives of the War in Kosovo." *Anthropology Today* 16, no. 1: 3–8.

Bryant, Rebecca. 2005. "The Soul Danced into the Body: Nation and Improvisation in Istanbul." *American Ethnologist* 32, no. 2: 222–38.

Carrier, James. 2012. Review of *Wall Street at War: The Secret Struggle for the Global Economy*, by Alexandra Ouroussoff. *Journal of the Royal Anthropological Institute* 18, no. 3: 703–4.

———, and Daniel Miller, eds. 1998. *Virtualism*. Oxford: Berg.

Carsten, Janet. 1995. "The Substance of Kinship and the Heat of the Hearth: Feeding, Personhood, and Relatedness among Malays in Pulau Langkawi." *American Ethnologist* 22: 223–41.

Chakrabortty, Aditya. 2011. "Athens Protests: Syntagma Square on Frontline of European Austerity Protests." *The Guardian*, June 19. Accessed June 26, 2011. www.guardian.co.uk/world/2011/jun/19/athens-protests-syntagma-austerity-protests.

Christie, Marie Elisa. 2006. "Kitchenspace: Gendered Territory in Central Mexico." *Gender, Place & Culture* 13, no. 6: 653–61.

———. 2008. *Kitchenspace: Women, Fiestas and Everyday Life in Central Mexico*. Austin: University of Texas Press.

Clarke, Allison. 2001. *Tupperware: The Promise of Plastic in 1950s America.* Washington DC: Smithsonian Institute Press.

Cockburn, Cynthia, and Susan Ormrod. 1993. *Gender and Technology in the Making.* London: Sage.

Counihan, Carole. 2004. *Around the Tuscan Table: Food, Family, and Gender in Twentieth-Century Florence.* New York: Routledge.

———. 2010. *A Tortilla Is Like Life: Food and Culture in the San Luis Valley.* Austin: University of Texas Press.

Cowan, Jane. 1991. "Going out for Coffee? Contesting the Grounds of Gendered Pleasures in Everyday Sociability." In *Contested Identities: Gender and Kinship in Modern Greece,* edited by Peter Loizos and Evthimios Papataksiarchis, 180–202. Princeton, NJ: Princeton University Press.

Cowan, Ruth. 1983. *More Work for Mother: The Ironies of Household Technology from the Open Hearth to the Microwave.* New York: Basic Books.

Crick, Malcolm. 1982. "Anthropology of Knowledge." *Annual Review of Anthropology* 11: 287–313.

Cronk, Lee. 1997. "Reciprocity and the Power of Giving." In *Conformity and Conflict,* edited by James Spradly and David McCurdy, 157–63. 9th ed. New York: Addison Wesley Longman.

Cruikshank, Julie. 2005. *Do Glaciers Listen: Local Knowledge, Colonial Encounters and Social Imagination.* Vancouver: UBC Press.

Daly, Ian. 2010. "Just Like Mombot Used to Make." *New York Times,* February 23. Accessed March 15, 2010. www.nytimes.com/2010/02/24 /dining/24robots.html.

Davis, Mitchell. 2012. "A Time and a Place for a Peach: Taste Trends in Contemporary Cooking." *Senses and Society* 7, no. 2: 135–52.

de Léon, David. 2003a. *Artefactual Intelligence: The Development and Use of Cognitively Congenial Artifacts.* Lund, Sweden: Lund University Cognitive Studies 105.

———. 2003b. *Actions, Artefacts and Cognition: An Ethnography of Cooking.* Lund, Sweden: Lund University Cognitive Studies 104.

DeVault, Marjorie. 1997. "Conflict and Deference." In *Food and Culture: A Reader,* edited by Carole Counihan and Penny Van Esterik, 180–99. London: Routledge.

Dilley, Roy. 1999. "Ways of Knowing, Forms of Power." *Cultural Dynamics* 11: 33–55.

Dimitriou-Kotsoni, Sybilla. 1993. "The Aegean Cultural Tradition." *Journal of Mediterranean Studies* 3: 62–76.

Diner, Hasia. 2001. *Hungering for America: Italian, Irish, & Jewish Foodways in the Age of Migration.* Cambridge, MA: Harvard University Press.

Dormer, Peter. 1994. *The Art of the Maker.* London: Thames and Hudson.

Douglas, Mary. 1992. *Risk and Blame: Essays in Cultural Theory.* London: Routledge.

Doumanis, Nicholas. 2012. *Before the Nation: Muslim-Christian Coexistence and Its Destruction in Late Ottoman Anatolia.* New York: Oxford University Press.

Downey, Greg. 2005. *Learning Capoeira: Lessons in Cunning from an Afro-Brazilian Art*. Oxford: Oxford University Press.

———. 2010. "Practice without Theory: A Neuroanthropological Perspective on Embodied Learning." In *Making Knowledge: Explorations of the Indissoluble Relation between Mind, Body and Environment*, edited by Trevor Marchand, 21–38. West Sussex, UK: Wiley-Blackwell.

Edwards, Elizabeth, Chris Gosden, and Ruth Phillips. 2006. "Introduction." In *Sensible Objects: Colonialism, Museums and Material Culture*, edited by Elizabeth Edwards, Chris Gosden, and Ruth Phillips, 1–31. Oxford: Berg.

Fajans, Jane. 2012. *Brazilian Food: Race, Class and Identity in Regional Cuisines*. London: Berg.

Farquhar, Judith. 2002. *Appetites: Food and Sex in Postsocialist China*. Durham, NC: Duke University Press.

Feld, Stephen. 2003. "A Rainforest Acoustemology." In *The Auditory Culture Reader*, edited by Michael Bull and Les Back, 23–39. Oxford: Berg.

Fernandez, James. 1986. *Persuasions and Performances: The Play of Tropes in Culture*. Bloomington: Indiana University Press.

Fertaly, Kaitlin. 2012. "Khash, History and Armenian National Identity: Reconsidering Post-Socialist Gender, Food Practices and the Domestic." *Identities* 19, no. 1: 81–102.

Finn, John E. 2004. "The Kitchen Voice as Confessional." *Food, Culture and Society* 7, no. 1: 85–100.

Freeman, June. 2004. *The Making of the Modern Kitchen: A Cultural History*. New York: Berg.

Galaní-Moutáfi, Vasilikí. 1993. "From Agriculture to Tourism: Property, Labor, Gender, and Kinship in a Greek Island Village (Part One)." *Journal of Modern Greek Studies* 11: 241–70.

Gefou-Madianou, Dimitra. 1999. "Cultural Polyphony and Identity Formation: Negotiating Tradition in Attica." *American Ethnologist* 26: 412–39.

Gelfand, Michael. 1971. *Diet and Tradition in an African Culture*. Edinburgh: E & S Livingstone.

Geurts, Kathryn. 2003. *Culture and the Senses: Bodily Ways of Knowing in an African Community*. Berkeley: University of California Press.

Goody, Jack. 1982. *Cooking, Cuisine and Class: A Study in Comparative Sociology*. Cambridge: Cambridge University Press.

Graeber, David. 2001. *Toward and Anthropological Theory of Value: The False Coin of Our Own Dreams*. New York: Palgrave.

———. 2011. *Debt: The First 5,000 Years*. New York: Melville House.

Grasseni, Cristina. 2004. "Video and Ethnographic Knowledge: Skilled Vision in the Practice of Breeding." In *Working Images: Visual Research and Representation in Ethnography*, edited by Sarah Pink, László Kürti, and Ana Isabel Afonso, 12–27. New York: Routledge.

———. 2009. *Developing Skill, Developing Vision: Practices of Locality at the Foot of the Alps*. Oxford: Berghahn.

Greenfield, Patricia. 2004. *Weaving Generations Together: Evolving Creativity among the Mayas of Chiapas*. Santa Fe, NM: School of American Research Press.

Grimes, William. 2004. "I'm Cooking as Fast as I Can." *New York Times,* September 15. Accessed October 3, 2004. www.nytimes.com/2004/09/15/dining/15FAST.html.

Haas, Roland. 2007. *Enter the Past Tense: My Life as a CIA Assassin.* New York: Potomac Books.

Hahn, Tomie. 2007. *Sensational Knowledge: Embodying Culture through Japanese Dance.* Middletown, CT: Wesleyan University Press.

Halberstadt, Alex. 2012. "Cooking Isn't Creative, and It Isn't Easy." *New York Times Magazine,* October 11. Accessed October 21, 2012. www.nytimes.com/2012/10/14/magazine/cooks-illustrateds-christopher-kimball.html.

———. 2013. "The Transformational Power of the Right Spice." *The New York Times Magazine,* April 7. Accessed February 22, 2014. www.nytimes.com/2013/04/07/magazine/the-spice-is-right.html.

Halkias, Alexandra. 2004. *The Empty Cradle of Democracy.* Durham, NC: Duke University Press.

Hallam, Elizabeth, and Tim Ingold 2007. "Introduction." In *Creativity and Cultural Improvisation,* edited by Elizabeth Hallam and Tim Ingold, 1–24. Oxford: Berg.

Harper, Douglas. 1987. *Working Knowledge: Skill and Community in a Small Shop.* Chicago, IL: University of Chicago Press.

———, and Patrizia Faccioli. 2010. *The Italian Way.* Chicago, IL: University of Chicago Press.

Harris, Mark. 2007. "Introduction." In *Ways of Knowing: New Approaches in the Anthropology of Experience and Learning,* edited by Mark Harris, 1–26. New York: Berghahn Books.

Hauck-Lawson, Annie. 1998. "When Food Is the Voice: A Case Study of a Polish-American Woman." *Journal for the Study of Food and Society* 2, no. 1: 21–28.

Hayden, Dolores. 1982. *The Grand Domestic Revolution: A History of Feminist Designs for American Homes, Neighbourhoods, and Cities.* Cambridge, MA: MIT Press.

Heller, Nathan. 2013. "Laptop U: Has the Future of College Moved Online?" *The New Yorker,* May 20: 80–91.

Hernandez, Michael, and David Sutton. 2003. "Hands that Remember: An Ethnography of Everyday Cooking." *Expedition: Journal of the University of Pennsylvania Museum* 45: 30–37.

Herzfeld, Michael. 1985. *The Poetics of Manhood: Contest and Identity in a Cretan Mountain Village.* Princeton, NJ: Princeton University Press.

———. 1991. *A Place in History: Social and Monumental Times in a Cretan Town.* Princeton, NJ: Princeton University Press.

———. 2003. *The Body Impolitic: Artisans and Artifice in the Global Hierarchy of Value.* Chicago, IL: University of Chicago Press.

Hill, Jacquetta, and David Plath. 2006. "Moneyed Knowledge: How Women Become Commercial Shellfish Divers." In *Learning in Likely Places: Varieties of Apprenticeship in Japan,* edited by John Singleton, 211–25. Cambridge: Cambridge University Press.

Hionidou, Violetta. 2006. *Famine and Death in Occupied Greece, 1941–1944.* Cambridge: Cambridge University Press.

Hirschon, Renée. 1998. *Heirs of the Greek Catastrophe: The Social Life of Asia Minor Refugees in Piraeus,* 2nd ed. New York: Berghahn Press.

———. 2008. "Bourdieu on Olympos: The Symbolic Character of the Karpathiko House." In *Proceedings, Karpathos and Folklore: 3rd International Conference on Karpathiot Folklore* (Καρπαθος και Λαογραφια Γ´Διεθνες Συνεδριο Καρπαθιακης Λαογραφιας 2006), edited by Minas Alexiadis, 565–79. Athens: Demos of Karpathos, Dodecanese Provincial Administration.

———. 2010. "Imported Individuals, Indigenous Persons: Changing Celebrations of Personal Identity in Contemporary Greece." In *Eastern Christians in Anthropological Perspective,* edited by Chris Hann and Hermann Goltz, 289–310. Berkeley: University of California Press.

Holtzman, Jon. 2009. *Uncertain Tastes: Memory, Ambivalence and the Politics of Eating in Samburu, Northern Kenya.* Berkeley: University of California Press.

Hoskins, Janet. 1998. *Biographical Objects: How Things Tell the Story of People's Lives.* London: Routledge.

Howes, David. 2003. *Sensual Relations: Engaging the Senses in Culture and Social Theory.* Ann Arbor: University of Michigan Press.

———. 2008. "Sensory Basket Weaving 101." In *Neocraft: Modernity and the Crafts,* edited by Sandra Alfoldy, pp. 261–24. Nova Scotia: Nova Scotia College of Art and Design Press.

———, ed. 2005. *Empire of the Senses: The Sensual Culture Reader.* Oxford: Berg.

———, ed. 2009. *The Sixth Sense Reader.* Oxford: Berg.

Hutchins, Edwin. 1995. *Cognition in the Wild.* Cambridge, MA: MIT Press.

Ingold, Tim. 2000. *The Perception of the Environment: Essays in Livelihood, Dwelling and Skill.* London: Routledge.

———. 2001. "From the Transmission of Representations to the Education of Attention." In *The Debated Mind: Evolutionary Psychology versus Ethnography,* edited by Harvey Whitehouse, 113–53. New York: Berg.

———. 2007. "Materials against Materiality." *Archaeological Dialogues* 14: 1–16.

———. 2011. *Being Alive: Essays on Movement, Knowledge and Description.* London: Routledge.

Inness, Sherrie. 2001. *Cooking Lessons: The Politics of Gender and Food.* Lanham, MD: Rowman & Littlefield.

James, Alice, and Loukas Kalisperis. 1999. "Use of House and Space: Public and Private Family Interaction on Chios, Greece." In *House Life: Space, Place and Family in Europe,* edited by D. Birdwell-Pheasant and D. Lawrence-Zuñiga, 205–20. Oxford: Berg.

Janeja, Manpreet. 2010. *Transactions in Taste: The Collaborative Lives of Everyday Bengali Food.* London: Routledge.

Jonaitis, Aldona. 2006. "Smoked Fish and Fermented Oil: Taste and Smell among the Kwakwaka'wakw." In *Sensible Objects: Colonialism, Museums and Material Culture,* edited by C. Gosden, E. Edwards, and R. Phillips, 141–67. Oxford: Berg.

Jones, Graham. 2011. *Trade of the Tricks: Inside the Magician's Craft.* Berkeley: University of California Press.

Kaufmann, Jean-Claude. 2010. *The Meaning of Cooking*. Malden, MA: Polity Press.

Keane, Webb. 1997. *Signs of Recognition: Powers and Hazards of Representation in an Indonesian Society*. Berkeley: University of California Press.

Keller, Charles. 2001. "Thought and Production: Insights of the Practitioner." In *Anthropological Perspectives on Technology*, edited by M.B. Schiffer, pp. 33–45. Albuquerque: University of New Mexico Press.

———, and Janet Dixon Keller. 1999. "Imagery in Cultural Tradition and Innovation." *Mind, Culture, and Activity* 6: 3–32.

Kirsh, David. 1995. "The Intelligent Use of Space." *Artificial Intelligence* 73: 31–68.

Kirtsoglou, Elizabeth. 2004. *For the Love of Women*. London: Routledge.

Knight, Daniel. 2012. "Cultural Proximity: Crisis, Time and Social Memory in Central Greece." *History and Anthropology* 23, no. 3: 349–74.

Landis, Denise. 2012. Notes from the Recipe Tester: Working with Phyllo. *New York Times*, April 10. Accessed April 26, 2012. http://dinersjournal.blogs.nytimes.com/2012/04/10/notes-from-the-recipe-tester-working-with-phyllo-dough/.

Latour, Bruno. 2005. *Reassembling the Social: An Introduction to Actor-Network Theory*. Oxford: Oxford University Press.

Lave, Jean. 1988. *Cognition in Practice: Mind, Mathematics and Culture in Everyday Life*. Cambridge: Cambridge University Press.

———. 1996. "The Practice of Learning." In *Understanding Practice: Perspectives on Activity and Context*, edited by Seth Chaiklin and Jean Lave, 3–32. Cambridge: Cambridge University Press.

———. 2011. *Apprenticeship in Critical Ethnographic Practice*. Chicago, IL: University of Chicago Press.

———, and Etienne Wenger, eds. 1991. *Situated Learning: Legitimate Peripheral Participation*. Cambridge: Cambridge University Press.

Leynse, Wendy. 2008. "Learning to Become a Culturally Competent Member of French Society through Food." PhD diss., New York University.

Lindstrom, Lamont. 1990. *Knowledge and Power in the South Pacific*. Washington DC: Smithsonian Institute Press.

Makovicky, Nicolette. 2010. "'Something to Talk About': Notation and Knowledge-Making among Central Slovak Lace-Makers." In *Making Knowledge: Explorations of the Indissoluble Relation between Mind, Body and Environment*, edited by Trevor Marchand, 76–94. West Sussex, UK: Wiley-Blackwell.

Malaby, Thomas. 2003. *Gambling Life: Dealing in Contingency in a Greek City*. Champaign: University of Illinois Press.

Mann, Anna, Annemarie Mol, Priya Satalkar, Amalinda Savirani, Nasima Selim, Malina Sur, and Emily Yates-Doerr. 2011. "Mixing Methods, Tasting Fingers: Notes on an Ethnographic Experiment." *HAU: Journal of Ethnographic History* 1, no. 1: 221–43.

Marchand, Trevor. 2010. "Embodied Cognition and Communication: Studies with British Fine Woodworkers." In *Making Knowledge: Explorations of the Indissoluble Relation between Mind, Body and Environment*, edited by Trevor Marchand, 95–114. West Sussex, UK: Wiley-Blackwell.

Mauss, Marcel. 1954 [1925]. *The Gift: Forms and Functions of Exchange in Archaic Societies.* Translated by Ian Cunnison. London: Routledge.

Maynard, Ashley, Patricia Greenfield, and Carla Childs. 1999. "Culture, History, Biology, and Body: Native and Non-Native Acquisition of Technological Skill." *Ethos* 27, no. 3: 379–402.

McCabe, Maryann, and Timothy de Waal Malefyt. 2013. "Creativity and Cooking: Motherhood, Agency and Social Change in Everyday Life. *Journal of Consumer Culture.* DOI: 10.1177/1469540513493202.

McFeely, Mary Drake. 2001. *Can She Bake a Cherry Pie? American Women and the Kitchen in the Twentieth Century.* Amherst: University of Massachusetts Press.

Meah, Angela. 2013. "Reconceptualizing Power and Gendered Subjectivities in Domestic Cooking." Spaces. *Progress in Human Geography* DOI: 10.1177/0309132513501404 (not yet available in print).

———— and Peter Jackson. 2013. "Crowded Kitchens: The 'Democratisation' of Domesticity?" *Gender, Place and Culture* 20: 578–96.

———— and Matt Watson. 2011. "Saints and Slackers: Challenging Discourses about the Decline of Domestic Cooking." *Sociological Research Online* 16, no. 2.6. Readers on institutional networks can access it at http://socres online.org.uk/16/2/6.html.

Michael, Mike. 2000. "'These Boots Are Made for Walking . . . ' Mundane Technology, the Body and Human-Environment Relations." *Body and Society* 6: 107–26.

Miller, Daniel. 1988. "Appropriating the State on the Council Estate." *Man* (n.s.) 23: 353–72.

————. 1998. *A Theory of Shopping.* Ithaca, NY: Cornell University Press.

————. 2005. "Materiality: An Introduction." In *Materiality,* edited by Daniel Miller, 1–47. Durham, NC: Duke University Press.

————. 2008. *The Comfort of Things.* Malden, MA: Polity Press.

Mintz, Sidney. 1985. *Sweetness and Power.* New York: Viking Penguin.

————. 1996. *Tasting Food, Tasting Freedom.* Boston: Beacon Press.

———— and Christine Du Bois. 2002. "The Anthropology of Food and Eating." *Annual Review of Anthropology* 31: 99–119.

Morozov, Evgeny. 2013. *To Save Everything, Click Here: The Folly of Technological Solutionism.* New York: Public Affairs Press.

Murcott, Anne. 1983. "'It's a Pleasure to Cook for Him': Food, Mealtimes and Gender in Some South Wales Households." In *The Public and Private,* edited by Eva Garmarnikow et al., 78–90. London: Heinemann.

Myers, Fred. 2001. "Introduction: The Empire of Things." In *The Empire of Things: Regimes of Value and Material Culture,* edited by Fred Myers, pp. 3–61. Santa Fe, NM: School of American Research Press.

Narvaez, Rafael. 2006. "Embodiment, Collective Memory and Time." *Body and Society* 12, no. 3: 51–73.

Norman, Donald. 2011. *Living with Complexity.* Cambridge, MA: MIT Press.

Ouroussoff, Alexandra. 2010. *Wall Street at War: The Secret Struggle for the Global Economy.* Cambridge: Polity Press.

Pachirat, Timothy. 2011. *Every Twelve Seconds: Industrialized Slaughter and the Politics of Sight.* New Haven, CT: Yale University Press.

Panourgia, Neni. 1995. *Fragments of Death, Fables of Identity: An Athenian Anthropography*. Madison: University of Wisconsin Press.

Papacharalampous, Nafsika. 2012. "'This Is Not Kolokythakia Tiganita!' or What Greek Cookery Books Reveal about Tradition, Nationality and the Localities." PhD diss., School of Oriental and African Studies, University of London.

Parr, Joy. 1999. *Domestic Goods: The Material, the Moral, and the Economic in the Postwar Years*. Toronto: University of Toronto Press.

———. 2010. *Sensing Changes: Technologies, Environments, and the Everyday, 1953–2003*. Vancouver: University of British Columbia Press.

Patel, Krina. 2008. "Thinkers in the Kitchen: Embodied Thinking and Learning in Practice." PhD diss., Harvard University.

Paxson, Heather. 2011. "The 'Art' and 'Science' of Handcrafting Cheese in the United States." *Endeavour* 35, nos. 2–3: 116–24.

Peet, Louise. 1975. *Household Equipment*. 7th ed. New York: Wiley.

Perley, Bernard. 2013. "Parsing Responsibility in Native American Language Revitalization across Generations." Paper presented at the American Ethnological Society Meetings, Chicago, IL, April 11–13.

Perrot, Martine. 1993. "The Domestication of Objects." In *Industrial Design: Reflections of a Century*, edited by Jocelyn de Noblet, 365–71. Paris: Flammarion.

Pink, Sarah. 2005. "Dirty Laundry: Everyday Practice, Sensory Engagement and the Constitution of Identity." *Social Anthropology* 13, no. 3: 275–90.

———. 2010. "The Future of Sensory Anthropology/The Anthropology of the Senses." *Social Anthropology* 18, no. 3: 331–40.

Politis, Nikolaos. 1969 [1914]. "Εκλογαί από τα τραγούδια του Ελληνικού Λαού" [Selection of the Songs of the Greek People]. 6th ed. Athens: Ekdoseis Ermis.

Pollan, Michael. 2009. "Out of the Kitchen, onto the Couch." *The New York Times Magazine*. August 2. Accessible at www.nytimes.com/2009/08/02/magazine/02cooking-t.html?pagewanted=all&_r=0.

Portisch, Anna. 2010. "The Craft of Skilful Learning: Kazakh Craftswomen of Western Mongolia." *Making Knowledge: Special Issue of the Journal of the Royal Anthropological Institute* 16, no. S1: 62–79.

Purbrick, Louise. 2007. *The Wedding Present: Domestic Life beyond Consumption*. Burlington, VT: Ashgate Publishing.

Pye, David. 1968. *The Nature and Art of Workmanship*. Cambridge: Cambridge University Press.

Rakopolous, Theodorus. 2014. "The Crisis Seen from Below, Within and Against: From Solidarity Economy to Food Distribution Cooperatives in Greece." *Dialectical Anthropology* 38: 189–207.

Relieu, Marc, Moustafa Zouinar, and Natalia La Valle. 2007. "At Home with Video Cameras." *Home Cultures* 4, no. 1: 45–68.

Riak, Patricia. 2012. "Fish Soup (Kakavia)." In *A Taste of Islands: 60 Recipes and Stories from Our World of Islands*, edited by Anna Baldacchino and Godfrey Baldacchino, 21–22. Charlottetown, PE: Island Studies Press.

Richards, Audrey. 1939. *Land, Labour and Diet in Northern Rhodesia: An Economic Study of the Bemba Tribe*. London: Oxford University Press.

Roosth, Sophia. 2013. "Of Foams and Formalisms: Scientific Expertise and Craft Practice in Molecular Gastronomy." *American Anthropologist* 115, no. 1: 4–16.

Rosaldo, Michelle. 1974. "Woman, Culture and Society: A Theoretical Overview." In *Woman, Culture and Society*, edited by Michelle Rosaldo and Louis Lamphere, 17–44. Stanford, CA: Stanford University Press.

Rowlands, Michael. 1994. "The Role of Memory in the Transmission of Culture." *World Archaeology* 25, no. 2: 141–51.

Salamone, S.D., and J.B. Stanton. 1986. "Introducing the Nikokyra: Ideality and Reality in Social Process." In *Gender and Power in Rural Greece*, edited by Jill Dubisch, 97–120. Princeton, NJ: Princeton University Press.

Scott, James. 1998. *Seeing Like a State: How Certain Schemes to Improve the Human Condition Have Failed*. New Haven, CT: Yale University Press.

Sennett, Richard. 2008. *The Craftsman*. New Haven, CT: Yale University Press.

Seremetakis, C. Nadia. 1991. *The Last Word: Women, Death and Divination in Inner Mani*. Chicago, IL: University of Chicago Press.

———. 1994. "The Memory of the Senses: Parts 1&2." In *The Senses Still: Perception and Memory as Material Culture in Modernity*, edited by C.N. Seremetakis, 1–43. Boulder, CO: Westview Press.

Shapiro, Laura. 1986. *Perfection Salad: Women and Cooking at the Turn of the Century*. New York: Farrar, Straus and Giroux.

———. 2004. *Something from the Oven: Reinventing Dinner in 1950s America*. New York: Penguin.

———. 2007. *Julia Child*. New York: Penguin.

Short, Frances. 2006. *Kitchen Secrets: The Meaning of Cooking in Everyday Life*. Oxford: Berg.

Shove, Elizabeth, Matthew Watson, Martin Hand, and Jack Ingram. 2007. *The Design of Everyday Life*. New York: Berg.

Silva, Elizabeth. 2000. "The Cook, the Cooker and the Gendering of the Kitchen." *Sociological Review* 48, no. 4: 612–28.

———. 2010. *Technology, Culture, Family: Influences on Home Life*. New York: Palgrave Macmillan.

Steinberg, Stephen. 1998. "Bubbie's Challah." In *Eating Culture*, edited by Ron Scapp and Brian Seitz, 295–98. Albany: State University of New York Press.

Stewart, Charles. 1989. "Hegemony or Rationality? The Position of the Supernatural in Modern Greece." *Journal of Modern Greek Studies* 7: 77–104.

Strasser, Susan. 1982. *Never Done: A History of American Housework*. New York: Henry Holt.

Sutton, David. 1997. "The Vegetarian Anthropologist." *Anthropology Today* 13: 5–8.

———. 1998. *Memories Cast in Stone: The Relevance of the Past in Everyday Life*. Oxford: Berg.

———. 1999. "Rescripting Women's Collective Action: Nationalist Writing and the Politics of Gendered Memory." *Identities: Global Studies in Culture and Power* 5, no. 4: 469–500.

———. 2001. *Remembrance of Repasts: An Anthropology of Food and Memory*. Oxford: Berg.

————. 2003. "Kollivo." *Slow: The Magazine of the Slow Food Movement* 42: 104–7.

————. 2006. "Cooking Skill, the Senses and Memory: The Fate of Practical Knowledge." In *Sensible Objects: Colonialism, Museums and Material Culture*, edited by C. Gosden, E. Edwards, and R. Phillips, 87–118. Oxford: Berg.

————. 2008. "Tradition and Modernity Revisited: Existential Memory Work on a Greek Island." *History and Memory* 20: 84–105.

————. 2010. "The Mindful Kitchen, the Embodied Cook: Tools, Technology and Knowledge Transmission on a Greek Island." *Canadian Material Culture Review* 70: 63–68.

————. 2011. "Memory as a Sense: A Gustemological Approach." Special Focus: The Sensory Experience of Food, with Carolyn Korsmeyer. *Food, Culture and Society* 14: 461–75.

————. 2013. "Review Article: Cooking Is Good to Think." *Body and Society* 19, no. 1: 1–16.

————, and Michael Hernandez. 2007. "Voices in the Kitchen: Cooking Tools as Inalienable Possessions." *Oral History* 35, no. 2: 67–76.

————, and Leo Vournelis. 2009. "Vefa or Mamalakis? Cooking up Nostalgia in Contemporary Greece." *South European Society and Politics* 14, no. 2: 147–66.

This, Herve. 2013. "Molecular Gastronomy Is a Scientific Discipline, and Note by Note Cuisine Is the Next Culinary Trend." *Flavour* 2, no. 1: 1–8.

Thompson, E.P. 1971. "The Moral Economy of the English Crowd in the Eighteenth Century." *Past & Present* 50: 76–136.

Trubek, Amy. 2008. *The Taste of Place: A Cultural Journey into Terroir.* Berkeley: University of California Press.

————. n.d. "Nutritional Gatekeeping: The Complexities of Navigating the Contemporary Food Environment." Submitted for consideration for publication in *Research Briefs for Journal of Nutrition Education and Behavior.*

Tuzin, Donald. 1997. *The Cassowary's Revenge: The Life and Death of Masculinity in a New Guinea Society.* Chicago, IL: University of Chicago Press.

Venkatesan, Soumhya. 2010. "Learning to Weave; Weaving to Learn . . . What?" In *Making Knowledge: Explorations of the Indissoluble Relation between Mind, Body and Environment*, edited by Trevor Marchand, 150–66. West Sussex: Wiley Blackwell.

Vernier, Bernard. 1987. "Filiation, règles de résidence et pouvoir domestique dans les îles de la mer Égée." In *Femmes et Patrimoine dans les sociétés rurales de l'Europe Méditerranéenne*, edited by G. Ravis-Giordani, 365–93. Paris: C.N.R.S.

Vournelis, Leonidas. 2013. "Lives in Pieces: Identification and Disidentification Processes at the Time of the Greek Debt Crisis in a Diasporic Community in Brooklyn." PhD diss., Southern Illinois University.

————, and David Sutton. 2012. "Yoghurt Projectiles: Food, Protest and Identity in Greece." *Anthropology News* 53, no. 1: 25.

Wajcman, Judy. 2010. "Feminist Theories of Technology." *Cambridge Journal of Economy* 34, no. 1: 143–52.

Warde, Alan. 1997. *Consumption, Food and Taste: Culinary Antinomies and Commodity Culture.* London: Sage.

Warn, Faith. 2000. *Bitter Sea: The Real Story of Greek Sponge Diving.* South Woodham Ferrers, UK: Guardian Angel Press.

Warnier, Jean-Pierre. 2001. "A Praxeological Approach to Subjectivation in a Material World." *Journal of Material Culture* 6: 5–24.

———. 2009. "Technology as Efficacious Action on Objects . . . and Subjects." *Journal of Material Culture* 14: 459–70.

Wasserman, Dave. 2011. "Will 2012 Be the Whole Foods vs. Cracker Barrel Election?" *OregonLive.com,* December 13. Accessed December 29, 2011. www.oregonlive.com/opinion/index.ssf/2011/12/will_2012_be_the_whole_foods_v.html.

Weiner, Annette. 1992. *Inalienable Possessions: The Paradox of Keeping-while-Giving.* Berkeley: University of California Press.

———. 1994. "The Density of Objects." *American Ethnologist* 21: 391–403.

Weismantel, Mary. 1995. "Making Kin: Kinship Theory and Zumbagua Adoptions." *American Ethnologist* 22: 685–703.

West, Harry. 2013. "Thinking like a Cheese: Towards an Ecological Understanding of the Reproduction of Knowledge in Contemporary Artisan Cheese Making." In *Understanding Cultural Transmission in Anthropology: A Critical Synthesis,* edited by Roy Ellen, Stephen J Lycett, and Sarah E Johns, 320–45. Oxford: Berghahn.

Whitehouse, Harvey. 1992. "Memorable Religions: Transmission, Codification and Change in Divergent Melanesian Contexts." *Man* 27: 777–97.

Wilk, Richard, and Persephone Hintlian. 2005. "Cooking on Their Own Terms: Cuisines of Manly Men." *Food and Foodways* 13: 159–68.

Williams, Brett. 1984. "Why Migrant Women Feed Their Husbands Tamales: Foodways as a Basis for a Revisionist View of Tejano Family Life." In *Ethnic and Regional Foodways in the United States: The Performance of Group Identity,* edited by Linda Brown and Kay Mussell, 113–26. Knoxville: University of Tennessee Press.

Wilson, Bee. 2012. *Consider the Fork: A History of How We Cook What We Eat.* New York: Basic Books.

Wrangham, Richard. 2010. *Catching Fire: How Cooking Made Us Human.* London: Profile Books.

Yanagisako, Sylvia, and Carol Delaney, eds. 1995. *Naturalizing Power: Essays in Feminist Cultural Analysis.* New York: Routledge.

Yates-Doerr, Emily. 2011. "The Weight of the Self: Care and Compassion in Guatemalan Dietary Choices." *Medical Anthropology Quarterly* 26, no. 1: 136–58.

Yiakoumaki, Vassiliki. 2006a. "'Local,' 'Ethnic' and 'Rural' Food: On the Emergence of 'Cultural Diversity' in Greece since Its Integration into the European Union." *Journal of Modern Greek Studies* 24, no. 2: 415–45.

———. 2006b. "Ethnic Turks and 'Muslims' and the Performance of Multiculturalism: The Case of the Dromena of Thrace." *South European Society and Politics* 11, no. 1: 145–61.

Author Index

Keyword Index

CALIFORNIA STUDIES IN FOOD AND CULTURE

Darra Goldstein, Editor